Carolann's Pathway

How to develop your clear vision and love your life on a pathway to spiritual freedom

GW00645408

**Carolann Frankie and
Roland Bush-Cavell**

Published by Mind Body Soul Development Organisation
Limited

For more information on our work, please visit
www.carolannspathway.co.uk or email
info@carolannspathway.co.uk

Contents

Disclaimer

This book is written with the purpose of conveying the author's perceptions of a spiritual universe which, it is our belief, can be accessed by all those who wish to do so. The nature of clairvoyance, or clear vision and indeed whether it exists in any of its forms is questioned by many and accepted by many more. It is not, therefore, our intention to prove anything to you, rather we offer here our perspective on a pathway that we sincerely wish could offer you methods by which you gain insight. Please remember that what might work for one person may not necessarily work for another and neither can we promise that you will achieve any of the abilities of clairvoyance we believe exist. Likewise, we cannot advise you to act upon what you perceive with your clear vision as your choices are yours alone. While we offer meditations on healing and discuss how to channel energies, nothing within this book is offered for diagnosis, prescription or treatment of any health disorder whatsoever. You should consult a medical practitioner for any complaint or medical condition, either diagnosed or suspected and no element of this book is intended to replace the advice of a competent healthcare professional. Faith, be it those of the authors or your own, can only be gained through personal experience and choice. It is your prerogative to believe as you wish, be it the nature of the beginnings of life on Earth, what pathway you follow, whether you recognise God and if you do, by what name you call Him.

About the authors

About Carolann

The originators and architects of my spiritual development are my teachers and guides in the spirit world, who first made themselves known to me over thirty years ago. With their arrival, for the first time in my life I felt the presence of spiritual beings that brought with them overwhelming feelings of unconditional love.

The first time I had a visit from spirit world was when they came to me a few months after my father's funeral. As I lay awake in bed one night, I became suddenly aware of a presence, as if a person was in the room there with me. Even though I could not see him, it felt as though my father was standing close beside me as I lay in bed. I knew he was there in the same way that you know if there is someone physically standing behind you; their presence is unseen but irrefutable.

Looking back, the fact that it was a family member and one who was so familiar to me, made this unexpected visit from spirit world so much easier to bear. That is why I believe it was he who was chosen, so I did not feel the shock it would have been to be visited by a complete stranger.

Immediately after this while still lying in bed and in a state of some wonder, a bright light came into my room. This time I felt the presence of a wonderful manifestation of love. From within this light came a figure I could just dimly perceive. A hand was laid on my head and saturated me with a feeling of awe and love that reached into my very bones. I remember thinking at the time that this could be death, so strong and unusual and deeply affecting was the sensation. But I was not afraid, the feelings were euphoric. I was filled with glory and it overcame any fear within me. I was lying there, overwhelmed with emotion and because the feelings were so all-consuming and I felt so wonderfully complete I even felt ready to die now that I had felt such immense love. It was not a fearful sensation, rather I was happy and content inside with nothing to be scared of.

Yet when I tried to get up the next day I found I was virtually immobile and totally unable to rise up from my bed. However, at the end of a week, this complete lethargy suddenly and instantaneously lifted away from me.

Thinking this experience and the visitations that came with it were over, I decided to focus on getting things back to normal. But normal is not a good way to describe what happened next. From that moment on and unbeknownst to me, my life was to change forever.

From that day forwards I received words, feelings and visions that lead me on a pathway of personal development. Up until then I had absolutely no knowledge, interest, schooling or contact with any of this kind of phenomena. It was a shocking revelation to find myself suddenly the subject of a wonderful spiritual awakening, which came literally overnight and with it the knowledge that was to begin a completely different way of viewing life.

Those whom I came to think of as my spiritual friends began the process of passing on their knowledge, helping me to recognise and develop my psychic gifts. This change was momentous and at the time all I could think as the incredible revelations were made was 'why is this happening to me?'

My life slowly turned around and improved for the better, while my spirit friends continued my tuition, schooling me so that I learned how to focus and to expand my clear vision. This tuition came in the form of lessons in visualisation and exercises to open and develop my mind, so that I learned the language of symbolics, the significance of colours and the meaning of our life here on Earth. As I developed, through their teaching I was able to use these same techniques to help other people, so that they could pass the teachings on to others and help them to develop and progress. These same spiritual friends are with me still, having created a bond of love and trust that continues to this day.

Many of the people I worked with in the early years became my friends; each of them learning, in turn, how to visualise, communicate and interpret the language of spirit world. I have now passed on this knowledge to those who wish to learn for decades and many of these people have progressed to use their clear vision to aid themselves and others.

Thanks to the instruction I have received from my friends in spirit world and the experience of working with many like-minded people, I am now able to teach others how to see clearly so that they can cope with the pressures in their lives, pressures that have always been there, but are more prevalent in the 21st Century as our everyday lives become increasingly hectic.

Through my teaching you can find answers to your problems, cope with stress, relieve depression, determine your own future and understand both the purpose and the part we play in life and how that fits within the bigger scheme of things. To me this pathway of clear vision, communicating with spiritual beings and being part of the universal energy is a natural part of my life. The words clairvoyance and mediumship carry numerous associations and beliefs, therefore we are presenting the pathway to you with a new term to help in developing a fresh perspective. This ability to see life outside of our own biased perception is (literally translated) called clear vision, for that is what it truly is.

Because it comes from a source beyond our human ability to reason, with the potential to take us to far higher levels of understanding, the power of this teaching is limitless. By following this pathway, we can recognise that life is precious and become better able to access and achieve the happiness we have within us. Through using this approach, we are able to understand life and by recognising and being accountable for our actions, to develop greater depths of inner peace. Your pathway to spiritual freedom begins here. It is in your own hands.

Look forwards and let your future begin now.

About Roland

For many years I have trained in this method of spiritual development. When I began my journey with Carolann, I had no aspiration to do anything spiritual with my life. I didn't have a religious background or any kind of spiritual understanding or insight. In short, the very concepts of clairvoyance or clear vision were alien to me and I had to start as a complete novice. So I began learning from Carolann, training in clear vision, with no inkling that one day we would be putting this pathway into a book so that others can share the journey.

I continue to learn every day on this amazing voyage, knowing that each of us can develop the same abilities and knowledge that Carolann has received directly from spirit world. Through Carolann's unique teaching of clear vision, we are able to provide you with all the tools you need to embark upon your own spiritual journey.

Throughout these years of learning I have benefitted hugely. From the beginning I was not only unaware of the ways in which spirituality could improve my life, but I was completely ignorant of what pursuing a spiritual path truly meant. Through Carolann's teaching, my eyes have opened to a more complete understanding of what life offers. I have received so much through pursuing the exercises and the benefits permeate all aspects of my life.

From my starting point where I was seeking a way of making sense of life, I now know of the bigger picture and how to pursue my own pathway within it.

With my growth has come the ability to understand myself and others more fully. I can relax far more easily than in the past and surprise myself at how good life feels. But the biggest gift has been receiving an understanding of what the spiritual side of life can offer. Learning about the energies that surround us has been truly fascinating. I have learned how incredible the universe is, that we can see far more deeply into it and into ourselves than many of us would imagine.

Clear vision has totally changed my perspective so that my innermost beliefs on the meaning of life and what we can hope to get out of it have been turned on their head, not because I have found a faith to cling to, but because I have seen the proof. I know too of many people who firmly believe they have had their eyes opened and now recognise just what clear vision can deliver. For me clear vision has provided a personal realisation of a wider universe, explanations for much unexplained psychic phenomena and broadened my mental horizons. This wider universe can be found through a deeper understanding and knowledge of our own spirituality and the pathway we are on. Once we have this perspective we can find our own way. Even if you are yet unable to define what spirituality means to you, this book can provide the tools needed to look directly into spiritual energies and incorporate what is good and true in the universe into your life. No one can prove the truth of this to you, you can only hope to discover it for yourself, when the time is right.

Perhaps unsurprisingly I am incredibly passionate about this method of teaching, having experienced it and seen what it can do for those who use it in their lives.

This pathway offers the prospect of continuous improvement, looking forward to each day, not solely because of what can be gained mentally, emotionally and spiritually, but because of the possibilities that can be found within life. The more this pathway progresses, the more fulfilling it can become.

I continue to see people growing and gaining fulfilment by incorporating these teachings into their lives, or benefitting from those who guide them with their own clear vision. From complete cynic, with no comprehension of what spirituality could add to my life, clear vision and spirituality are now a growing and central part of my world, a world that continues to widen as I continue to open my mind.

We decided to embark on the journey of writing this book, with myself as writer and Carolann as teacher and source of knowledge. Knowing that what Carolann teaches is unique and comes in an unadulterated form from her teachers and guides in spirit world, we wanted to share the possibilities with everyone.

Introduction from Carolann

I have been conversing with spirit world for over half my life, working with their energies of purity and goodness that are available to us all and yet so few of us know how to fully access. To those who have not yet encountered or come to terms with this world of spirit, my daily reality of communicating with what is a far wider universe will seem extraordinary. In this book I would like to share the benefit of decades of direct experience as a teacher, clairvoyant, medium and healer, who has been taught exclusively by spirit world.

All of what you read here is true to my experience of it. Everything in this book has been taught to me by the world of spirit. The knowledge and the exercises can help you to develop your own understanding through the very best method of learning, which is to experience it for yourself.

The goal of this book is for you to develop a greater awareness of yourself, your spirituality and of the role that your emotions play in your life. By using the exercises herein, you can develop a clearer vision that can serve as a vehicle towards personal enlightenment, so that you are better able to help yourself and others.

Spirituality is a subtle journey. This book seeks to capture the essence of that journey in language we are all able to relate to, so that self-understanding is readily available within it.

Within this book we will develop your clairvoyance or clear vision and use these natural gifts to guide us on a spiritual pathway to enlightenment.

After reading this book and experiencing the exercises within it, you may find your thought-patterns changing so that you are turning your life around for the better. It comes to you with the strong wish that you will find your spiritual pathway and the hope that you will gain knowledge of the way forward. By allowing yourself to open up to the road of self-discovery and self-knowledge presented herein, our aim is to help you find a better quality of inner life and heart-felt personal rewards. The aim of this book is to awaken you so that you may find peace from within, peace that can then extend outwards into your life.

Love has a purpose, in that it is the foundation of our spirituality and with love in your heart all things are possible. In its widest manifestation it does not come alone, it comes with the act of acknowledging that there is beauty that surrounds you and that all are equal in the eyes of God. By opening your mind you create room for a far wider love that can transform your outlook and your life.

Presented within is a spiritual understanding of life, together with exercises and meditations that can enable you to develop and open your mind to the prospect of a better existence, both for yourself and those around you. Our wish is that you will read this book, be open to the possibilities it can create and recognise the impact that practising the exercises and understanding the messages herein can have upon you.

Life is what we make it. Each of us has our own reason for being here in this world and opening your mind to the spiritual pathway can lead you to self-discovery and enable you to find your purpose and niche. We are presenting herein an alternative way of thinking that, should the time be right, can enable each of us to recognise and respond to the beauty in existence and achieve harmony within it.

We invite you to imagine what life could be like, knowing that you were happy both with yourself and within yourself, in peace and harmony, at one with everyone and everything. This book shows you how you can embark upon this journey towards enlightenment.

On this journey there are sometimes changes to be made for our own personal well-being and these can take many forms, such as teaching ourselves that spiritually it is better to love than hate; that it is better to give than to take and better to forgive than to seek revenge.

Each of us has the potential to recognise how to bring happiness into our own space and act upon that recognition. By progressing and learning along this pathway we can gain a sense of belonging. Most of all, by gaining the knowledge that we are not alone, that each of us is part of a bigger picture, a bigger plan, we can find that we all have a purpose and a right to experience all the joy that life has to offer. Experiencing this wider universe comes as you develop spiritually and no amount of preaching, instruction, or reading can lead you there until you are ready for this awakening. This book is here to help you develop your clear vision and provides you with tools to help you gain a greater understanding of who and what you are and what the bigger picture is.

Life can be like a Pandora's Box offering both positive and negative experiences as part of our journey. The majority of us are here to learn from the choices we make from within our options, whereas some are born into this life with the ability to set examples for us to learn by. Yet all of us can learn how to tune into the circumstances we might find ourselves in and the choices available to us.

By living our lives honestly and spiritually, we become at one with ourselves, developing a feeling of fulfilment, self-worth and happiness. From this point of self-knowledge, we can see who we are, what will best fulfil us and in what direction happiness lies.

Chapter One - Clear Vision

Clear vision is clairvoyance, used for the benefit of yourself and others as part of your spiritual pathway to greater enlightenment.

There are many ways of developing and living a spiritual life and many spiritual pathways and religions have truth within them. The pathway of clear vision offers you one means of gaining access to this spirituality. Put simply, if you develop clear vision, you can become more aware so that you develop your own insights. Alternatively, you can receive the benefit of this insight from someone who has already developed clear vision for themselves, such as a clairvoyant or psychic. It is for you to develop your own perception of what is true, for no matter what you are presented with, your own belief will dictate what is true for you.

Clear vision gives you the ability to see beyond the obvious, beyond the usual thought-patterns that colour and define our minds. By working on our clear vision and attaining it for ourselves, we can naturally develop an ability to see what is necessary to help us and others through life. Developing this gift lets us widen our state-of-mind. It allows us to appreciate another person's point of view because we are able to experience directly what life feels like for them and we naturally become more open and flexible. Clear vision helps us to look beyond the limitations of our own perception and see other possibilities. Without clear vision, life can otherwise seem like a factual black and white landscape of circumstances. Without it, we have to create or adopt our own rationale for the world. Learning through experience in this way is not a bad thing, in fact it is what life is all about. However, if we are brave enough to put our own solidified opinions to the side for a while, clear vision can accelerate our learning in a way that is unique.

Without clear vision, we live in a world restricted to our knowledge of what has come before; we operate from a point of view reliant on our past experiences and how much we are willing to allow into our lives. If, rather than what we 'know' from our viewpoint, we tune into the energy that permeates life, then we receive our own direct knowledge. In other words, unless we both allow our minds to be open and develop our inherent intuitive gift, we will live in a world of the immediate that is defined by the boundaries of who we are and how we think.

We can be going through life blind to anything other than our own perception and even if we listen to those around us, we cannot necessarily 'know' the bigger picture; instead we use logic and experience to guide us. This means that there is nothing other than these in life we can trust to give us the bigger picture and of necessity we live in a limited orbit, blind to the spiritual universe we live within. All we have to guide us is our sometimes narrow perspective and the opinions of others. What we are conditioned to feel as a result of our experiences, may be right for us, but much of what we learn from life will in effect be governed by chance. If we learn fear and do not challenge our own ignorance, we can become trapped by outside circumstance in a life of limited reward. If, instead of relying on the opinions we have formed to guide us, we use our clear vision, then we can develop an insight that if properly used, can guide us to a life that accelerates our development, both spiritually and emotionally.

When we use clear vision it is like looking into a clearer level of reality. With it comes the ability to develop a 'knowing' that shows you the outcome of events and situations in your life. Another way of explaining it is that it is like looking through a window of the room you are in so that you can see what is truly going on outside. Past all the noise in your mind, beyond the confusion of opinion and advice, once you find your clear vision, it will offer solid answers. While our minds can change seemingly minute by minute, all of us can develop an insight that does not change with our minds, because it is a clear perception of the truth.

Clear vision won't necessarily show us everything about life and it takes a while to master it, but once you have it, it will never lie, nor will the ability leave you. Instead, it will take your mind wider, so that you are able to appreciate and relate to the viewpoint it allows you to work with. It gives a heightened level of understanding that means you will always have a way to look forward into your own life and the lives of those you wish to help.

Chapter Two - The Art of Relaxation and Meditation

Developing on this pathway, we need to learn to work with a mind that is calm and peaceful. A relaxed state-of-mind will help us develop quickly as well as bringing benefits in its own right. Yet relaxation is an art in itself and for many of us it does not come easily. There can be many reasons why we find it hard to relax; it can be because we are thinking too hard, our minds are too active, or perhaps we have too much stress in our lives.

The stress we are experiencing may not even necessarily be our own, it can be in the environment around us. If we are sensitive to the anxieties, traumas and life dilemmas of others, we can pick up on these feelings, react to the problems of those around us and even take them on board. In this way we can, in turn, make the problems of others our own and absorb their negativities into our lives.

Whatever the reasons for our experiencing stress, meditation is one way of dealing with it. Meditation is the foundation for developing equanimity and clear vision, as well as learning to achieve a greater calmness within. It can also provide a greater flexibility so that we find alternative ways of looking at things or even increase our ability to cope.

If you are overly sensitive, meditation can lend you a far greater inner strength and likewise, if you find you have trouble in relating to your emotions, meditation can develop your insight. In this way the knowledge you develop using the exercises in this book can even help convert situations that are potentially stressful into fuel for your self-development and a better understanding of life.

There are a number of meditations presented. Some will develop and stretch our minds and others will help us to switch off, while others still allow us to understand more about the mind itself. There are many types of meditation; some of the exercises allow us to recognise our stress and develop a greater understanding of it, while others offer us an effective and immediate way of relaxing. The meditations and exercises can show us how to identify and therefore avoid sources of potential stress in our lives. This is an essential stepping stone in allowing us to develop clear vision for ourselves.

Meditation also enables us to be at one within ourselves and with the rest of life. This means that we are less influenced by self-doubt and we can gain a greater ability to focus. It gives us a feeling for just how strong we can be, not succumbing to life's pressure and allowing it to overpower us. We can develop a greater ability to relax, refresh ourselves and become calm within a vision of strength, unity and self-honesty. In this way we can become whole.

When you start to meditate, you might initially find that there are aspects you find difficult. It is quite common to experience pitfalls, such as becoming tired and falling asleep, or the mind racing away so that you feel frustrated and unable to relax. However, this is all part of your development. Eventually, through practice, you can find that meditation will open up to you like a window, so that you are immersed within the experience.

Relaxation is both the key to, and the result of, a good experience of meditation and yet it can often elude us. There are many reasons why we find it difficult to relax within meditation or indeed even find the time to meditate. It can be, for instance, that our minds are conditioned to be active and we are not used to just sitting without outside stimulus. Yet, we may not be used to putting ourselves first. We may find it difficult to prioritise our meditation above the chores of everyday life, even to the extent that we feel guilty for taking the time to meditate. Alternatively, we may not be bothered with meditation, not understanding how working at it can benefit our life and the lives of those around us. Being able to put yourself into a meditative state no matter how you achieve it, can help enhance your life and help you deal with its demands. Once we understand this, if we choose, we can gradually learn the art of meditation and can use it to free ourselves from the cares and worries that trouble us. Meditation doesn't just help our mental state, it can also give us greater energy and strength and allow our bodies to heal, enhancing our life and balancing our health.

If, as many of us do, you have a busy lifestyle governed by time constraints and commitments, it is most beneficial to establish meditation as a positive habit and find a consistent time within your daily or weekly routine to practice this life-enhancing skill.

Once you have taken the step of allowing yourself this regular time, you may find a way of prioritising or becoming more flexible as to when and how you meditate. As we become familiar with meditation, it becomes easier for us to fit it into and even integrate it with our lives. Like time spent playing, just five minutes in the morning or evening can become a liberating part of your day.

Meditation may initially be something separate from our lives, there may be a distinct difference between the feelings and experiences we are having in meditation and those we are having in our day-to-day lives. As we develop we can begin to benefit from what we learn and experience in meditation, applying it to day-to-day situations and achieving a greater integration, so that what previously challenged us now becomes easier to accept or overcome.

In order to start meditating, we may firstly have to learn to put ourselves first just for a moment. It may be that we want to start taking a regular moment to relax in a way that familiarises us with switching off our usual thought-patterns without sitting down to meditate and in this way prepares us for the state-of-mind we are looking to achieve through meditation. We should choose whatever method is best for us, it could be taking a hot bath or reading a book, or being in good company, chatting over a pleasant meal, listening to relaxing music, gardening, or walking in a natural environment. All of these can provide a break, by allowing ourselves to become absorbed in the moment. Setting time aside for a gentle activity helps us move towards developing the art of meditation for ourselves.

However we do it, if we take the time to enjoy what is around us, by taking a walk in the woods, observing the flames in a fire, watching children laugh and play, or wondering at the natural beauty of a flower, we can observe and learn to appreciate life and what it offers. Taking the time to walk by the sea, watching the waves coming in, standing on a hilltop, or in an open space can all open us up to the natural spirituality within everything around us. If we take a moment to alight from the express train of life, we can get a clearer mind and become more receptive, understanding where we are headed and why.

The best things in life are free. if we only take the time to enjoy them. If we are able to lose ourselves in the enjoyment of the moment, then we have captured some of the feelings that can act as the inspiration to begin walking a spiritual pathway, teaching us that a calm and open state-of-mind can offer rewards in itself. If we are not there yet, we are missing so much of what life is offering us.

Wherever we find ourselves, meditation will allow us to develop an ability to experience the spiritual nature of life. It teaches us to look for and naturally experience the best in everything and can bring joy, exuberance and beauty. The best place to start is with a meditation that teaches us how to relax, because a relaxed state-of-mind allows us to do our best work.

Preparing for meditation

In setting ourselves up for meditation, we need to put aside time that is dedicated totally to this pursuit, to find a time and a place that is special to us.

You will need to make the environment around you as conducive towards meditation as possible, in the way that suits you best. Your aim is to find a quiet place, free from distractions, with soft background music or silence according to your preference and a niche with a comfortable chair or place to sit in. The important thing is to find a place that is right for you and where your body is as relaxed as it can be.

The meditations in this book are predominantly visualisations that will develop your mind, opening and refining your abilities as you progress. As you develop and your concentration increases you may wish to build up the time spent in meditation. Remember that every meditation has a purpose and it may not be necessary to meditate for a long time. Relax and go with the flow so that you develop in a way that is best for you, growing each and every time you practice.

Many people initially find one place suits them best. Ensuring you have no disturbance from outside is always a good idea, although as you develop you will find that you can meditate despite interruptions. You can make it a special place and a special occasion when you meditate, or you can choose to meditate just about anywhere you like.

Meditating is one of the most positive things you can do for yourself because it will develop you and it will provide you with a means for future development also. This is the foundation of your developing clear vision, which can benefit you and others in many ways. The most important thing is that you are relaxed and that how you choose to meditate feels right for you.

Once you have settled yourself into a comfortable position, take some nice deep breaths and close your eyes. Allow your whole body and mind to relax. Move your mind-energy to the backs of your eyelids and, keeping your eyelids closed, look through them with your mind into the darkness beyond.

Letting your shoulders relax, breathe peacefully. Take a few moments to enjoy this peace. Let go of your Earthly vision and any distracting sounds. Focus your attention outward into the darkness and allow your mind to clear of all thoughts and worries. You can use this preparation to ready yourself for any of the meditations in this book.

Distractions within meditation
It is best to remember that whatever you experience on your pathway of spiritual development, it is all part of the journey and until you have developed some familiarity with meditation, it is quite common to have distractions and reactions. These may take the form of such things as coughing, itching, twitching or even strange noises from your digestive system as your body relaxes and opens!

There are also numerous ways in which we can become distracted or seemingly diverted from what we want to achieve in our meditations. Common pitfalls are that we strive too hard, that we are too self-critical or that we have bodily discomforts and reactions. If you are experiencing any of these natural reactions, just gently return to your meditation; the gentler you are with yourself the better.

Your own thoughts can distract you from meditation, but you should not let this worry you. Meditation is initially like taking a car out of gear and allowing it to coast. As long as our foot remains on the accelerator pedal, it will seem as if the mind has become even noisier, racing away with nothing to occupy it. So if you feel like your mind has become busy or distracted, or if your mind wanders, don't let it worry you, simply return to the point where you drifted from the meditation. The experience and the benefit of meditation comes from relaxing into it while allowing your mind to let go of the physical body so it can instead work with the calming effect that meditation can bring. Likewise if you can meditate right the way through the distraction, then you are also developing your ability to focus in meditation and in everyday life.

Meditation for relaxation

Purpose
The purpose of this exercise is to allow ourselves to relax our mind and body so that we are better able to meditate without mental or physical distractions taking over and ultimately feel better during and after each session. Relaxing into this meditation will give us greater clarity of thought, improved ability to focus and generally help our health and well-being. This can help our body and mind to regenerate itself so that we are better able to manage our everyday lives.

Preparation
Put yourself in a place where you feel at ease. Sitting comfortably or lying down, put on some relaxing music. Take some nice deep breaths and close your eyes. Move your mind-energy to the backs of your eyelids and, keeping your eyes closed, look through them into the darkness beyond. Letting your shoulders relax, listen to the music and breathe peacefully. Let go of your Earthly vision and any distracting sounds around you. Focus your attention outward into the darkness and allow your mind to clear of all thoughts and worries.

Meditation
Let yourself sink into a feeling of total relaxation, as if you were lying on a soft and warm feather quilt. Be aware of how comforting and secure it is; wherever the quilt touches you, you

feel nurtured, safe and loved. In your mind there is no place like it.

Allow your mind to float freely, let go of everyday thoughts and feelings and let yourself become spacious and free. Feel your body in your visualisation become as light as a feather, as you are at once supported and comforted. There is just you and the warm quilt.

Become aware that the quilt is beginning to drift gently as if on a breeze, floating out into space, still cradling you in its sumptuous embrace.

Feel yourself rising with the quilt, still cosseted and safe, slowly floating outwards into the wide open space that is all around you, seemingly infinite, without borders or limits.

Let yourself relax even more; fill your mind with thoughts of peace and openness. Breathe in the wonderful tranquillity. How gentle you feel in this infinite void, at once free and yet totally absorbed within it. How clear your thoughts have become, with nothing for your mind to touch or your eyes to see! Just you and your feather quilt drifting in openness. Peace and harmony all around you.

Allow yourself to become totally immersed within this meditation, connecting with the feelings you are experiencing. When you are totally immersed in the warmth and feel the sense of freedom, just allow yourself to drift along in peace as you become increasingly relaxed.

Let these feelings flow, until you are refreshed and feel ready to emerge from your meditation. Then in your own time becoming aware of the space around you, allow your eyes to open gently and arise from meditation.

This meditation is all about learning to let go of stress. It will provide you with the ability to relax and feel some freedom from your everyday worries. Practising this meditation will help you gain a greater ability to let go of life's pressures, so that you are more flexible and better able to switch off. It will also enable you to refresh yourself so that you feel less tired in a very short space of time. In this way you gain greater control over your own mind. Initially this may be for just the brief period of the meditation and as you progress you will find this sense of relaxation can carry over into your life. Taking this time out is a very positive step and can provide a way of strengthening yourself when day-to-day life is getting the better of you, or you simply want to devote some time to improving yourself. It can be used as a small break that you may well deserve.

Chapter Three - Visualisation and Increasing Our Awareness

The meditations and exercises in this book are presented to help you develop your clear vision to the best of your ability and to allow you to expand your awareness so that you further your progress on your spiritual pathway.

To move forward on this journey, each of us needs to recognise our emotions, how they affect our experience of life and what we receive from that life. At times, we can find that our emotions are controlling us rather than serving their true purpose of guiding us. If this is the case, then we can feel powerless to change ourselves or the situation we find ourselves in. If we experience feelings such as anger or frustration or any number of negative reactions as a result of what is happening around us or to us, then that is not in itself unhealthy or a problem. If we work with our mind enough, we can reduce the effect that frustrations and annoyances have upon us. What we are initially seeking is the freedom in our mind to recognise these negative emotions for what they are. Recognising the negative feelings we have is the first step in gaining freedom from them and we can then point ourselves in a positive direction so that they no longer control or hinder us.

When our emotions rule us and function unchecked, we can be out of control of ourselves and respond instinctively without self-guidance and thought. If we do not have our emotions in perspective, the way in which we act is in effect governed by our individual experience of life and how our particular personality has evolved. If we are in this situation, then we can feel very confused, the purpose or meaning of our life can elude us and we find that there are seemingly no answers within, only the option of reacting to life. If we instead gain the freedom to be guided by our clear vision combined with a developing insight, then we become the captain of our own ship, steering our course using our intuitive senses, looking at possibilities rather than living in fear of limitations. As we gain experience in using our clear vision, the feeling of knowing what is right for us grows, as does confidence in our own intuition. In this way, our innermost intuitive feelings become our guiding light, rather than the conditioned emotional responses we have learnt to adopt.

Meditation enables us to recognise emotions and understand what our options are, before the emotions take control. Our emotions can then assume their correct role as guides as to what is the right path for us, as well as becoming signposts for our development.

One of the goals we set ourselves on a spiritual pathway is to have a positive outlook and experience of life and this is possible, in part, because we recognise, rather than ignore, our emotions. If, instead of this recognition, we push our emotions away from ourselves, we can feel lost and empty inside. So if we are true to ourselves and learn to understand our emotions, they will be true to us. In this way, how we feel can act as a guide and rather than placing obstacles on our pathway, our emotions act as signposts. Emotions should not be ignored, they are an integral part of our personalities and when they are in balance we have the ability to not only deal with life, but create something from it. We can then effectively paint our own canvas, understand ourselves, life and everything within it, so that we gain an independent perspective and our picture is then complete. Clear vision illuminates a pathway of understanding that enables us to achieve more from life by balancing our emotions. Because clear vision expands our perception, we can see things that much more clearly and this allows us to develop spiritual understanding and grow as an individual.

Clear vision is like a third party viewpoint, a viewpoint that is free of our own emotional hang ups and negativities, such as our impatience, our bias, or our unwillingness to see another point of view. So if it is our fears that are colouring our judgement and stopping us from acting, having clearer vision will mean we are better able to both see and understand these fears. If, on the other hand, our negativities make us feel so bad that we don't want to move forwards, or we perceive ourselves as too limited to progress, then with our clear vision we are better able to see how these adverse emotional states stop us from enjoying life. Whatever our position, developing clear vision provides us with a pathway to follow and an increasing ability to see the most beneficial directions to take and choices to make.

A building block for our clear vision is the ability to visualise. Developing this ability connects us with the language of the mind, which helps us gain independence from our mental obstructions. In this way, visualisation helps us develop both our clear vision and our practice of meditation.

Visualisation allows us to put our mind in a beneficial place. For instance, we might choose to see ourselves on a beach or in a garden and in so doing we begin to develop our mental faculties, allowing our mind to stretch and strengthen. By developing visualisation techniques, we can become aware not only of the visual elements but also of the sounds, tactile sensations and even the feelings we pick up in these visualisations. The ability to see, feel and sense in our meditation grows and we gain a more complete experience of what is happening on that beach or in that garden. We can see the sky, feel the air, smell the flowers and hear the sea. As we progress, we can become confident in our abilities, relax and fully immerse ourselves in what we are experiencing.

Therefore, visualisation stretches our minds, while giving us a greater awareness. It also increases our ability to work with and understand the symbolic meanings of what we see with our mind's eye and this greatly benefits our ability to use our clear vision.

With enough practice, eventually we will understand the whole language of symbolism and interpreting images can become second nature to us. These images need not necessarily be interpreted solely by what they visually represent; with each image we receive can come a feeling. That feeling can play a great part in revealing the meaning of the image we are interpreting. Seeing a white dove with our clear vision may not initially tell us all we need to interpret and understand what it represents, but if we receive a very powerful feeling of peace alongside the vision, then we know that the dove itself is there to indicate peace. Therefore our ability to visualise and interpret images works alongside our ability to recognise emotions and feelings and is a key element in our clear vision. There is more information on images, symbolics and interpretation in later chapters.

Your current mind-set may restrict you in many ways and visualisation will help you to recognise opportunities, free from your mental limitations. Visualisation helps you gain perspective and gradually teaches you how to paint a colourful canvas with the many opportunities available to you in life.

Clear vision offers us a method for gaining a totally independent and positive perspective and visualisation helps us by strengthening and refining our abilities. Where our logic and emotions cannot guide us, our clear vision can. That clear vision is developed by using the meditations we present in this book. Meditations that help us develop an independent intuitive ability and in fact take us nearer to the person we are inside, the person who entered this life with a goal in mind. We are then better able to see these goals and take steps towards achieving them.

By developing our awareness, we can see how our negative thought patterns affect our lives and recognise how our attitudes and emotions affect not only how we experience life, but also how they affect what we aim for, receive and become.

Being able to see clearly the role our emotions play in cluttering our thinking can make a vast difference to our lives. We can then choose a pathway towards a positive outlook, so that we can find the positive within our past, present and future experiences. This helps free our minds from clutter and see life in an entirely different way, making it so much clearer, enjoyable and vibrant. To connect with ourselves in this way is possible for each and every one of us.

The meditations in this book can help take us beyond merely clearing our minds of obstructive thought and towards developing an outlook that is also free of emotional clutter. We can become capable not only of clearing things for ourselves but also of understanding how emotional states affect those around us.

The next thing we can recognise is how, once we are free of all of these conflicts and clutter, we are able to write our own agenda for life. Life is a journey and we can receive so much from it, no matter what our circumstance, it is within the grasp of each of us to find the positive learning and the positive experience within it.

Many of us are looking for either meaning or a goal in life, or we exist without it and may feel a nagging lack of fulfilment or inner value. Whether we see our glass as half-empty or half-full can be dictated by our outlook and circumstances. By understanding ourselves, we take a step towards finding our role and goal in life, so that we can see the glass is half-full. By continuing to develop our abilities of clear vision, we each of us have the potential to see that glass as it fills and runneth over.

The meditation in Chapter Two can help us clear the clutter from our emotional landscape. A meditation for relaxation enables us to gain greater clarity in life and the room to fill the picture of our lives with colour and excitement. With this clearer perspective we can recognise what we do have in our lives and the benefits of having challenges that enable us to learn and grow.

The following chapters include many meditations, exercises and visualisations that can help us enhance this ability to paint our own colourful picture of life.

Chapter Four - Opening Yourself to the Universal Energy

Once we have taken the first step in our development by gaining some experience of meditation, we now have a tool for gaining a more relaxed state-of-mind and wider awareness.

The ability to relax is a stepping-stone and the next step on our spiritual pathway is to open ourselves to a better understanding of who we are, the situation we find ourselves in and our purpose in life. As explained in the previous chapter, the process of visualisation is essential in achieving this clarity; with clarity comes a positive outlook that is the natural outcome of knowing just who you are.

Our goal in opening ourselves is to understand our own emotions better and therefore gain greater perspective of the people and situations around us. At the same time we gain greater freedom from negative emotions, while understanding the role of our positive emotions, how they can be an asset and how our intuition can guide our development.

We are now learning to open and recognise the universal energy that is a pathway to individual guidance. Developing our openness takes us another step towards developing the ability to work directly with this energy.

Initially, some of us are closed and find ourselves emotionally blocked or standing still in that we cannot move our lives forward. This is a very uncomfortable and potentially frustrating place to be (that many of us can relate to!). In this kind of situation, we may feel suffocated or in a state-of-mind where the joy of life is diminished.

By closing off, we block ourselves from reaching our full potential for happiness. If we are governed by our limitations we find ourselves stifled. There are many reasons for this type of situation arising. It can arise because of the stresses we feel coping with everyday problems or situations, or we may be restricting and denying ourselves the right to be who we really are, which can bring about feelings of frustration, emptiness or loneliness. By acknowledging and bonding with the bigger picture, we can eliminate our own fears and frustrations and achieve satisfaction and happiness within.

Through opening and recognising our situation and looking beyond our own problems, we can develop:
- A positive outlook
- Faith in our own abilities
- The ability to look at everyday situations as challenges
- The ability to understand what we can learn from our challenges
- The freedom to respond in a way that allows us to grow
- The confidence to be one with ourselves
- Openness and an acceptance of life

There are many reasons why we close ourselves to our emotions and some of us may be more closed than others. We may be stubborn in clinging to our existing views, or it may be that we have developed a need for control that has allowed us to function in difficult situations. We may be closed to change because of fear of the unknown or of negative thinking, or conditioning may have trapped us emotionally, while insecurities play a great part in obstructing us and stopping us moving forwards. Wherever we start from and whatever our state-of-mind, meditation will allow us to open up.

By opening ourselves we are naturally more able to go along with the flow of life. Along with the feeling of going with the flow we know intuitively what is best for us and with this intuition, we get the feeling of being naturally satisfied and content. It is not something we necessarily have to strive to achieve; through practicing meditation and the visualisations in this book we can allow the thoughts and elements that conflict with this flow to dissipate. By taking a gradual approach our thoughts and the good elements in our lives fall into place more readily, rather than our having to force the attainments and conclusions we want.

That is not to say that effort is not needed to achieve these goals. Clear vision can take us into incredible areas of knowledge but thankfully teach us that ultimately life is very simple. We can expand our minds to confront our own thinking and to listen to and test viewpoints that may not initially be in accord with our own, or even make sense, or seem possible. By keeping an open mind and testing the exercises in this book, we will see how we develop. The proof of the pudding is in the eating.

Below are three meditations that help us to develop our ability to open ourselves up within a visualisation.

Meditation - The Beach

Purpose of the meditation
This meditation teaches us to tune in to a naturally relaxing beach scene and we can use it to become familiar with feelings of relaxation and openness. Through regular practice, we can both engage our senses of sight, touch, smell and hearing and discipline ourselves to be consistent so that we are able to maintain our focus for longer periods of time. This ability to concentrate will help us to maintain our focus in life.

Preparation
Put yourself in a place where you feel at ease. Sitting comfortably or lying down, put on some relaxing music. Take some nice deep breaths and close your eyes. Move your mind-energy to the backs of your eyelids and, keeping your eyes closed, look through

them into the darkness beyond. Letting your shoulders relax, listen to the music and breathe peacefully. Let go of your Earthly vision and any distracting sounds around you. Focus your attention outward into the darkness and allow your mind to clear of all thoughts and worries.

Meditation

In your mind's eye, move your attention to your feet and recognise that they are on an open sandy beach that stretches into the distance on either side.

See the sand all around you and look forwards to the ocean in front of you, aware of its vast expanse. As you feel the waves rolling in, breathe in a nice deep breath and as you feel them roll out, breathe out – allowing your mind to travel over the sea to the horizon where it meets the sky.

The sand is warm and golden. Feel your feet sink into its softness. Stretching your thoughts, allow your mind to open and be aware of the beach, sea and sky. Expand until you can sense the scene all around you. Feel the warmth on your face, the gentle breeze and the sea rolling onto the beach making the sand wet and dark. Visualise the waves on your beach, advancing and retreating. Now take your thoughts to your breathing. As each wave comes in, breathe in and as each wave goes out, breathe out. Become one with the beach and water and feel the space and openness all around you. Join your mind with your vision to become one with the splendour of the beach, the sea and the wet firm sand. Feel the freedom that this brings within you. You are now one with your spiritual senses, your mind absorbed in the vision of your meditation.

Take your mind's attention to the right and see the sea as the sunlight shimmers on the water. As you turn, see the tide bringing the sea onto the beach. Look once more at the soft dry golden sand where you are standing. Look to the left and see the wet firm sand stretching all the way along the water's edge. Focus on the horizon where the sky touches the sea, once again you are tuning yourself in to the vision of the beach, the wet firm sand and the sea rolling in and out. You are one with the vision – you are one with the gentle breeze that blows over your face and body. Hold onto the feeling and the energy that this vision brings; you are relaxed and comfortable on your beach. Enjoy this feeling of oneness for as long as you wish, until you naturally feel it is time to arise from your meditation.

Allow yourself to sit quietly and when you are ready, open your eyes and arise from meditation.

Meditation - The Horse in the Field

Purpose of the meditation
This meditation helps us to let go of past conditioning. Allowing ourselves to give up control within our meditation, releasing us from the constraints of logic and programming. Free from these restrictions we open the doorway to our senses and we are more aware.

This meditation allows us to directly experience another perspective, joining with new energy. Free from our reasoning minds we are better able to let go of the analytical thought that can sometimes constrain and hold us back.

Preparation
Put yourself in a place where you feel at ease. Sitting comfortably or lying down, put on some relaxing music. Take some nice deep breaths and close your eyes. Move your mind-energy to the backs of your eyelids and, keeping your eyelids closed, look through them into the darkness beyond. Letting your shoulders relax, listen to the music and breathe peacefully. Let go of your Earthly vision and any distracting sounds around you. Focus your

attention outward into the darkness and allow your mind to clear of all thoughts and worries.

Meditation

Move your mind-energy all the way down to the soles of your feet. Feel them on the ground and visualise yourself standing in front of a revolving door. This is an old fashioned revolving door made from highly polished wood and glass, with a brass rail on each segment, which you have to push with your hands in order for it to move.

Now visualise yourself stepping into the revolving door for the first time; let your mind feel your hands on the bar, pushing the door around with your entire body. Push the door all the way around and back to the point where you started.

Now take another deep breath and, for the second time, see yourself standing facing the same revolving door, but this time your hands are behind your back.

Focus on the door in front of you and on the brass rail. This time push the rail and revolving door with your mind alone. You are pushing the door once more all the way round, but this time without touching it. Push it all the way through a full rotation and back to where you started.

Now for the third time approach the door. Step right into the revolving door and push at it again with your mind alone, but this time you will not return to where you started. Instead, step out half-way around so that you emerge on the other side. This time you step out into a field, a green field bordered by a tall hedge that keeps everything within it safe.

All around us is the field and we are standing on lush green grass. Looking outward and over to the right of the field, focus your mind on a white stallion you see grazing there.

The stallion sees you and lifts its head. You approach it slowly, walking across the field. You now find yourself in front of him. You reach out, feeling pleased to greet and touch him.

Stroke his neck and feel how strong and powerful he is. Realise now how real the horse has become. Go round him, all the way and feel the tail and hair and its coarseness. The horse turns its head towards you at the feel of your touch. Feel your way from the tail along his flanks until you touch the mane and the ears. Move all the way round to the front and feel the horse, see its eyes and sense its breath. Offer it something to eat from your hand and watch the jaw in motion as it begins to chew.

This horse is magnificent and you have bonded with him. You now feel free to walk with him. Turn and lead the horse by allowing him to follow you. Walk and feel the power and strength and gentleness as he walks beside you.

Ahead you see a wooden box. The horse walks to it and stands expectantly beside it. Knowing that you have been invited, you use this box to step up on to the horse and sit high upon his back.

Gently you pat the horse and command him to walk forward on the grass. Hear the sound of his hooves as they move on the grass below you, vibrations running through his frame. Encouraging him with your heels, you command your horse to go forward in a gallop. Feeling strong and safe you will move forwards, getting faster and faster. Feel the exhilaration as you both begin to rise, leaving the field, climbing up into the sky, carrying you quickly into the clouds. You are now very high and, with the sky all around you, be aware of the sense of freedom that the power and the strength of this animal is giving you.

Pause for a while and enjoy this liberation. Let the horse be your guide as you explore the sky together for as long as you wish. Looking down, become aware of the clouds below beginning to clear. Far below you can see fields, forests and houses, resembling a patchwork quilt that stretches to the horizon. Totally immerse yourself as the wind rushes through your hair. See the colours, the greens of the trees, the striking blue of rivers and lakes, the contours of the hills and feel the vast open depth of the sky between you and the land below. Take in every detail and allow the scene to build in your mind, becoming one with all that you experience.

When you are ready, prepare to return to the field where you began your journey. Pat the horse on the neck and ask it to descend to the fields below. As you get lower, you see the fields becoming ever closer, the green of the grass and hedges getting nearer, until the horse's hooves contact the ground of the field from which you began your journey.

The horse walks you to the box that you used to climb onto his back. Stepping down onto the wooden box and then the grass, hug and thank your horse for carrying you on this spiritual journey.

The horse will return to grazing contentedly. When you are ready, leaving the horse in the field behind you, walk away until you see the revolving door ahead. Step forward once more and enter the door. Using your mind only, turn it until you return to where your journey began, bringing with you the exhilaration of the spiritual freedom you have experienced.

Allow yourself to sit quietly until you are ready to open your eyes and arise from meditation.

This exercise allows us to let go of the conditioning that tells us we must work through actions alone to achieve our goals. By allowing ourselves to be fully immersed in the vision, to trust the horse and to experience the sensation of letting go, we are able truly to fly freely. This prepares us to work with the input of outside energies, without seeking to manipulate them for our own ends. What this means in practice is that we can learn to open up all our senses to energy that would otherwise be unknown to us. We can trust what we find with our clear vision and free our spirit to react on the basis of what we find rather than what we fear. In this way the horse in the field helps us to let go of our preconceptions and accustomed patterns of thought.

Group Exercise - The Jigsaw Puzzle

Purpose
This is a fun visualisation exercise designed to get a group of family and friends working together. The jigsaw puzzle will help us to develop by bonding with like minds tuning in to the same story. Initially we will be developing a story that is in all probability fictional and drawn from our own imaginations. From this beginning we can progress and develop the ability to link our minds with others. Joining together in this way we receive information as one, as if we are all reading the same story.

Preparation
This is a fun group exercise suitable for children from six or seven years old upwards to adult. For this exercise you will need at least two people. A group of four or five works well and even larger groups can use this exercise too, the more the merrier!

Make all the usual preparations for meditation as a group to ready yourselves for the exercise. Put yourselves in a place where you feel at ease and as this is a team exercise, it is not necessary to keep your eyes closed. At the outset, you may believe that the information you are receiving is coming from your imagination. If carried out correctly, the aim is that the group will eventually find that they are on the same wavelength and what each member of the group perceives will fit together like the pieces of a jigsaw.

How it works
You will need to select a leader to guide the group. It is the job of the leader to keep the group together, so that they are tuning into

the same story, and to decide where the group should be going based on the information received. In case of the group or the story becoming fragmented, it is the leader's job to look at the images that each member of the group has in their mind. We do this initially by allowing the group to voice what they are seeing.

The leader visualises a jigsaw box and in their mind, takes the box and empties it out on to a table in front of them. They then ask the group to visualise the pieces and describe them. The first task is to identify whether they are large or small. The individual members of the group voice how they see those pieces. The leader goes with the majority decision of whether they are big or small pieces.

Then each individual in the group will take one element of the picture. For instance, one person will take the sky, one will take the centre of the picture and one will take the foreground.

The member of the group reading the sky will visualise it in their mind's eye and will voice what they perceive. They may see it as blue with few clouds, or overcast. For example the person reading the foreground may have seen a wood, a lake or a stately home. The individual elements will fit together into one complete picture. The foreground will match the sky that we have already seen and the centre will bring them both together. Once you have read each element of the picture in this way you will see that it is now a complete whole.

Once the picture is complete, the leader now puts the rest of the group in a position within the picture. In their mind's eye, every member of the group puts themselves into the scene that has been created and the group leader will now lead them on a journey into the picture itself.
Each individual, in turn, will voice where they see themselves and describe the situation they find themselves in.

As an example, they walk past the lake and through the trees up to the stately home. They will go up to the door and knock and someone will open that door to them. They let their journey and findings be known, voicing them as they go along. They then pass to another member of the group and that person will take us into the entrance of the home, into the reception hallway and lead us further into it, describing it as they go in. Then, another member of the group will take us into the living room or elsewhere within the home. In turn, each member of the group describes everything they see as they move forwards into another area of the house, going into the other rooms, bedrooms, kitchens, larders and into the servant's quarters. All of the group should remain tuned into the speaker in their minds, so that they all see the same picture. All the time the leader of the group will be checking the information spoken by each member of the group against what they are seeing in their mind. It is the leader's job to keep the group together. They ensure that each person is describing the same house and focusing on the one place they find themselves in at any given time. In this way no one wanders off and the group maintains its focus.

It is up to the group now to identify who lives in the house, how many people are there and who they are. You then move on to how the people feel, to get a taste for their personalities and how they interact with each other. In this way, you will build a story of people's lives, gaining an understanding and a feeling for their actions, emotions and motivations. This story will unfold to the group. It may be any type of tale that unfolds, a chaotic saga with emotions that are running wild or a tale of everyday lives, all dependent upon how you find it. It doesn't have to be a house, any scene or situation can be tuned into and related; a village, an Indian reservation, a haunted house, a castle, a pirate ship; anything is possible.

This exercise can last for twenty minutes or for hours. You will reach a natural point of conclusion. When you feel you have reached this point you can agree as a group to conclude the exercise and discuss what you have found together.

The jigsaw puzzle is an exercise that helps our minds to tune into a common source, reading the story as it unfolds, working together, bonding as a team, learning to trust our feelings and going with our intuitive first impressions. This enables you to link with like minds and act spontaneously. Treat this as a fun exploration, enjoying the act of using your imagination and developing your gifts, all at the same time. By practising in this way, you will be better able to receive and understand images and feelings. The jigsaw puzzle also helps you to become used to voicing what you find with your clear vision. It exercises your ability to read using your clear vision in unfamiliar situations, especially where you have no previous experience of what you are encountering, so that no matter what you come across you are better able to read and relate to it.

Chapter Five - Developing Our Clear Vision

If we want to develop our understanding of clear vision, then it might be helpful to know that we will all at one stage or another have experienced it without necessarily recognising it for what it is. Common examples of this are, knowing that the phone or the door bell is about to ring, or for instance knowing who is on the other end of the phone before they have spoken. When this happens, it is your intuition or psychic senses informing you so that you know something directly without the aid of your physical senses.

Other examples of our clear vision coming into play are when we get 'gut feelings' about a person or a situation, or when we have an instinct, a 'knowing' felt deeply within that tells us what is the best course to pursue. There are many stories of people who have dreamed of an event before it happened and then read of it in the papers or saw it on the news the next day. Many of these are also examples of our psychic senses expanding beyond what can be explained logically.

Clear vision as we define it is the ability to use our intuitive senses to perceive images, messages, feelings and sometimes smells and sounds within our mind to reveal that which we may not otherwise know or recognise. Our intuition is a major part of this process and no matter how intuitive we are, developing our ability to perceive psychically increases our intuition and vice versa. By developing clear vision, we are opening all of our senses to receive information from a dimension other than this physical reality. The dimension from which we are receiving this information is the domain God and it is the universal energy which he radiates that contains all information about what has happened and what is yet to happen in the lives of each and every one of us. As we develop, we get a greater ability to access this energy, but our access is never absolute, we do not have a total and unlimited comprehension of everything that is happening in time, whether it be in the past, present or future. That ability is God's alone. Because of our limited perspective, we are often assisted by spiritual beings who have chosen to take on the role of guides to those who seek to develop this pathway.

The ability to receive images and information is the first step in developing our clear vision. The next step is to learn to interpret these images and understand the language of the mind and that ability comes from learning to interpret the symbolic images we receive.

What we perceive through our psychic senses manifests subtly. It may come as images, or as a very faint whisper heard with our inner ear. To distinguish that inner perception from our own thoughts, we need to learn to differentiate between the feeling we get when we are thinking and the feeling we get when we find our clear vision. This is very important, as it helps us to discern between what is clear vision and what is information from our own subconscious or our imagination. The ultimate goal is to instinctively tell the difference between the two. The meditations and exercises in this book are designed to open this pathway to you to help achieve this goal.

Every one of us is able to learn how to use our mind to access clear vision and to interpret what we perceive with this heightened awareness. Clear vision comes through on a frequency that we are all born with and have the ability to tune into.

From a logical perspective, we might look at this psychic potential that we all enjoy and question how we can we have free-will if the future is already written? This can seem to be a contradiction, being able to see potential events and yet being able to dictate how we act now and yet from a spiritual perspective this is the essence of life. From God's perspective, life will continue as it is meant to continue and He can see the beginning and end of everything that is born and dies. But we have not yet developed so that we have anything like the perspective of God. Even if we develop our clear vision, we are able to see only so far ahead and have a finite perspective. Even so, if we use our gift, we move closer to the essence of the universal energy and if we act upon what we see our life is far more in tune. We are physical beings with a physical viewpoint and if we are able to guide our free-will from an unclouded spiritual perspective, it can help us to move forwards in the most beneficial way possible.

Clear vision

Each of us is born with natural gifts, be they the ability to be creative or to think analytically and logically, or physical gifts like beauty, strength and physical prowess.

The ability to see things clearly through our mind's eye is another such gift that each of us is born with and possess throughout our lives. This ability is the basis of all psychic skills, be it clear vision (or clairvoyance), mediumship or any other skill that enables us to see into other areas beyond the physical.

An essential element in developing these skills is to learn to distinguish between the evidence and input of our physical senses and that of our psychic senses. What comes in from our mind's eye is, in fact, far clearer a vision than that we get from our own eyes, hence the name clear vision. It is our eyes that show us things from our own singular perspective. However, eyes will only penetrate to the level of the visual, seeing an arm or a person's face for instance. Clear vision on the other hand, can go beyond the physical to see a person's situation and feelings, perceiving far more than if we rely on our eyes alone. It also transcends our reliance on logic and our own limited perspective. This gift allows us to perceive far more lucidly; by looking into the dimension of the universal energy, we are able to gain glimpses of our past, present and future, clear of our own thoughts and preconceptions.

How many times have we thought to ourselves or wondered out loud "why is that person acting in that way – I just don't understand?" Clear vision can provide us with a key to greater understanding, not through attempting to psychoanalyse or through applying logic, but by directly perceiving a person's situation and understanding their viewpoint. Likewise if we are wondering why we are feeling uncertain, we have an alternative way of looking at things, which can give us tools to begin to understand ourselves better.

Clear vision sees beyond a personal situation and allows us to gain insight into anything and everything around us, becoming a part of the bigger picture. This, in turn, gives us a direct knowledge and serves to expand our minds into other dimensions, other realms and beyond. By seeing the physical world alone or choosing to see things from a singular viewpoint only, we could be restricting our options and our potential to learn. Allowing that there may be other possibilities and choosing to develop so that we can understand them, opens up a pathway that can widen our perceptions to include the world beyond.

Clear vision is a gift we are born with and that we can develop. It is a function of our ability to tune into the energy around us and the energy of those around us. By tuning in to these energies we can see clearly for ourselves and for others. The insight we then gain means we are able to develop ourselves, our wisdom, our compassion and truly understand others and where they are coming from.

Once we have taken steps along the path to clear-seeing, the next stage is to develop our ability to communicate with and be guided by spirit world. This gift is the gift of mediumship.

Any element of the psychic is a contentious subject for those who have had no direct experience of it. Proof of the existence of life after death and of God is only available to each of us personally though belief and by being open to personal proof through our own perceptions. If you choose to develop your clear vision, then you can build your own experience and know what is possible for you; from that viewpoint you can develop your own opinions and beliefs. Ultimately, for those who do not believe, there is no absolute proof that mediumship or clairvoyance exists, because we can always rationalise what people say to us, or argue that they are receiving their information from elsewhere, that it is so general that "it could be for anyone" or even that solid verbal evidence by its nature is a lucky guess. So, even information that is irrefutably correct could be rationalised away as circumstantial or obtained other than by psychic means. Names of those that have passed over, even if they are correct can be said to be common, emotions when they are identified by a clairvoyant or medium are always subjective and without an open mind we might disregard that which is in fact true.

What is presented here is based on personal belief of the authors from our own direct experience. You are free to decide for yourself what it is you believe. We take issue with no religion and present the principles contained herein as being true because our own personal experience tells us it is so. The testimonies in this book presented by our other contributors are authentic and witnessed by those who have experienced real benefits in their lives by allowing themselves to be guided by clear vision, whether it is their own or someone else's that has put them on a spiritual path. What you choose to accept is up to you, we only ask that you keep an open mind. Try it for yourself and you may become living proof.

Clear vision is the basis of all psychic development. In the same way that wheat is needed to produce flour and is the basis for many dishes, so it is the basis for all our psychic gifts. Incorporating it into our lives helps us to make the right choices, to develop and avoid unnecessary and avoidable stresses, dangers and strains by taking the direction that is right for us. This enables us to trust our feelings within a spiritual context. Rather than being ruled by our emotions, or cutting them off and ignoring them, we are able to trust our own inner voice.

In this way, we can go beyond what we see with our fallible eyes, to look beyond the obvious. As we develop on the path, we will increasingly see the bigger picture. By this, we mean that we can gain a greater perspective, free from negative emotion and self-interest.

Healing and clear vision are intuitive functions that operate independently of our logical minds and thought-patterns. A question that is inevitably asked early on in training is how we differentiate between our imagination and our clear vision. Both our imaginings and our clear vision are played out and received in the mind. Yet our imagination is a creation of our mind alone, while our clear vision comes with a different feeling and we can prove to ourselves that it is separate by using it for ourselves and others.

Imagination is a wonderful gift; we can paint pictures and scenarios in our minds and if we focus on imaginary situations, we can invest our energy in building them up until they seem almost real. However, when we receive images, symbols and information psychically, they have substance and come from an outside source. We can see an elephant in our imagination quite easily, just think it and it is there. We could choose to see it in any scenario we wish, just by thinking we could put that elephant in a circus or a jungle. However, if we perceive the image of an elephant with our clear vision, it will have meaning. It may be a symbol for us to interpret and once we have identified this meaning, it cannot be changed. With clear vision we have no choice as to what we see, only in what we look for! If we see the elephant on top of a hill, we will not be able to change it by thinking it is in a valley. Likewise if the elephant comes with no background or situation around it, we will not be able to put one to it in our mind. Each element of our clear vision has substance and meaning that cannot be changed by our will. Instead, with clear vision, what is given to us is what we get. Our job is not to change what we receive, but to look into it so that our understanding deepens.

So our clear vision has substance, whereas what we imagine or make up in our minds does not. When we use exercises and get consistent answers, it is one guide that we are using our clear vision correctly. If we continually get the same answer when looking at a situation, then this tells us we are on the right wavelength, until such time as the situation changes, in which case so will the information we receive.

We cannot expect to understand this all at once, practice truly makes perfect and each of us needs to persevere if we wish to get continually better results.

Our clear vision comes to us in many ways; we may receive sounds, images or feelings or we may even eventually just be aware of the truth within a situation. Typically, the feelings are the first things that we perceive and from these we gain our information. Thereafter we may start to develop images and then sounds. Eventually, this can develop into a direct knowledge of situations. This direct knowledge will come on a particular frequency of thought, like listening in a particular direction for our doorbell or the telephone; we come to recognise when the information is coming from our clear vision and when it is merely a flight of fancy or a passing thought.

Because we are dealing with energy and thought, the information we receive can initially be difficult to differentiate from our imaginings. Relaxation will enable you to become more familiar with your state-of-mind and how you are feeling so that you are better able to distinguish between information that is coming from 'you' and your own imagination and that which is coming from 'outside' and your own clear vision. In this way any self-doubt we may initially experience in our development can be overcome through practising using meditation and visualisation and you will be better able to receive through all of your spiritual senses.

Chapter Six - Unconditional Acceptance and Going with the Flow

Each of us is born with something that is uniquely us. We have a wealth of experiences from previous lives that have built us into the people we are. We are born with abilities and the potential we need to fulfil our journey, while our personality and attitudes develop from this starting point to create who we are today.

Whatever personal goals for happiness we set can be achieved all the more readily if we learn a spiritual attitude. We are then able to learn to accept life for what it is and find what we can achieve within it.

No matter who we are and how we entered life, no matter what we have experienced, be it positive or negative, limiting or liberating, by learning this central spiritual attitude, everything else in our lives becomes far easier to deal with and develop.

Acceptance and patience are essential. They are the remedies that help us focus on life's wider journey, even if we are dissatisfied with the way things are and therefore developing our unconditional acceptance means we are better able to go with the flow of life. The reason we need to develop acceptance is that without it, we can become frustrated and even angry. These reactions are not unnatural, they prompt us to recognise that something is wrong or out of balance, but sometimes they can just be signs that things are not going the way we want them to. If we stubbornly cling to our own interpretations, bias or viewpoint then this can hinder our progress on the spiritual pathway. Our will can serve us if it is used to further our growth, or work against us if we are stubbornly denying alternative answers to life's meaning.

Learning to go with the flow is a good remedy for frustrations and will help us to feel better about what we cannot change while we are deciding whether it is important enough to us to take action. For those things that we cannot change, it will help to keep us stable, our minds free of unnecessary worry and allow us to weather life's storms all the better by maintaining our perspective.

The concept of going with the flow is very subtle and being able to live in the flow of life is a result of pursuing a spiritual journey. We all have limitations as to what we can accept and what causes us pain. There will always be something in life that we need to accept, despite wishing that a situation was different. Learning to live in this way will stand us in good stead and help us steer a pathway through life's challenges.

We may feel we are already an accepting patient person (and we may be right), or we may feel that what we do not accept is beyond the endurance of anyone and that it is natural to reject it (and again we may be correct). A spiritual pathway offers us the option of deepening our acceptance so that we feel better about life. Going with the flow means that we can take greater joy in what we receive. Like a good meal that is laid out in front of us, life can be bolted down and rushed or we can enjoy it all, savouring every morsel. The one thing in life that is finite is time. Going with the flow means we are more able to enjoy every minute and allows us to realise our ambitions in the most positive way, giving everything in life the very best that we can.

This allows us to achieve the things that are right for us, progressing with less hindrance and developing positive personality traits as we do so. In that way, we can feel so much better as people. It doesn't mean that life will be served to us on a plate, or that we won't have to put in anything less than all our effort; patience and perseverance are part of the spiritual journey. If we go with the flow, we can see that much of what is there in life can sort itself out without our reaction. By allowing our negative emotions to pass without acting upon them and by treating life's lessons as opportunities for growth, we can be who we are meant to be.

Going with the flow is the process of learning to tune into what we perceive to be the universal energy and allowing it to guide us to what we deserve and what we need. Maintaining this approach, we open ourselves to what is right for us and the negativities and insecurities, that might otherwise dictate to us, have less opportunity to breed disharmony in our lives.

By learning to accept difficulties and obstacles on our pathway and learning from them, we develop the ability to accept what is right for us and what life is offering to us. Taken to its ultimate conclusion, this acceptance of life can become unconditional, while our goals are discovered through this spiritual approach.

Our lives are like a journey upon a flowing river and we are in a boat that is guided by the current. The boat is all the abilities we are born with and the river is the universal energy that is leading us in the right direction. Letting the boat go as the current directs, we can let the day take care of itself. We have the ability to steer ourselves to keep our direction and this is much easier if we follow and go with the current, rather than fighting it. So, by letting go, we are developing a trust that, come what may, while we may have to make adjustments to our course, everything will be alright within the bigger perspective of life. That is not to say that another boat passing won't disturb us, like a speedboat that rushes past and rocks us, or where the stream is crowded with other boats trying to make their own way, they might make it difficult and uncomfortable for us to move forwards. These other boats are people making their own way in life, each seeking to achieve their own goals for happiness. A speed-boat could be someone who is discordant, or merely rushing headlong to pursue their own goals, oblivious of another's presence. A crowd of boats could be people seeking fulfilment in areas that aren't appropriate for them and encroaching one on the other. Alternatively, it may just be that circumstance has thrown people together to learn. These situations teach us that things come and go. A speeding boat will pass, leaving us rocking and perhaps momentarily thrown off course. So it is not to say that by intending to pursue a spiritual pathway we don't have problems and cannot be affected by others. In adopting this approach, we need to be true and honest with ourselves and to face the obstacles and fears that restrict us or delay our moving on. However, by having a wider perspective, we are more able to go with the flow and we are less disturbed by what is around us and the situations we find ourselves in. Each of us is already living within the natural order of things. We are meant to be here, we are meant to learn from what we experience and on this pathway of clear vision, we have the flow of the universal energy to guide us, if we so choose.

We are all entitled to work to have our needs met on a spiritual pathway. However, wants and needs are two different things, they are separate. We can fulfil our needs without getting lost in them, whereas we can get lost in our wants. If life is a constant striving for status and position and material excess then our cup is half-empty and we are working against ourselves. If however our cup is half-full, then we know that we already have everything we need to enjoy life purely through experiencing it. It is when our attitude to life is one of acceptance that our cup fills and overflows with positivity, providing us with more inner happiness than fulfilling our wants could ever achieve.

On a spiritual pathway we challenge ourselves. Clear vision helps us to see our behaviours, reactions and emotions so that we find our limitations and by being accountable to ourselves, discover who we truly are. When we have adopted this clear sighted approach, we are better able to go with the flow. Because we know we are honest to ourselves, we can be true to other people and to life.

If we find ourselves in situations where we are blocked and unable to overcome our negative emotions or fears, it may be because we have not developed this openness as fully as we might. Often these blocks come from negative thoughts due to disappointments from our own past experiences. In being true to ourselves and what we are, we can free ourselves from our emotional problems and limitations. Until we have overcome these problems generated by our past negativities and the thought processes we adopt, we may find ourselves time and again confronted with the same type of obstructions. Learning to go with the flow helps us to break this cycle and try another way of reacting.

Another common obstacle that many of us encounter is that we feel we are living our lives to meet the expectations of others. If you feel this way, it is probably because you are subordinating yourself to someone else and it can feel like life is an act. Be it in work, relationships, at home, or anywhere we feel insecure or under pressure, if we are not true to ourselves we can get caught in a trap. That is not to say that we should not help those who are in need, but we are letting ourselves down if we are not true to our own self. If we are not able to be honest with ourselves and we are diverted from our own pathway, then we need to firstly recognise that this is the case. Any relationship that forces us into acting out of fear can cast us in a role that is alien to our nature.

If we are in this situation, then we should not blame ourselves for it, circumstances can dictate that we put on a brave face or meet the needs of others to ensure we have a position in life, or so that we may keep the peace. Additionally, sometimes we have to accept and work within our own fears and limitations until we are ready to move on. It doesn't matter necessarily that we feel we are not being true to ourselves, as long as we recognise that we are behaving in this way, keeping sight of who we are and taking opportunities to express that elsewhere in our lives. What is important is to develop ourselves and our spiritual life until the situation resolves itself or we are able to release ourselves from it.

By learning from the past and the blocks it may have generated within our thinking, we can move forward. In learning not to repeat the same mistakes we can move on to opening new doorways, accessing new areas of experience and development within our lives. Life then becomes a pathway of learning from the present and living increasingly in the moment. We can also become more generous and take joy from seeing others achieve their own goals, secure in the knowledge that we know who we are.

If we are going with the flow, then we can learn to have order and balance within what we do, but life itself is not something that we can control. For instance, if we receive bad news, such as our job being taken away or a relationship being threatened, then if we are allowing life to flow, we are better able to react positively and look for what the situation is telling us. Perhaps our job is not the right one for us or we need to reassess our relationship, looking to what we are putting into it and what we are receiving from it. If, instead, we react negatively, only conscious of the negative effect this is having on us, then we may feel ourselves to be a victim. By looking for the lessons in what we are experiencing, we grant ourselves options for change.

By living spiritually, we move towards a sense of wholeness. This means that we know what we want to achieve within life and what we are willing to put into it. We know who we are and what is acceptable to us and what is beyond those boundaries for acceptance. With this sense of oneness comes freedom and a far greater sense of comfort. Because we are guided from within, we have far fewer causes for regret and therefore we are far less likely to be caught up with the past and instead our minds are far more able to live in the present. We also have much more mental freedom to value the moment and appreciate what is happening with us at any time. Our priorities are far more settled and we become more self-aware. We know what is important and what isn't. A bigger car or house may no longer be our priority, rather we choose to work towards inner happiness, a home filled with love and a vehicle that gets us where we need to go. This is because we value things for their function and not for the level of status they provide. There will also be a greater sense of value in the things we achieve from our effort. Valuable things such as true friendships achieve their correct significance because they are amongst the things that money cannot buy.

Even while we are seeking to let life flow, fears and insecurities can create false reflections that make it seem like a house of horrors. Clearing negativities frees us from the false reflections that they create. Being at peace with oneself and who we are frees us from the maze of self-doubt. When we confront situations for what they are, this distorted reflection of life is removed.

When our thoughts are not limited by our fears, we gain a greater mental freedom and we are clearer and better able to deal with situations as they present themselves. In this way, our challenges are genuinely external ones and not our internal phantoms.

Another benefit of a spiritual approach is that we can genuinely feel a better person for having confronted life in the right way. Instead of having staked our view of ourselves on material achievements, competing with others to beat them, or the pursuit of power, rather we have developed internally.

Without a spiritual approach, we may feel we want more than we have and therefore never have enough to satisfy ourselves. Fulfilling our wants is like trying to fill a bottomless pit, which is constantly getting deeper and deeper. No matter what we fill this pit with it, will never bring us satisfaction because we are seeking to fulfil ourselves through ownership and consumption. We can mistake the good feelings we receive from the ownership of material objects for the objects themselves, this can make us shallow. The good feelings we receive from ownership will not last long because a beautiful house or car is not ultimately capable of fulfilling our inner needs. If we are taking this material approach, then no matter what we have, very soon we will want to improve upon it. In contrast, the good feelings from a spiritual pathway far outweigh and outlast material rewards because they are always there within us.

We may also feel that we need status and position and power in comparison to those around us. If we are dependent on the good opinion of others to feel good about ourselves then we must be empty and lonely within. It is fine to have the recognition that comes with achievement, provided one has a balance, but status and power cannot fulfil us.

A spiritual perspective allows us to learn the difference between our wants and our needs, we can then learn to appreciate the people around us and the life we are living. This is why faith is so important, not just faith in a spiritual side to life but faith in oneself. If we have faith that there is a spiritual side to life, then we can be motivated to move in the right direction. This, in turn, means that we can have a greater faith in ourselves because we cannot doubt that we are seeking to do what is for the best. This in turn means that we will develop spiritually and personally because our effort has been well considered and when we achieve our material goals we can see them as a well-earned bonus and value them for what they are, rather than for what they signify.

Whether we are the type of person who looks at a glass as half-empty or as half-full and whether we are positively or negatively minded affects how we look at things. Two people can see the same situation and what they feel can differ greatly. Likewise, we may look at our own personal situation and feel we need a whole host of material things to make that situation better. There is nothing wrong with wanting comfort and security and to feel as though we have achieved something with our lives. However, there are many things we buy that we feel we need (the empty bit of our glass) that in fact we could well do without. We will not all be able to have everything we want and riches that only the few enjoy. Some people have the level of income or the money to have everything that they desire and to enjoy many indulgences and some people have not. This world of haves and have-nots is the material and not the spiritual world. Material things bring temporary relief, or can relieve us of the stresses of not having enough food on the table or a roof over our heads. Material things can provide us with a life of excitement and luxury, but they do not bring the internal contentedness we are seeking. It is not a case of either we do or do not have material things, rather it is the case that our internal happiness originate from a different source.

Regardless of the material aspects of life, developing clear vision enables us to look around at the wider options available. If we are depressed, lonely, or feeling hopeless and helplessly lost, if we have no faith, nor the ability to look outside of our own perspective, then viewing life from this narrow outlook, we can see neither hope nor help. If we are trapped in this way, then we might end up throwing ourselves into any situation that offers hope, but could be drastically wrong for us. This escape route could be a relationship, or anything we see as a lifeline. If we act out of desperation, then we may not consider what our lifeline could lead to. Clear vision allows us to look forwards on our life journey so that we can better understand what we are getting ourselves into. It therefore gives us choices that help steer us nearer to the life that is meant for us.

Likewise, on our wider life journey we may end up in situations that are wrong for us. Even if we are not desperate and only seeking fulfilment, we may be motivated by the material safety nets of money and status. If this is the case, then we may put all our efforts into something that will satisfy only those material desires and not give us the feelings of fulfilment we are seeking. The desire for comfort isn't bad, but it can drive us in the wrong direction. We may not find our right direction immediately; it may take time, while clear vision puts us on the route to becoming our own guide so that whenever we are lost or seeking direction it can provide the answers that elude us. If life is lacking in colour, it can point us towards growth. If we feel mystified as to what direction to take, it can help us gain insight and choose our own goals. So clear vision, working with our ability to go with the flow, can put us on the best possible path.

Steering your pathway

On the pathway of clear vision we are seeking to see life from the clearest perspective open to us and each of us is responsible for how we live our lives with the benefit of that clearer vision. As our vision expands, so will our potential for insight and our awareness that there are far more options in how we choose to think and act than we might imagine. Clear vision is offering us the choice of how to live our lives within the situations we find ourselves in and ultimately it will help us to find the best situations for our growth and happiness.

Learning to steer your own course using clear vision can teach you to think in terms of the bigger plan of your life. It can help you to trust in your feelings, keep your mind open, have faith that there is more to life (even beyond your own current understanding) and to believe that what you learn from each outcome will be positive. On this journey, and any other, what direction we take is up to us. Recognising that like attracts like and that karma is as much about what we are doing, as what has happened in the past, helps us to choose the way forward. By abandoning our negativities and thinking and acting in terms of what is best for all concerned, we will have a happier life.

Steering your pathway is about letting go of all doubts, fears and insecurities and seeing difficulties as a challenge that you can learn from. It is recognising that everything you are learning will help you in difficult times, in the future and beyond. So when you feel worry and anxiety, realise that you are not alone and that problems or hurdles could be here to strengthen you. If you have faith that help and guidance from above will shine through and that strength, understanding and clarity will come from trusting and opening your mind to it, then that trust will be rewarded. These rewards come in learning how patience, honesty, love and giving will make you feel so much better in every second of your life and that you will attract like-minds and find friendship with yourself and others. With this, comes the benefit of an uncluttered mind, a clear conscience and the ability to focus on what you want from life, free from the worry that you are contributing to its woes and knowing that you are adding something positive and good to it.

To believe that this is possible may be difficult; many of us walk in the dark and have no sight to understand or see the outcome of the individual situations in our life, let alone those of the bigger life plan we are here to fulfil. If all of us saw the bigger picture, we could feel the joy in our lives that much more readily, because we are better able to realise that if today doesn't work out the way we want it, or if we take a wrong turn, with the right attitude we can find what will take us forward in a way that makes us happy and unencumbered by baggage from the past.

Only with clear vision can we perceive the whole picture and truly understand that there is a method in the way in which life develops. Nor are we always put here for an easy life. How would we develop and grow if life came easy. We would not be able to enjoy the good times because they would be the norm. Difficult times provide perspective and therefore teach us how to enjoy life and find fulfilment. Looking for more quality and purpose and seeking the positive in everything we do provides us with structure and depth within ourselves. By changing our perspective, we will learn to let go of stress caused by our doubts and insecurities, have more mental resources to think positively and spend more time doing the things that make our life productive and fulfilling. If we believe that our best is good enough, then we can realise that is all that is asked of us and be free to try our utmost in everything we set our mind to. By being entirely who we are, we can avoid wasting our energy trying to be what we are not. Through learning and letting go of our mistakes we can find peace of mind and serenity.

Meditation for going with the flow - Skating on Ice

Purpose of the meditation
This meditation aims to teach you to work gracefully and fluidly and to both feel and accept outside input, using your mind to stay in sync, while you learn to flow in this difficult medium. It helps to tune you in to the energy of spiritual help and the universal energy without obstruction so that you gain familiarity and learn how to work with them both. You can feel the support outside energies offer and learn to accept how much easier it is to work with them than force yourself against guidance. In this way, the meditation will help you to follow the course that is both just and right for you. It can help you find the ability to steer through problems and lead you to be at the right place at the right time.

In practising the meditation your goal should be to awaken yourself to appreciate the difference between imposing your will and accepting guidance from a source you are learning to trust.

You will be familiarising yourself with the feelings that come with the universal flow of energy that is guiding us all. This both allows us to work with an energy other than our own and allows us to feel its influence and if we choose, to be guided by it in our lives. Another benefit is that it will help you to recognise the subtle feelings and intuitions we all experience from time to time that are available to us when we most need them.

Preparation
Put yourself in a place where you feel at ease. Sitting comfortably, or lying down, put on some relaxing music. Take some nice deep breaths and close your eyes. Move your mind-

energy to the backs of your eyelids and, keeping your eyelids closed, look through them into the darkness beyond. Letting your shoulders relax, listen to the music and breathe peacefully. Let go of your Earthly vision and any distracting sounds around you. Focus your attention outward into the darkness and allow your mind to clear of all thoughts and worries.

The meditation

In your mind's eye, visualise yourself standing at the edge of a large skating rink that stretches out before you. By your feet are skating-boots in your size for you to wear. Put the boots on your feet, lace them tightly and step out onto the ice. Be aware of the feel of the surface beneath your feet, feel its smoothness and the solid support it offers. Holding on to the side of the rink, look across and see a person coming across the ice to join you. Feel the approaching presence of this person as they skate ever closer, eventually coming to a halt and taking hold of your arm. Then allow them to lead you out onto the ice-rink.

Now feel the sensation of being guided, of your feet gliding forwards. Push with first one foot and then the other, together in unison with the person who is teaching you how to skate with them. Allow yourself to go with the flow and experience the sensation of being led by your partner on the rink. Feel the relationship between their movement and your own. Allow them to guide you through subtle movements and sense the direction they are steering you across the ice. Enjoy this sense of freedom and let it all happen, knowing that you are totally safe. With your partner's guidance you are a fantastic ice skater, moving in complete co-ordination. With their help you become filled with exhilaration as you perform ever more intricate moves. Jump, turn, twirl, race, feel the coolness emanating from the ice below and the air on your face as well as the ever-present partner by your side. Have fun with this meditation, recognising the sound of your skates as they cut the ice and feel the rush of air as you speed forwards.

When you have experienced everything you wish and you feel the time is right, allow things to slow down and you will be taken smoothly back to where you started at the edge of the rink. Here you may pause and remove your boots, leaving them where they are for a future time. When you are ready, allow yourself to arise from your meditation, knowing that you can return to this exercise at any time.

Learning to understand yourself

Understanding yourself is all part of the spiritual journey and by understanding ourselves we become free to choose our direction unencumbered by doubt or negativities. The ability to relax and go with the flow is available to the extent we are able to trust our inner feelings and vice versa. Without this insight our ability to let events take care of themselves or to be flexible is dependent on blind faith and trusting that things will work out for us in the end. Many of us do not have the level of faith that allows us to trust the future to this extent nor believe that it will ultimately work out for us. Therefore it is essential we develop the insight to understand how our motivations can affect our lives and our own role in the seemingly independent situations around us. Life can progress beautifully without our controlling or fighting for our vision of the future. Therefore if we know who we are and have an open mind, we can recognise what is right for us and let it into our lives.

Understanding yourself means finding your motivations and your needs for fulfilment, not on some superficial level but from deep within. The meditations in this book will help you to achieve this as you tread the spiritual pathway to an enlightenment that gradually opens you up to life and to yourself.

This greater self-knowledge is the stepping-stone to happiness. By looking at yourself and your life situation free from negativities and bias you will find this inner understanding. From this vantage-point, you will then be able to see what it is you want to get out of your life and what it is that truly fulfils you.

To understand yourself, you must first discover where you are at this moment in time and how you identify with yourself, finding what your thoughts, feelings and opinions of life and your role within it truly signify. In other words, the first step is to develop a level of insight.

This insight comes from looking into your life with your clear vision and your clear vision develops by learning to understand your own mind and the language of your mind. Once you have learned this language, you can interpret your own feelings and where they originate, so that you can live with far more consciousness, understanding what is the most beneficial path for you to tread.

Many of us will have tried to make sense of life's purpose and to increase our self-understanding, but knowledge is a pathway that cannot be forced. Even if we try our hardest, it can still feel like we are lost. The first and very important step on this spiritual journey is to learn to let go and relax, so that you can begin to go with the flow. Likewise, going with the flow brings the positive state-of-mind that allows you to achieve this sense of relaxation and therefore the space to realise the possibilities that are open to you. From there, you can develop your understanding and rid yourself of negativities and insecurities. These attributes naturally build with your clear vision, because it is your clear vision that shows you how false all your self-doubts are and teaches you how to see through your negativities and live in a way that rids you of their burden. There is a greater spaciousness and an openness that comes from understanding how wide life can truly be and the choices you have within it and this understanding naturally helps us to work with a long-term view.

When you achieve this level of understanding of yourself; when you can see into your thoughts, wants, needs and desires, you have a starting point from which to move forward and live life to the full, knowing that any obstacles are a teaching and every success you fully deserve.

Wherever any of us are on the pathway, the more we go with the flow, the more we are able to act in accordance with our true inner self. This means that the more we let go, the more complete we can feel and the greater our self-understanding. As you move onto a path that is at one with all of life, you can gain a far greater sense of solidity and a oneness, both within yourself and your spirituality. Alongside this, you will become increasingly aware of your limitations and how far you are able to go in any area of your life before your shortcomings manifest themselves. This in turn allows you to look more positively at challenges and understand that there is the potential for development and reward as well as failure within everything you do, but that neither is the be-all and end-all of life, because life will continue.

Each of us has the capacity to develop into someone who trusts their feelings and uses their instincts to steer them around the obstacles of life, knowing that whatever it inflicts upon us, the outcome will be growth. By accepting situations for what they are, there is a greater ability to relax. Sometimes merely taking this approach of accepting what life is presenting to us will provide the answer, then the challenge we perceive is taken away from our pathway. Because we are being flexible, more options become apparent.

Stability is a product of understanding life, living it to the full, helping and aiding others and giving your best to everything you do. By forgiving ourselves for our own mistakes and forgiving others for theirs, we can learn to see beyond the obvious and understand that everyone is making a journey through life. In this way, we can see everyone as equal and accept people for who they are. Understanding shows us the responsibility we have for our own emotions and that we can gain even greater stability through realising the positive role we can then play in working with life.

Steering our pathway using our clear vision is all about making choices that are right for you and for those around you. This is because being a spiritual person isn't about 'me', 'I' or the ego – it is more about 'us' and 'our' and 'all.' Learning to understand the bigger spiritual picture helps us understand life and how we fit within it so that we live with respect and have the faith to go with the flow, no matter what life's challenges. Put simply, it is looking to both the bad and the good and deciding what you should do based on what is good.

Chapter Seven - Developing Clear Vision and Becoming One with All

Each of us is here on this Earth to develop and an essential part of this journey is learning to understand ourselves and each other. The more we understand, the more we can identify the good traits within each and every one of us and understand our own and others failings. Working to develop ourselves in this way will naturally increase our happiness, because understanding and forgiveness help us overcome frustrations and disappointments. This type of spiritual development is made easier if we are able to develop the natural intuitive talents we each possess. Every one of us is born into this world with a 'box' of such gifts that we can learn to access. We call this box of gifts our spiritual lunch-box, full of abilities that can sustain and nurture us. Within this box are our feelings and emotions (to guide us) our clear vision (to show us how things are) and our healing abilities (to enable us to heal emotionally and physically). Because we have these gifts, our potential for development is without limits.

In the same way that we are born into the world with physical bodies that enable us to function, moving and creating as we wish, our spiritual lunch-box enables us to access modes of thought that gives us a totally refreshed view of life. While some of us open and use the gifts within this box and others do not, we are all able to access them if we choose to and this offers up possibilities far beyond those which our five senses alone can comprehend.

Clear vision is a way of looking at things by directly tuning our mind into either our own selves or those around us. What we then see is far more accurate and clear than if we attempted to reason our way through situations, consulted with friends or used what we refer to as our 'common sense'. All of these other routes may help, but they do not access the unadulterated perspective that our clear vision can bring. The passport to developing our clear vision is an open mind.

An essential part of developing our clear vision is to learn to access and trust our feelings, to tune into our inner voice and tune into our conscience. If we are able to do this, then we become open to so many more possibilities than we currently possess. Instead of being bounded in by our preconceptions, opinions and perhaps our negative emotions, we are able to tune into everything around us. This growing ability to tune-in helps us to become more completely at one with the whole of life. We are opening our senses, our feelings and our minds to the bigger picture and we are using our clear vision to allow us to walk the right pathway. Becoming 'one with all' in this way enables us to steer our lives according to what is right for us.

So how do we achieve this? How do we enable ourselves to differentiate and make choices that take us in the right direction? The first step is to meditate; the bigger picture opens to us through meditation. From this relaxed state-of-mind we can then tune into higher energies by using meditations that allow us to merge with them. Familiarising ourselves through practice, we gain an increasing experience of becoming at one with what we encounter in those meditations, immersing ourselves in the experience. Typically we use exercises that tune us into nature and enable us to encounter spirit world, so that we become familiar with the feeling of these energies.

Eventually, when we have developed this ability to immerse ourselves totally in a meditation, we can say that we are at one with all, because our sense of self disappears and our consciousness is absorbed in the object of our meditation. Having this ability means we aren't so wrapped up in our own thoughts and opinions and allows us to gain a far wider perspective than the one we currently hold. It is like moving from a situation where previously we could only look straight ahead, to one where our blinkers are removed and, for the first time in our lives, we are able to look forward to the future and see what it can hold for us. The shift in mental attitude that we may gain from using techniques in this book helps us gain a fresh perspective and we are better able to understand what path we are treading and what kind of an environment we are in, be it negative or positive.

The exercises in this book can show us how to sense and feel potential obstacles on our pathway and help us to find whether it is the right one for us. With this clarity of vision, we can develop our understanding and a spiritual perspective that helps us to move forward with a feeling of unrestrained personal liberty. As we increase our ability to become one with all, we are freer to see the wider picture around us.

As we progress we will develop our own abilities, find ourselves able to listen to our inner voice and use our clear vision to identify any obstacles on our pathway. We can then recognise a purpose in what is happening around us and we will develop a sense of balance and understanding, so that no longer are we moved or guided by negative emotions. Instead, we can see if we are going to fit in with any given situation, for instance how we fit in at work or what a new relationship might hold for us. As we build our experience of meditation and especially clear vision, we will also become aware that we are never spiritually alone, because there is a level of communication other than the physical that is accessed by our clear vision and this opens the potential to communicate with the spirit world where countless opportunities for support, help and camaraderie are available to us.

For many of us, how we perceive life is dictated by how we are reacting, how we might feel at a given moment. If, instead, we look at situations and try to understand how they help us on our pathway of understanding and spiritual development, our perspective widens naturally and we have more options as to what view we take. So, spirituality is a journey of awakening to who we really are. It is a journey from confusion to meaning; from fear to faith. It is not feeling alone in a hostile world and it is being at one with everyone and everything. To become one with all in this way we wake up to the bigger picture, we gain perspective, discover that the situations we find ourselves in are teaching us important lessons and understand whether where we are going in life is right for us.

Meditation - Connection to life and energies

Purpose of the meditation
This meditation teaches us to use what is commonly called our 'second sight' or our 'third eye' to tune in with our mind-energy to other energies and spiritual dimensions. This can help us to understand that outside energies are available to help each and every one of us.

This meditation simply stretches our minds to make them more flexible, training ourselves to relate to things without depending on the physical senses. We are not reaching for any particular spiritual destination or goal. Instead, we are just learning to accept what we experience within the meditation and relax without questioning or analysing what we find.

What we experience in the meditation will present itself in our mind as if we were using our senses. With training, the experiences gained can become as vivid as those we have in the 'real' world and we will see, smell, touch, hear and taste. However, all these experiences will be had through our mind alone. We then begin to learn the difference between input from outside and what we feel within. This helps us become more flexible and to learn to separate outside situations from our inner reactions. This, in turn, helps us to recognise our own feelings, the role they play and also to clear away our negativities. With time, we will have created for ourselves a clearer vision that will aid us in every situation we encounter in life.

This meditation also allows us to recognise an opening to an area of life that may be entirely new to our understanding. It is a training and in the same way that an athlete limbers up and breathes to prepare their muscles, this meditation is preparing our minds to accept input from beyond the physical world.

We may not yet know what it is like to merge our mind with an energy other than our own. When we merge with Spiritual Energy we will find ourselves at peace and feel totally free of our physical body and thoughts and emotions that might cloud our perceptions.

This meditation takes us wider than just the input of our own senses and our everyday experience, connecting us beyond the natural physical energies that surround us and going wider to the Spiritual Energy of the universe. This serves as a preparation to develop a spiritual perspective on life and increases our flexibility to accept and learn from what is around us.

Preparation
Put yourself in a place where you feel at ease. Sitting comfortably or lying down, put on some relaxing music. Take some nice deep breaths and close your eyes. Move your mind-energy to the backs of your eyelids and, keeping your eyelids closed, look through them into the darkness beyond. Letting your shoulders relax, listen to the music and breathe peacefully. Let go of your Earthly vision and any distracting sounds around you. Focus your attention outward into the darkness and allow your mind to clear of all thoughts and worries.

Meditation
Allow your thoughts to travel to your feet and imagine you are sitting on a park bench in a large park on an open flat area of grass. Use your clear vision and visualise the elements of nature all around you, a vibrant landscape of trees, grass, water, plants and all manner of animals.

Place your hand on the grass and feel your connection with the Earth. What is the grass like? Is it short or long? Can you see how green it is? Look at everything around you, can you see the myriad colours in your mind's eye? How deeply are you experiencing each? Do not worry if it does not come immediately; go with the feel of it. The most important thing is to relax and enjoy relating to everything around you.

Be aware of the firmness of the seat beneath you, the sensation of the air on your face. Feel the cool smoothness of the grass. Allow the sensations to come through. Can you hear bird-song and noises around you? Look for the smaller animals, squirrels, dogs and birds. Focus on a plant or the silhouette of a tree against the sky.

Can you feel the freshness of all the living plants? Be aware of the expansiveness of the sky above you and the solidity of the Earth. Feel the smooth wood of the bench. Feel your feet on the solid ground beneath you. Take time to look in every direction, learning and absorbing; stretching your mind and your abilities. Relax in this natural scene and allow yourself to observe the moving play of life.

Then, when you are ready, gradually bring your awareness back into your body and allow yourself to arise from the meditation in your own time.

Comment

The simplest of all spiritual practices are often the most profound. This meditation, practiced correctly, allows us to open up to everything around us, so that we can take notice of that which we are experiencing and may currently take for granted. Therefore, we can recognise that life is not solely about what we are perceiving or what is in it, but how we choose to perceive it. The meditation also prepares us to use our mind-energy to look deeper and to become conscious of the different levels of energy around us. With a heightened awareness, we can become conscious not only of the different aspects of nature but also of the energies present in our fellow humanity. It prepares us to sense the feelings of others as well as identifying with the differing sensations we feel in people's lives and personalities. Therefore, we can recognise atmospheres and changes within what is happening around us, so that we have a firm grounding in sensing with our clear vision. This simple practice can provide us with much of what we need to develop our clear vision.

Meditation - Becoming One with All

Purpose of the meditation
The purpose of this exercise is to allow us to open our minds and then to identify and merge with the universal energy.

The goal is to become intimate with this energy, to be absorbed within it and to feel it intuitively so that we trust and allow it to guide and lead us in the best way. The meditation lets us experience opening and joining with everything, with all of creation, so that we develop positive familiarity until it becomes a natural process. We can then use the intuitive grasp we develop within the meditation to bring this feeling into our life. Guided by this feeling and being in tune with this energy helps us to go with the natural flow.

This meditation provides us with a way of practicing so that we can access a clearer view of life. Learning to see in a way that is independent of our familiar thought-patterns allows us to be free of our usual mental distractions so that we can gain a different perspective on the best way forward. This meditation familiarises us with letting go and relaxing while connecting with the energies around us, literally going with the flow. If we perceive life in this way, free of mental clutter, we are better able to recognise and progress along the journey we were born to.

Preparation

Put yourself in a place where you feel at ease. Sitting comfortably, or lying down, put on some relaxing music. Take some nice deep breaths and close your eyes. Move your mind-energy to the backs of your eyelids and keeping your eyelids closed, look through them into the darkness beyond. Letting your shoulders relax, listen to the music and breathe peacefully. Let go of your Earthly vision and any distracting sounds around you. Focus your attention outward into the darkness and allow your mind to clear of all thoughts and worries.

Meditation

Send your attention down your body, from the lungs, through your stomach, all the way to the soles of your feet and feel them on the solid ground. Now, in your mind's eye visualise your feet on springy green grass at the edge of a lakeside.

Looking down, you see a small open boat in the water. It has no oars and is full of soft, comfortable, satin cushions of many colours; emerald green, deep pink, purple, orange, blue and yellow. Allow yourself to go down to the boat and get in, stepping from the shore onto the boat's deck. Once you are in the boat, find the rope that is holding it to the shore and untie it. Then find yourself a comfortable place amongst the cushions, lay yourself down so that you are relaxed and look up to the sky, feeling the movement of the boat as it gently drifts away from the river-bank with the current, moving further and further from the bank. Trees growing out from the river-bank frame the sky and you notice the silence as you drift gently further into the lake, watching the clouds pass by as you travel to the lake's centre. Trail your hand over the side of the boat and let your fingertips feel the water. It is cool and silky, caressing them like velvet on the skin. Feel the energy that surrounds you emanating from the sky and the trees that hang over the banks of the lake. Look into the cool deep shadows cast by the trees on the water.

You feel a desire to stand up in the boat. Raising yourself to your feet, stand and lift your arms, stretching them out above your head, so that your body and arms make the shape of a capital 'Y', your face turned to the heavens, becoming one with everything around you. Connect and become one with the water, the trees and the open sky. Open every fibre of your being, so that you are absorbed within the scene. Be alive to the energy of the universe and allow it to permeate, filling you from within.

When you feel the time is right, lie down again and continue your journey. Allow the boat once more to glide on the lake with the current, allowing it to take you where it will.

Eventually you return to the grassy bank. Standing, you step up from the boat and onto dry land once more. You turn to find a large tree and walk towards it. The tree is leafy and green and you sit at its base, with its trunk behind you. Leaning back so that you are supported by it, you look up through the canopy. There you stay, completely connected and at one with all. Allow your mind to merge with the entire scene, feeling the river and the river-bank, the tree and its solidity at your back. Allow yourself to totally rest in this feeling. Then, when you are ready, and in your own time, arise from your meditation, knowing that you can return to this place whenever you wish.

Chapter Eight - Mediumship

To understand clear vision and spirituality fully, it is necessary to understand mediumship, what it is, how it functions and its purpose in connecting us with the world of spirit. In this book we will not be looking to develop mediumship, merely to understand how and why it exists. Therefore, this chapter is dedicated to providing the reader with an overview, so that there is an understanding of this next stage of clear vision. This chapter is also intended to help you understand the difference between your clear vision and mediumship and to explain how it works from a spiritual perspective.

There is much debate as to the nature of what survives this life; many would have it that we exist here in a physical form and that is the only dimension to us, our humanity contained within our physical being and ceasing on the death of this physical body. Yet there are those who believe that by developing the ability that is commonly referred to as mediumship, we can connect with an element of a once living person that can communicate their personality, knowledge, likes and dislikes, as well as information that only they could be privy to.

Mediumship can provide us with what many recognise to be details of a departed loved one's life and elements within it, as well as seemingly insignificant information such as personal mannerisms and even ways of thinking. In this book we are not going into an in-depth discussion on mediumship or how to develop it, nor are we categorically stating what it is that survives physical death. The authors have their own perceptions and beliefs, based on personal experience and we ask you as the reader to form your own opinions.

Messages from loved-ones can be especially comforting to the bereaved when there is a sudden or unforeseen parting, where there is unfinished business, or messages of love to give and receive. Once they have had the opportunity to communicate, invariably it helps the bereaved to move on with their own journey, perhaps with a wider understanding of the process of life and death.

The purpose of mediumship is to provide proof of the endurance of the human spirit; that within us that survives physical death, both for those who have a belief in the after-life and for those who don't. For those who choose to believe the evidence, mediumship provides the proof and bestows the knowledge that there is a life for us beyond the physical. Along with this if we choose to investigate it, we can see that there is more to us as human beings than we may suspect; each and every one of us can be so much more than we are.

Distinct from mediumship, clear vision is the gift that allows us to develop and use our own skills to read the pathway, situations and journey of life, either for ourselves or for other people. To do this, we work with our own energy and the energy of the person for whom we are reading. In this respect, clear vision does not depend on outside influences, nor help from any other source, to achieve its purpose.

Once we have a level of clear vision, mediumship is the next natural step along the pathway. As we know, it is the ability or skill to connect with those who have passed over and then convey messages from them to the living. When we connect with the soul of someone who has passed over, we are acting as the mediator between Heaven and Earth, connecting someone in spirit world with those who remain. This is what a medium does, acting as the middle man (or woman!) for messages to be delivered. In this way, we can find and identify evidence that some part of us survives physical death. The part of us that survives is the soul, the profound depth of our being and it contains information from our entire life here on Earth, as well as our life in the spirit world.

It is important to understand that different definitions of the word 'spirit' are given and understood by many people involved in clairvoyance, mediumship and spirituality. Nevertheless, for the purpose of this book we understand the spirit to be the energy that animates us here in this life, as it is the spirit that feeds the soul and therefore makes human life possible. The soul is the ultimate depth of our being, while our spirit is the energy that joins our spiritual life force and our body together in any one lifetime. It is the link between the two that enables both soul and body to survive on the physical plane. Therefore, in this book we do not talk about 'spirits' or someone's 'spirit' in the sense that it is the spirit that survives death. Rather we look upon it that the <u>soul</u> is the continuing element of us beyond physical death and it is the soul that we communicate with through mediumship. The spirit is the essential energy that joins body and soul together and at the time of death that energy has passed. When we refer to spirit world we are using the term that is most readily understood, yet in reality spirit world is the spiritual plane where our <u>soul</u> survives.

In the same way that our bodies are sustained by food, so the food that sustains the soul is spiritual energy. The spirit that we bring into our life here on Earth is the energy that sustains both body and soul and to nurture this energy we can meditate, pray and develop concern for those around us, strengthening the spiritual side of our nature.

Mediumship is at this moment very prominent in the press and media. There are numerous Mediums who have become well-known for their readings, even to the extent of having their own television shows, books and websites.

With this media attention and heightened public awareness, there is a place for the accomplished medium in the public eye and yet with this fame comes pressure to deliver consistently good messages and perhaps spectacle to go alongside their work with spirit world. While some Mediums are entirely genuine, still others will feel pressure to deliver the volume and quality of messages that regular television and media coverage can demand. Mediums are human too and may want to achieve fame and fortune. This means that along with those who are genuine and spiritually motivated, as in all areas of life, we may find those who seek to deceive, or inflate their shows, so that they include showmanship that is entirely unnecessary in conveying a message from a loved one in spirit world.

Inevitably, the mediums who exaggerate or even seek to dupe the public are generally caught out, while those who are genuine continue to do the best that their abilities allow them. It is important to say that there are both mediums who may provide great comfort by providing information the bereaved can identify with and people who call themselves mediums who seek to play on a person's vulnerabilities for financial gain. For so often when a bad apple is identified, the public reaction is to assume that all Mediums are motivated by greed, when nothing could be further from the truth. For every medium who has achieved national recognition, there are hundreds of naturally talented Mediums who have never achieved or perhaps sought the wider public eye, many of whom perform their services on a one-to-one basis or in theatres and halls throughout the world and faithfully serve spirit world to deliver messages to those who have lost loved-ones or are seeking proof that life continues after physical death.

It is important to understand the nature of a Mediums work. Even the best Mediums are simply a channel for communication and while they usually spend years, if not a lifetime, developing their ability to interpret and access spirit world, they have no control over what information is initially available to them. Some connections with deceased loved-ones will be strong and easy to grasp for the medium, while others will be vague and therefore the reading may seem unclear with limited depth. The point of mentioning this is so that you can recognise that the same difficulties that exist for Mediums can happen with your clear vision when you are reading for someone who is still alive.

Another criticism Mediums receive is that their messages are vague, repetitive or too general. This will be because the information coming through is limited or difficult to decipher; not every soul communicates well! The same can happen when we are using our clear vision. When this happens, there can be a temptation to read more into the information you receive from your clear vision than is actually there. The rule is to only speak what you find and nothing more.

To understand why these gaps occur in mediumship we need to appreciate how and why messages come through in the way that they do. To understand the process, we need to recognise that it is as difficult for those who have passed over to contact us, as it is for us to contact them.

A medium giving a reading will be seeking to tune in and establish communication with the soul of a person who has passed over and a medium, when delivering messages in front of an audience or even one-to-one, will seek to connect with the energy or soul of a relative or friend, someone that is known to the recipient. While a medium could connect with any random soul, there would be no recognition and no knowledge of whether the information given were correct or not, so a medium will seek to find someone linked with a member of the audience or for whom they are connecting for, so that the information will be relevant and recognised. Invariably, the information we receive from the other side will be from someone with whom we had a strong link, or someone we can relate to, or who cares for us. Should we be open to receiving this information, it can for some serve as proof that there is a greater existence outside that of the human form and even put them on the path to a more spiritual view of life.

Mediumistic communication is received through the mind and it is extremely rare to actually hear a spirit with our physical ears because of the huge amount of energy required to make noise from thin air. This mind communication is a two way process with both the medium and the soul on the other side seeking to connect their energy through thought. Typically this thought will be received by the medium as images, impressions and feelings and perhaps even words, phrases and sounds that were familiar to the person who has passed over during their lifetime. Importantly, the medium can recognise only things that they personally are familiar with. So, for instance, if a medium is shown architectural drawings as evidence that someone who has passed over was an architect, the medium may not recognise them as such, they will just see a drawing of a building. It is then up to the medium to interpret the feeling that comes with this reference. Likewise, if a particular ailment was experienced by someone who passed over, the medium may experience the feeling of that ailment or see the part of the body that it affected. There are numerous pitfalls, problems and difficulties encountered in trying to interpret these feelings thoughts and energies. They are, after all, merely impressions in the mind. The medium might see the architectural drawing for instance and have the feeling of drawing and conclude that the person who passed over was an artist. If all we hear is that information, we may wrongly conclude it is of no value. That is why it is so beneficial to understand the process and how it works.

If we look at someone who has passed over, they will only have the attributes on the other side that they had in this life. So, for instance, if we take the example of someone who had very little emotional awareness in their physical life or was not a great communicator, perhaps finding it difficult to express themselves, when they pass over, we cannot expect them necessarily to become a great source of information for the medium. Communication in this instance may be very limited and restricted to references as to what that person did for a living and perhaps a feeling for what their personality was like in this life. That is why we may see a medium referring to personality traits, such as stubbornness, a lively outgoing personality, or someone who kept themselves to themselves. Someone who was giving in life, with a generous, open and loving heart and who had a great ability to communicate would be a much easier subject for the medium to receive and recognise. Here the medium is likely to have a stronger link and a greater wealth of information.

Likewise, those who had strong minds and will in their physical life would have a better chance of communicating with a medium when they pass over than a weaker minded person.

Whilst the information conveyed in a sitting is only as good as both the medium and those who have passed over can convey, similarly, a lot depends on the person who is there to receive information from the medium. There are those who wish to believe and those who do not. In either case, the person who is receiving the information is best advised to keep, at the very least, an open mind.

Many go to a medium seeking information from one particular relative, friend or lover who has passed over, perhaps because they were very dear to them or they wish to be reassured by a message from that person. However, a medium is not in control of who comes through to communicate with us. Therefore it may not be the particular person we want to hear from who comes through in any given reading. This is the same with clear vision; what we want, expect or even feel we will receive for a person may not be what we find through our clear vision.

Likewise, if we are addressed by a medium, we should be open to the type of information that comes through. We should remember that a person who has passed over is now made of energy and has no physical form. Theirs is now an entirely different existence to the one they have most recently known. This person now has information from the whole of their life to choose from but they are in an unfamiliar form and situation, in soul form with a memory link to their life here. To achieve communication they will need to identify and convey that which is relevant to the person who has come to see the medium. We may be seeking a particular message or reference as proof that there is a genuine connection. Some may have agreed a key word or pet name that will prove life after death. Yet, what is memorable to the departed may not be at all memorable to us. They may convey what are distant memories or perhaps what we feel are trivia or irrelevant and therefore in a reading we may receive information that we see as being inconsequential. To those on the other side it is not.

Those who have passed over can also communicate events they have witnessed since their physical bodies died and receiving information of this type, that no one else has witnessed, can act as proof that they are still interacting and part of our lives.

To understand what it is like to communicate from spirit world, imagine that it is you who has passed over. Visualise what it is like to communicate when you have no body, no voice, no touch and no ability to speak and make yourself physically heard. How would you make yourself known and understood by someone who is close to you? How would you achieve this when the only avenue open to you is to convey thoughts, images, emotions and words through your mind-energy? To do this you would need to focus your mind and convey those mental images, ideas, associations and feelings, not only so that you were transmitting clearly, but also so that they were recognisable to the person you were trying to reach.

Therefore to form a link with their loved one, someone who has passed over needs a way of transmitting and being understood and will communicate through the path of least resistance. The best type of person to for them to contact therefore is someone who has trained as a medium.

However, not everyone will visit a medium after a passing. In the absence of a medium, a departed loved-one can effectively communicate with us, only when our minds are quiet and receptive. Typically, this may be when we are relaxed, asleep and in a dream state, when we are meditating, distracted or half awake.

For this reason, we are at our most receptive when we are in environments that put us in a relaxed state. Listening to music, gardening, walking in a natural environment such as woodland, by the sea, or relaxing in the bath or shower; in these situations we can flow into a similar frame of mind to that of a working medium. There is a 'gap,' a pause in our thinking that allows outside information to come in. The only difference between us and a medium is that a medium will be deliberately entering this state and know how and where to direct their mind so that they are consciously seeking a connection and have experience in recognising and interpreting the information they receive.

When someone with no tuition or experience is contacted by a departed loved one, they may just have impressions or the awareness of their presence but because they have not learnt to distinguish between their own thoughts and information that comes from 'outside', they may therefore remain unsure or uncertain of the encounter. Many of us may have had this type of experience and we either brush it off as just a flight of fancy, or perhaps we carry on with our lives and put the experience down to something 'unexplained.' A third option is that we look further into this exciting field.

Losing a loved one is perhaps one of the most emotionally painful things that can happen in our lives. Whenever we lose someone, it can cause us to question how it can be right for such a thing to happen and to question 'why?' The primary purpose of mediumship is to provide the living with reassurance of the survival of their loved-ones. Seeing that there is the possibility of a far wider existence is a key to faith in spirituality. If we are therefore open to spiritual thought, we can begin to appreciate that there is a continuity of life beyond the physical and beyond death. This is in itself an affirmation of faith and an opening into developing our lives along spiritual lines, not because we are told to, or feel we should, but because we 'know'. Once we know for ourselves that there is more to life, we can grow, blossoming into a spiritually aware person and if we choose to take this awareness deeply into our lives, we can realise our widest potential.

To truly 'know' what this is like we need to develop ourselves and our own skills to be able to tune into these energies. As soon as we have achieved the first step of having some clearer vision, then we will know that there are possibilities far beyond what we currently understand and if we wish, we can investigate mediumship for ourselves. If we decide to take our interest further, it is advisable to seek out a recognised and recommended tutor to assist us in developing in this area and it is not recommended for anyone to develop mediumship without the supervision of such a guide.

Chapter Nine - Healing

As we develop on a spiritual pathway, inevitably we will learn more about ourselves. As life becomes clearer, so we can recognise our automatic ways of reacting and responding, perhaps questioning what our role in life is and who we really are. If we have internal barriers, as many of us do, then we must learn to overcome them so that they do not restrict us and we are able to move on. Clearer insight allows us to recognise our past hurts and current fears and once this inner landscape is revealed, we can let go of our blockages and truly heal. Overcoming our own problems helps us to understand those who find themselves in similar situations and therefore healing from within is essential if we are to help others.

It is up to each of us to decide what place healing has in our lives. We can choose to accept what emotional healing comes our way as a result of our spiritual growth, or we can seek to develop healing gifts for ourselves. Regardless of what pathway we tread, there are many ways of attracting healing, taking energies and channelling them to heal ourselves and others too.

Spiritual healing enables us to channel energy either into ourselves or others while prayer enables us to ask for healing for whoever we feel is in need. However we choose to connect, we can observe the healing influence that our journey on the spiritual pathway can have on ourselves and even those around us. Healing can come in the form of emotional, spiritual and physical improvements; feeling better about ourselves and better able to cope with life. These improvements can have a direct effect on the lives of others we come into contact with, improving our relationships with them and perhaps helping emotionally and spiritually too. If we are sending someone spiritual healing, then this, in turn, may help, even if it is just to make that person feel better, in the knowledge that someone cares enough to make the effort.

As we progress on the pathway of clear vision we can develop the ability to recognise energy and feel its presence. By meditating we are mentally working with positive energies and allowing them into our lives. Because we are already becoming familiar with recognising and exploring energies with our minds, we have an excellent starting point from which to develop the ability to heal spiritually. From this foundation, it is easier to learn how to access healing energy and channel it so that it can then aid and enhance us physically, spiritually and emotionally. There are numerous methods and names for the ways in which we can work with spiritual energy. 'Channelling', 'hands on healing', 'faith healing', 'distant healing', 'angel healing' and 'universal energy healing'.

Even though the methods and energies we are working with may differ, all of these are methods of healing with assistance from the spiritual universe. In this chapter we are going to look at healing, its place within our journey and how to develop the ability to heal ourselves and others.

Spiritual Healing
Universal energy emanates from God like an aura that encompasses the entire spiritual universe and there are numerous ways in which we can draw on that aura of energy. Like the yolk of an egg, our physical bodies sit within the nutritional egg white of the universal energy, which feeds and nurtures us. The egg shell is the entire universe of spirituality which has no beginning or end and is almost too vast for our minds to comprehend. So it is entirely natural for us to access this spiritual energy and use it to sustain our spiritual growth. God is like the power station and by putting our minds to Him through simple exercises we can learn to tap directly into this energy in its purest form. From this energy comes healing. Alternatively we can join our minds with angels or

healing guides, who act as intermediaries out of their love and compassion for us.

The benefit of using angels or healing guides is that they are already connected to God's energy and by merely tuning into them, you will be able to receive and pass on healing to others. To tune into the guides and angels, we need to be able to find and recognise them in our minds and submit our will and allow them to do their work. If we choose, instead, to tap into God's universal energy directly, we become the conduit to healing energy ourselves.

Regardless of what method we use, universal energy can rejuvenate and balance the emotional and the physical within us. By achieving a greater balance and spiritual harmony within our lives, we can create space for our spiritual development and encourage our own growth. Regardless of what our lives are like physically, we have the ability to create space so that we can develop and strengthen ourselves. Our emotions and spirituality are as essential to us as the physical elements of our body, such as the bones, muscles and organs. So, however we use healing, it has the potential to help every aspect of our lives.

When we are not physically manifesting here on Earth, we exist in spirit world in our soul energy forms. There we are able to access universal energy freely because we are part of it and obviously there is no need to heal the physical because it does not exist. To access healing here in our physical forms we must direct our attention towards the source of healing, tuning-in with our mind so that it is then available to us. If we learn to do this then we gain the ability to focus this positive energy with our intention, directing it wherever it is needed and in this way healing can be sent to individuals or groups of people and even situations.

Healing the emotions

Everything we do in life is an expression of our will, our conditioning, or our emotions, but despite them influencing what we do, very few of us have our emotions in perfect balance. Commonly, we block them and carry on regardless of how we are feeling or we are too influenced by them and we act out the extremes, so that life feels like an emotional rollercoaster. If we are used to blocking our emotions and find ourselves feeling upset, dispirited or depressed, we will not be able to see why. Locked up in our feelings in this way we can become overwhelmed. Whatever way we deal with our emotions, rarely do we allow them to guide and inform us as they should.

There are numerous reasons why we become emotionally blocked. It may be we are not achieving anything with our lives and we cannot stand the truth as it brings with it too much pain for us to bear. Alternatively, our upbringing or events in our life may have led us to ignore our emotions. Whatever the reason, if this is the case, our emotions won't be doing their job of informing us and guiding our actions, because we are blocking them from affecting us.

Without emotional guidance and clarity, we may find we have chosen a life that isn't right for us or sacrificed our inner needs for an outer goal. Instead of listening to and working with our feelings, we have gone in the opposite direction and ignored our intuition.

It isn't unusual for people to do this. Perhaps we needed to get our life going, or for whatever reasons we felt we had to act against our feelings. Yet, if we have chosen this route we can become blocked, because we can become trapped in a negative feeling and lost to our own emotions. If we have lost our inner guidance, we may instead try and 'think' our way out of this feeling, but without emotional clarity, the direction we take may not be the right one for us.

It is only possible to fully know which feelings you should trust when you know yourself and recognise that you do not need someone else to bolster your weaknesses and you are strong enough to separate your desires from your intuition. A common example of how difficult this can be is when we have intense feelings for someone, typically at the beginning of a relationship when we are unable to separate our intense desire from our inner truth. Overcome by strong feelings, we can end up with a partner that is wrong for us. We may fall madly in love with someone who fills our areas of weakness, or brings us the kind of stimulation that is hard to abandon, despite knowing on some level that this person is incompatible with our needs.

Unless you are truly in harmony and happy with yourself, then you cannot know what is totally right for you and to achieve a state of greater equilibrium you will have to live with trial and error, sampling life until you have hopefully learned enough to put you on a path that gives you what you need.

Therefore to achieve happiness, each of us has a need to recognise our emotions and how we deal with them. We need to understand whether we are suppressing and subordinating our inner needs to meet our desires, or whether we are being too closely affected by our emotions and the way they are making us feel, so that we over-react to life. Happily, this isn't an intellectual exercise, it is something we can learn to feel from within and once we have learned to sense and feel what is right for us, we need only do it once

To better understand this, we can take the example of a person who, despite having no obvious or major problems, feels little joy in their existence. Looking for happiness, they spend their time thinking about things they don't have; an attractive partner, a better car or a life of luxury and ease. If we are constantly wanting more and feel life is lacking, living the kind of existence where we are dissatisfied and yearning creates a negative environment. If someone is living like this, perhaps hoping for something such as a lottery win or someone to come into their life and make them happy, their mental energy is pointed in the wrong direction. Where we find ourselves dwelling on our material desires in this way, perhaps yearning for a life we do not have, it can seem like happiness is forever out of our reach.

Someone trapped in this cycle of discontent may not see what is right in front of their nose and instead focuses on what they think is missing. But what is missing is not outside, it is within. Their attitude creates a vicious circle, because through discontent we empty ourselves of hope and without hope we are lost and alone. If we are in this situation we may not recognise that we can change the way we think and flourish through self-realisation.

Ironically, if we are looking for happiness from material things, when we do get a better car or a more attractive partner, it makes us temporarily feel better, but soon we will want just a little bit more and our dissatisfaction will begin to grow again. If we are not enjoying living purely for the act of living itself then like a rolling stone we will continually need new pastures and new stimulation, for if we stood still we would only have our feelings of need to keep us company.

If we are like this, always wanting more, we can become a negative person and if we remain in this state for too long we can fall into a downward spiral. Without their fantasies fulfilled, many in this situation can lapse into depression and may not have the skills or knowledge to get themselves out of it.

Naturally, we need a level of comfort within our lives, otherwise meeting the needs of our day-to-day survival would rule us and override any other consideration. Yet much of society focuses on the material to the exclusion of all else, so that it is in danger of becoming our overriding preoccupation. Learning what we need and what we can live happily without is part of life's journey, yet at any point on our journey, if what we own becomes the most important thing in our lives, then in reality we are losing out. We owe it to ourselves to focus on our spiritual needs, taking the time to learn, to understand and like who we are, so that we can believe in ourselves and love what we are, faults and all. Balancing the needs of our spiritual nature with the material side is key if we are to be fulfilled. If we have a good relationship with ourselves, we will have fewer gaps to fill within and won't stray into excessive consumption in an attempt to make ourselves feel better.

If we know and like ourselves and are comfortable with who we are, free from insecurities and fears, then our inner happiness is not dependant on gaining material reward. If we have a rich inner life then we do not need more money than we can spend. If we love ourselves, then we are not dependent on relationships to feel good about who we are. If we are friends with who we are and have warm feelings for others then we don't need friendships as a crutch or salvation. We become truly strong, able to state with conviction what is right for us and identify that which is wrong. Conversely, if we have conflict within, what happiness we own may be short-lived or superficial because we lack the inner authority to guide ourselves on our pathway. A person who is in a good state materially may still have a negative outlook and insecurities. Yet being rich doesn't mean we are miserable, rather it is what aspect of life we focus on that determines whether we can maintain our inner equilibrium. Happiness cannot be bought, but inner peace can be earned through effort.

That is not to say that if bereavement or loss has affected us and made us feel we are a negative person and should feel guilty, we all feel sad from time to time and often with good reason. Yet, if we have a positive outlook and are working towards a goal, we will receive feelings of achievement in the work we do because we recognise that everything we experience and everything we do can serve as fuel for our development.

If, at the other extreme, we are negative in our outlook, then we will neither have a sense of value in ourselves nor our achievements. If we have a positive outlook, we become much more able to determine what we want from our lives and what we are gaining from them. We are able to distinguish between negative and positive thoughts. If we are working hard and we are positive, we can recognise the benefits of our labour.

By learning from the past, with a spiritual understanding of who we are, we can overcome our lingering fears and negativities. This removes limitations and we can gain a greater inner clarity which opens us up to many more possibilities. Knowing who and what we are gives a sense of belonging and we do not need to make demands on life because we already have an opportunity to be at one with everything around us. This inner liberation is true spiritual healing, knowing our place within life means we have discovered its meaning and everything we then do can become a source of healing to ourselves and others.

There are numerous emotions that exist within us, both the positive and the negative. The negative emotions are a problem because they cause us pain. Loneliness, fear, insecurity, jealousy, resentment, bitterness, hatred and even anger are troubling because they show that something is wrong in our lives. If we understand these troubling feelings, their presence can serve as a catalyst for change. But, if we are trapped in any negative emotion, we can be blind to its causes and they can then be hugely difficult to unravel.

It may be our pain is caused by situations that are seemingly immediate and apparent to us, something that is hidden deep within, or it may have its root cause in our childhood. Of course, it is widely accepted that what happens early on in our lives can shape us and even cause disharmonies that we cannot deal with in our adult life. If we do not have the skill to deal with our hurts, they may linger and refuse to leave us, overwhelming our existence.

If we develop our clear vision, we can better understand negative emotions and their innumerable causes and this is the first step in being able to deal with them. Clear vision gives us a way of identifying the root cause of our problems and therefore enlightens us so that we can find a resolution. Healing can help us by working on the energy within, cutting through to our pain, soothing and allowing it to be released.

Healing the physical

Healing can affect the physical condition of our bodies, both by giving us energy where it was lacking and encouraging that energy into balance.

By understanding ourselves on a spiritual pathway we can understand that our emotional landscape either enhances or suppresses our physical well-being. Because our emotions are often what prompt us into action and therefore express themselves through our behaviour, any emotional disharmonies can create blockages that have a corresponding effect on our bodies. When we look at our physical state, we can see that it reflects what is going on with us emotionally and vice versa.

Our bodies naturally grow, support and sustain us, but our physical well-being can suffer for a number of reasons other than just our emotional outlook. With age, our bodies naturally slow down and eventually decay and along the way we may pick up various physical ailments through injury or the strains of ill health. Likewise, a positive outlook and emotional environment encourage positive health, but by denying emotions, or acting on negative impulses we have a negative effect on our physical state.

For instance, we may find that we have many responsibilities or carry a heavy burden in life, we experience back problems, or, if we are unable to move forwards in our lives, that we suffer problems in our legs and joints. Likewise, if we have problems with our eyesight, we may have a narrow perspective of life, or if we do not listen to our own emotions, that we suffer problems with our ears. We should not, however, imagine that every physical ailment is caused by an emotional block, as it is natural for our bodies to age, just as we can suffer problems from the physical strains of life independent from what is going on with us emotionally. Alternatively, we may be born into a body with genetic traits or physical problems that leave us predisposed to certain illnesses. Therefore, we shouldn't think that we have caused every bodily ailment we have, nor feel guilty for it. Guilt, in particular, is another emotion that can cause disharmony in the body! Rather, the point of knowing that we have direct influence on our physical state allows us to engage in activities that have a positive effect on our lives. A physical ailment isn't something we should blame ourselves for, but it is something we can direct healing towards, alongside the more conventional treatments available to us.

If we look now at some emotions that can cause blockages, we need to firstly appreciate that of themselves they are not necessarily 'bad' or to be avoided, rather it is what we do with those emotions that is important. Guilt, for instance, if there is a good reason for it, can prompt our conscience to redress the balance in whatever way is open to us. If we do not, then we carry our guilt as a burden and we experience its effects. However, we cannot necessarily seek out every person that we have slighted or wronged in some way and we need to be able to release the feelings of regret for the petty errors we may have made by learning to forgive ourselves and deciding not to make the same mistake again. For the bigger things, such as when we have acted vindictively and deliberately caused someone long-term harm, we should listen to our conscience and find whatever opportunity we can to make amends. In this way, we can overcome the negativities and turn them into positive emotions and positive outcomes.

Therefore, healing does not come solely from working with energy; healing comes from being in tune with our emotions and life. Any activity that takes us closer to ourselves, to nature and to the spiritual side of life can bring harmony and our clear vision allows us to understand and direct this process.

The universal energy flows in waves and at the same time it follows lines throughout the universe that intersect with the planets and all physical bodies. In the same way that electrical energy will earth itself or seek the line of least resistance, universal energy can be tapped into by putting our mind to it. By making ourselves available by whatever means works for us we can act like a lightning rod, drawing energy from the source so that it can then be directed within or used to help others. Our bodies too have lines or channels within them that allow our own energy to flow freely. However, emotional blocks and stress that cause tension within us can disrupt this flow, causing the energy to stagnate. This can, in turn, lead to physical problems and ailments.

There are a number of ways of working with the energy that is around us and within us, so that we become sensitive to the harmony of life, increasingly familiar with what it feels like to have balance and also what it feels like when this equilibrium is absent. The spiritual energy of the universe can be brought into our lives and into our bodies to enhance our energy level, expel negativities and unblock our emotions. In whatever way we work with this energy, the experience is wonderful, a source of joy that is freely available to everyone who is aware of its existence and open to its effects.

Learning how to heal

The deepest form of spiritual healing comes through living a spiritual existence. This, in turn, allows us to be a part of the bigger picture of life. Some of us are born to live in this way, while for others we have to learn to incorporate a spiritual feeling into our lives. If we choose this pathway, then we need to understand and work with our emotions. To do this we need to find an approach to life that enables us to achieve purpose within it. In this way, a spiritual life heals whoever lives it, helping us to feel safe and emotionally stable, because we understand who we are, where we are and where we are going with our lives.

Wherever we are on our spiritual journey, we can learn to heal by accessing Spiritual Energy and sending it to ourselves and others. Spiritual Energy can aid the process of physical healing by directly working with the energy of our emotions and the energy of our body, using different levels of energy to put our own back into balance. In this way, both our feelings and our physical health are strengthened where they are weak and blockages to health removed.

To talk about healing it is essential that we look at what it is within our lives that requires it. When we are lost and alone in life, we can become negative. Whenever we experience these negative periods, we can let our emotions effectively take over and this will put us in a far worse position than if we had a positive outlook.

In contrast, with a positive outlook we can address life's problems openly and doing this allows us to make changes that let us pursue the journey that is right for us. Healing can allow us to access this pathway because we are able to identify and gain perspective on the negative emotions that can otherwise overwhelm us.

Taking a spiritual perspective allows us to learn from our mistakes in the widest possible sense and to recognise the positive elements in our lives. This, in turn, enables us to free ourselves from our negative emotions because we can learn forgiveness, throw off old guilt, see the positive learnings in our past and, once we have taken these truly to heart, we can take joy in the positive change we have achieved. Taking this wider perspective helps us to understand ourselves and others. We are then able to understand the essence of who we truly are.

Healing is a product of the spiritual pathway and as much as it helps others, healing helps heal the healer because they are a conduit for the energy passing through them.

If we think loving and healing thoughts towards those around us it will work on many levels. It will serve to get us used to sending healing, loving thoughts; it will break mental patterns of negativity and also serve to give us a direct experience of what it feels like to work positively for the benefit of ourselves and others. By engaging in unconditional, loving, healing thoughts, we clear our minds of negative elements such as animosity, jealousy and day to day frustrations. By removing neutral or negative thinking we create space, so that we are then able to allow concern for others into our consciousness.

Meditation - Loving thoughts

Preparation
Put yourself in a place where you feel at ease. Sitting comfortably or lying down, put on some relaxing music. Take some nice deep breaths and close your eyes. Move your mind-energy to the backs of your eyelids and, keeping your eyelids closed, look through them into the darkness beyond. Letting your shoulders relax, listen to the music and breathe peacefully. Let go of your Earthly vision and any distracting sounds around you. Focus your attention outward into the darkness and allow your mind to clear of all thoughts and worries.

Purpose of the meditation

Practicing this meditation helps us to expand our thinking and recognise how limited our mental horizons can become. It can also give us a comparison and to see how thinking positively and sending warm feelings towards others can compare to what may be our current indifference. Through whatever barrier holds us back, be it shyness or lack of concern as to what is going on in other's lives, we can challenge it by thinking positively and with love, so that we become more accepting of other people.

The Meditation

Focus on someone you love, be it a friend, parent, child or lover and send them loving, healing thoughts. Really put your mind to it, feel the affection you hold and become absorbed in it. In your mind, send this feeling directly to them.

Now try focusing on a stranger, a neighbour or someone you have no thoughts for at all. Send them the same loving healing compassionate thoughts and wish them well. Wish the very best for them and be aware of how that can sometimes meet a mental barrier within. Relax and project as much love as you are able.

In many areas, this world has become a 'keep ourselves to ourselves' place because of the indifference we hold for each other and even the threat of violence that exists. Instead of getting involved with others we keep our barriers high and this standoffishness can become a way of life.

By projecting love to a stranger, we learn to reach beyond these boundaries and to break our mental habits. By focusing our thoughts, at the very least we are reaching out to others while mentally and emotionally broadening our horizons, clearing the clutter of negativity and indifference from our minds and stretching ourselves to bond with those we may not yet be sure of. Love breeds love and violence breeds violence and it is our choice what we wish to increase in our lives.

Now focus on a person you have quarrelled with or who you feel has wronged you. Extend your feelings of kindness. This will help us to work through situations within our own lives. Once we have used kindness instead of our usual reaction we will feel the difference. We will feel how much better it is for us as well as others to generate these positive feelings, as opposed to our usual human reaction of defending ourselves or counter attacking those who act badly towards us, or use unkind or ill-considered words. Again, we are creating familiarity with a way of acting and reacting that will give us a positive outlook on life, space for better relationships and a sense of emotional balance.

Love and loving thoughts open us up to the possibility of friendship, so that when we engage with other people it can be on a friendly basis.

The last part of this meditation is to focus on ourselves. Extend the same good feelings to yourself that you have sent to others. Cherish your good points and recognise the good in you.

The reason we need to take time to study ourselves is to see how far we have developed and how far we have come in dealing with the situations we encounter in life. In this way we get to know ourselves and develop our self-worth. Without this, how could we hope to know our inner essence and meaning? We can reject the habits of a lifetime while we strengthen our self-esteem and self-worth and engender a positive outlook on life. At the same time, knowing ourselves will help us to understand how far we can go and how far we can allow people into our lives. For each of us is a human being and we should not expect to be perfect, but rather to do the best we can with our individual gifts. That alone is the first stepping-stone to becoming a spiritual person.

Meditation for Healing – Using the universal energy

Purpose of the meditation

The purpose of this meditation is to provide healing directly to you and to those you choose to include.

Preparation
Put yourself in a place where you feel at ease. Sitting comfortably or lying down, put on some relaxing music. Take some nice deep breaths and close your eyes. Move your mind-energy to the backs of your eyelids and, keeping your eyelids closed, look through them into the darkness beyond. Letting your shoulders relax, listen to the music and breathe peacefully. Let go of your Earthly vision and any distracting sounds around you. Focus your attention outward into the darkness and allow your mind to clear of all thoughts and worries.

The meditation
Take some nice deep breaths and focus on your breathing. Take your mind-energy from the backs of your eyelids all the way down to the soles of your feet. In your mind, visualise yourself on a beach. Feel your feet bare footed on wet firm sand, watching the waves as they approach and retreat in unison with your breathing. As each wave approaches, you breathe in, and as each wave retreats, you breathe out. Now, as you breathe out, take your mind out over the water to the horizon where the sky touches the sea. Focus on the horizon and visualise a light upon it. This light now begins to shine within a cloud that, in turn, begins to roll over the water towards you. Closer and closer the cloud moves, bringing with it a source of divine universal energy. This healing energy shines within the cloud. Eventually it moves close enough to envelop you. You are now inside the cloud, surrounded by healing energy. Feel your body, mind and breath relax and let it come into every element of your being. Be aware of the sensation of the energy energising you as it passes through you. You are breathing in a cloud of pure positivity, absorbing it into every fibre of your being. Eventually, any remaining energy you have not absorbed disperses and you are ready to repeat the exercise.

Now, once again focus on the beach, the sensation of your feet on wet, firm, sand, breathing with the movement of the waves and turn your attention once more to the far away horizon. See the pin of light on the horizon as it forms itself into a cloud, approaching you filled with energy for you to absorb. Only this time the energy is stronger still. Watch the energised cloud and feel it as it surrounds you, moving until you are totally enveloped. Allow this greater energy into you, feel it permeate you and absorb every drop of energy that this cloud has brought to you. Watch again as this second cloud dissipates and you are once more standing on the beach with your feet still on the wet firm sand.

Now, for a third and final time, begin to breathe in time with the movement of the sea, breathing in as the waves approach and out as they move away from the beach. For the last time, see a point of light on the horizon forming into a cloud. This time a cloud forms that holds a greater energy than before and moves from the horizon across the sea towards you. Once more you are surrounded by this beautiful energy that comes flooding into every fibre of your being, exhilarating you with each and every moment you spend within it.

Now you have absorbed the energy three times, each time feeling how much stronger it has become.

Once more feel your feet on the wet firm sand, feel your mind's energy move up from your feet to the backs of your eyelids. Begin to focus on the physical room around you. Aware of how you now feel from your universal energy healing, sit quietly until you are ready to return from your meditation.

If you wish to perform this meditation for someone else, you can visualise them alongside you throughout the meditation and see them receiving the same benefits that you yourself are receiving. By directing it in this way, the healing will automatically be sent to the person you have in mind.

Meditation for Healing - The Lighthouse

Purpose of the meditation

The purpose of this meditation is to provide healing directly to you and to those you choose to include. The lighthouse provides you with directed, controlled universal energy and allows you to experience it in a focused beam. It will also allow you to feel the measure of the amount of energy you absorb, so that you learn to maintain your focus on that healing energy while it is being received. This also allows you to differentiate between when the healing is present and when it is absent in the meditation and gives you a greater degree of control.

Preparation

Put yourself in a place where you feel at ease. Sitting comfortably or lying down, put on some relaxing music. Take some nice deep breaths and close your eyes. Move your mind-energy to the backs of your eyelids and, keeping your eyelids closed, look through them into the darkness beyond. Letting your shoulders relax, listen to the music and breathe peacefully. Let go of your Earthly vision and any distracting sounds around you. Focus your attention outward into the darkness and allow your mind to clear of all thoughts and worries.

The meditation

Focus your attention on the backs of your eyelids. Taking some nice deep breaths, allow your mind-energy to go all the way down to the soles of your feet. It is night time and you are standing on a sandy beach within a cove. To your left at the rocky end of the cove stands a white light-house, piercing the sky with a beam of light. The sea dashes itself against the lighthouse's base sending huge sprays of sea water over the rocks and into the air. Great plumes of frothing water wash themselves all along the beach, reaching nearly as far into the cove as your feet. You can hear the sea as it pummels against the rocks where the light-house stands.

See the piercing beam of light shining from the light-house as it searches around, pointing out into the dark sky and moving across the waves around to your right, all the way around the cove illuminating everything within it. As the beam of light sweeps around and shines directly upon you, feel it's pure energy saturate you and hold the beam of light for a few moments until it sweeps around once more.

Feel the beam moving away, continuing its sweep of the bay, over the rocks once more, out onto the horizon, searching across the water and then circling back around the cove until the light is shining directly upon you where you stand. Again you hold onto the beam, this time for a slightly longer period. Feel the energy!

Repeat the exercise as many times as you wish, feeling the beam of light as it continues its sweep and returns to shine directly upon you.

Allow yourself to become familiar with the feeling of holding on to the beam of light, aware of the difference between when the light is shining upon you and when it is not. Recognise what it feels like to have this energy filling your body and what it is like when that energy is absent.

When you are ready, allow your attention to return to the soles of your feet and feel your mind's energy returning to the backs of your eyelids. Begin to focus on the physical room around you. Aware of how you now feel from your direct energy healing, sit quietly until you are ready to return from your meditation.

As well as using this healing meditation for ourselves, we can use it for someone else's benefit. They do not need to be physically present, you can simply visualise the person alongside you on the beach. A better way of including someone else in this meditation is to be physically present with them. Place them on a chair in front of you, while you stand behind, your hands on their shoulders. Then start the meditation. Because you are in physical contact, a connection is established, and while you are focusing on the energy beam, the other person will receive that energy too. You need do nothing more than keep your hands upon them while you complete the exercise.

Meditation - The Healing Energy Room

Purpose of the Meditation
The Healing Energy Room is a meditative visualization that provides you with a way of working with your own energies and allows healing to take place. At the same time, it encourages positive energy to come into your life because your mind is open to it. In this way, you benefit from two types of positive influences. There are no limits to the healing you can receive during this meditation. We can open ourselves to self-healing for every type of condition, be it physical, mental or emotional. In no way is this a replacement for medical advice or for any treatment you are receiving from a qualified medical practitioner. You should consult a medical practitioner before making any change to an ongoing course of treatment.

Preparation
Because the brain takes such an active role in this meditation, it is very important that you do not have interruptions. Put yourself in a place where you feel at ease. Sitting comfortably, or lying down, put on some relaxing music. Take some nice deep breaths and close your eyes. Move your mind-energy to the backs of your eyelids and, keeping your eyelids closed, look through them into the darkness beyond. Letting your shoulders relax, listen to the music and breathe peacefully. Let go of your Earthly vision and any distracting sounds around you. Focus your attention outward into the darkness and allow your mind to clear of all thoughts and worries.

The Meditation

Visualise a door. It is made of solid oak and, upon it carved in simple letters that you can trace with your fingers are the words 'My Healing Energy Room'. Underneath, engraved in the same simple lettering, is your name. There is a brass lock on the door with a key in it. Turn the key and the door will open outwards, away from you and into the room.

Walk into the room. You will see that there is a bench to the right with shelves behind it. Slightly to your left and facing you is a large and very comfortable fireside chair. Further away at the back of the room is a wooden staircase that leads upwards. The entire room is made of wood, a wooden floor, wooden paneled walls and a wooden staircase. On the bench stands a glass and a jug of water and alongside is a pad of adhesive labels, paper and a pen.

On the floor by the bench is a large wooden box of full empty bottles in a variety of shapes and sizes.

Knowing that you are here to receive healing, walk into the room and over to the bench upon which stands the jug of water. Take the pen and the pad and write on a label "Healing for 'my condition' (and insert the name of your condition)." E.g. "A healing for my headache."

Take a bottle from the box and stick the label around it. The bottle will now fill up with the remedy that is appropriate, whether it be liquid, tablets, cream or whatever is right to aid healing for your condition.

Pour some water from your jug into your glass and if your medication is a pill or liquid or any other remedy you swallow, take it now and wash it down with water from your bottle. If it is a cream or a gel, administer it as you would normally in whatever manner you feel is most appropriate.

Be aware that the medicine is beginning to take effect. Replace your bottle or tube of cream on the shelf with the remaining remedy within it, ready for a return visit.

Now cross over to the fireside chair and sit comfortably in it. Feel the support it offers your body, be at ease in its soft, warm comfort and allow yourself to relax totally.

Now be aware of your healer approaching you. He or she will arrive on the stairs and descend. You sense them approaching, across the room. Your healer places his or her hands on your shoulders. Tune into the pressure and then the energy that is coming from their hands. Feel the energy enter you, targeting that which you wish to be healed. Be aware of its positive effects, allowing your whole being to receive it. Remain seated for as long as you feel the hands on your shoulders and be aware of the sensations you feel as this healing takes place.

Upon completion and when you are ready, your healer will take their hands from your shoulders and after a pause, return to the stairs and exit the room.

In your own time, you rise from your chair and leave your Healing Energy Room, retracing your steps and locking the door on the way out.

Remember that you can return to the Healing Energy Room as often as you like.

Comment

The Healing Energy Room is an exercise that you must complete in its entirety. Therefore it is essential you are not interrupted during it. If, for whatever reason, you have to break off from the Healing Energy Room meditation, you must go back to the beginning of the exercise and start again.

Chapter Ten - God and the Spiritual Universe

God's realm encompasses the spirit world and the denser physical plane of the material world which we live in here on Earth. It is His energy that permeates all of creation and it is this that we refer to as the 'universal energy'.

Spirit world is comprised of energy, occupied by the souls of those who have passed over from a physical life. Each soul contains the thought-patterns of all a person's past-lives lived here on Earth. In short, that within us that carries on after death is our soul and it is as much a part of us as our physical body, in fact more so, because our soul survives our physical death. If someone we know or love passes over, it is their soul's connection with its most recent life on Earth that we can relate to. In other words, what we think of as their spirit, is their soul relating to us through the memory of its most recent life and the connection they enjoyed with us.

Some of these spirits are yet to be born into future lives here on Earth, some are dwelling in-between lives, while those who have progressed to the higher spiritual state of being are permanent presences residing in spirit world.

The spirit world is formed of numerous levels and our spiritual fulfilment comes from pursuing a curriculum of learning, so that we earn the right to progress ever higher up those levels. Eventually, our souls reach a stage where they are ready and able to manifest in human form in spirit world. Reaching this state can take millennia and is only achieved by those who have worked through their karma and are enlightened enough to choose whether they are born back into human form on Earth as a physical being, or remain in the world of spirit. If we choose to live in spirit world, from that point forwards, our lessons are learnt on that spiritual plane. Up until that point, our thought-patterns in spirit world are increasing in coherence. Finally, we reach that point where we are complete and ready to live an existence in God's realm. We are then able to manifest a spiritual image of our chosen human form, fully conscious of our life in the world of spirit and of our past experiences on Earth.

The spiritual universe is populated by both souls and angels. Whilst angels are here to help us in our human development, the more progressed souls can take on any number of roles. In the same way that we have options as to what we do with our physical body, so our spiritual world contains the same choices. Amongst those spirits that have progressed higher are those that have chosen to take on the role of Guides, helping those of us on the Earth plane who wish to learn and develop.

Much of our connection with spirit world is through our mind's ability to sense psychically, so we 'see' and 'hear' through our minds. Yet those who inhabit the spirit world and who have developed far enough are able to manifest here in the physical plane. This could be by actually appearing so that we can see them with our physical eyes, or creating noise vibrations so that we hear them with our ears. However, it takes a huge amount of concentration and energy for a spirit to do so and so this form of communication is so much rarer than connecting through our mind-energy. Here on Earth, we are connected to God's Energy because it surrounds us. Therefore to connect with spirit world, we use our mind and our clear vision to connect with its energy, not our physical senses. However, sometimes this mind link is so strong that it can feel as though we are physically seeing or hearing what is projected from spirit world to us. Therefore, when we hear of someone having 'seen a spirit', in reality, they will most probably have received a communication directly with their mind from spirit world.

In spirit world we are free to move within our current spiritual boundaries with no physical ties. Here on Earth our soul is connected to our physical body, so that the two are mutually linked with a strong magnetic-like force and our soul remains within our body, only permanently departing when our physical body dies.

Therefore, here on Earth, our soul lives within us; introducing itself to life on this planet through the vehicle of our body, while we are in the womb.

Our body is governed by our brain and without a brain we would not be able to function on this planet. Therefore to us the brain is the god of our bodily existence, facilitating control of the universe that is our arms legs, skin, bones, organs and enabling us to move, think and operate as human beings.

What we think of as God, the God of the wider universe, exists outside of the body and it is God's realm where our soul originates. God radiates universal energy in the same way that our bodies radiate bodily energy and because this universal energy radiates through us, God is as much within us as he is without.

Learning to connect with God through our soul allows us to go beyond the idea that our brain is the only guiding force. Taking this spiritual approach helps us go beyond what we think is reason and logic, yet is in reality the current boundary of humanity's understanding.

Regardless of our attitudes and choices, not only are we observing and learning through our life here, but our soul is also learning, connecting with the lessons it is receiving through us and the lives we live. In this way, the mistakes we make are as much learning for the soul as are our achievements, for it is through our mistakes we learn. If we are able to quieten ourselves and listen, our soul can communicate with God and is better able to guide us through life.

Our spiritual life journey

We are a spiritual energy within a physical body; and without the physical, the soul could not take its journey into this world. When a soul decides to manifest in the physical plane, it departs from its origins in spirit world and arrives in the chosen foetus. With it comes an inner knowledge and awareness of its previous existence. The memories of all its experiences come with it, including knowledge of all its previous lives on the Earth plane.

After fertilisation, the egg leaves the ovary and starts its journey down the fallopian tube. At the same time the soul that is destined to be born here is leaving a higher level to join and unite as one with the embryo. Embryo and soul unite at the moment the embryo attaches itself to the womb. The cycle of life now begins. It is a bonding, a partnership between the spiritual soul and the physical body.

Our driving force is our soul and the body is its physical vehicle. Once the joining of physical and spiritual has taken place, with the embryo and soul united together, the period of growth in the womb allows our physical body to grow and ready itself for the world.

The next stage is birth; the journey from the womb to the outside world. After birth, we have arrived in the physical world and the physical side of life now takes precedence, in the sense that we need to take care of our physical needs for food, sleep etc. As our life develops and we progress, we are later able to awaken to our spiritual identity and until then our physical side needs to be our primary concern as our body grows.

We come into life with full knowledge of where we have come from. That is to say that we have brought with us the knowledge of the lessons we have learned and the impact of the experiences we have had. There is an understanding within us all, of what life was before we were born into this body. Yet it is mainly a memory, a feeling of what we are, rather than what we have done in previous lives.

The purpose of our being here is to experience the lessons we have chosen to learn. Learning intellectually however is totally different to the way in which we learn the lessons our soul has chosen. For our soul to learn we must experience life's lessons through our physical journey so that they truly become a part of us. By allowing ourselves to experience these lessons, life becomes a journey of learning. During this time, the brain manages our bodies and learns what we need to survive and progress in the physical world. This makes our brain the God to our body, because it directs it through a physical journey, while we learn to clothe, feed and fend for ourselves. The soul however learns the lessons we have come to experience on a spiritual level, interacting with one another and learning patience, acceptance, generosity and love.

The physical body is born into this world to enable the soul to develop, to provide a vehicle for the soul within and through which to gain experiences. By being here, we are open to innumerable joys we cannot find in our energy form. Our soul comes into this body with its spiritual knowledge, it's beauty, splendour and a huge love of life within it. It is this feeling of joy and exultation that we are here to experience and we should expect from life. Life is the big adventure we are all here to take part in. Experiencing a physical body and all of our five senses opens us up to the pleasures of a human existence. Yet, for so many of us, this is not how we feel life to be and it can be of course, that our soul must journey through hardship to appreciate the inner wealth of experience. No one is saying that we must feel joy if we are living through physical pain or restriction, yet our soul may have taken this path to understand what it feels like to be in those circumstances, or perhaps to understand mankind and its failings. Living through any aspect of hardship means we can empathise with those who are suffering in similar circumstances, because we know what it feels like for ourselves. Therefore, experience can help us evolve into patient, forgiving beings of compassion, love and understanding.

Life is a journey of the soul, but that is not to say that we do not need the brain. Our physical body and the ability to control it is essential to our needs and to the journey we are taking. It connects us to reality and allows us to interpret the world around us, to think and to guide and feed our bodies. Without the brain there is no way we could survive.

Without the brain, the body deteriorates and if the soul knows that the brain is dead, it will leave the body. So, the soul within us knows when it is time to come into this world and when it is time to leave. Like a bird that knows it is time to emigrate, the soul will fly and go back to its origin, there to start its journey once more. In the case of a body where the brain is totally without activity and thought, where it is said to be brain dead, then at this point the soul has already left the body and taken its journey back home. In the instance of somebody who is in a coma, their brain may be on a temporary 'sleep' pattern. If they subsequently awaken, then during the time of this sleep, the soul will have continued its existence both within the body and on the spiritual plane, reunited at the point when the brain awakens into the body once more. In either example, the soul contains the knowledge of what we have experienced and learned and in this way our cycle of development continues.

The role of choices within our spiritual life journey

At the time we unite our soul with its body, we have chosen conditions that will be helpful to our journey. We have selected particular parents, in a particular place as a stepping-stone on our road of development. The soul is like a blueprint and from the moment a child enters this world, the physical takes over. As we develop, with our five senses all providing input directly into our brains, the memory of where we have come from, or our previous lives, quickly fades.

After our birth, we are entirely dependent upon our parents or whoever cares for us. Care and attention offered with love is the best kind of start for a child, as it gives us the inner stability we need to move forward in life. Without these, we can become lost and stray from our pathway of development until we are able to find ourselves once more. If we have a spiritual background and know that love and caring are always available, it means that we need never be lost to life.

At the same time, it is our choice how we choose to live our lives. The reality that we experience is partly dependant on how far we are willing to open our mind. With a spiritual outlook, if we find ourselves in a situation that is not to our liking then, recognising the options we have, it is our responsibility to choose what direction we take. If we like where we are, then we can learn to enjoy it all the more because we appreciate what life has offered us. In either situation, we can ask to grow and develop spiritually or we can stay locked into our viewpoint. Spirituality offers us the option of looking beyond that which we consider as fact, so that we have more options than we currently understand.

A spiritual life journey can have many outward forms. So whatever situation we are in, we can ask for help from above to increase our understanding, patience and ability to love and accept, as well as understanding our own current position and feelings. If we choose to widen our minds, then we can say that we are on a conscious spiritual life journey. Yet without this conscious decision to appreciate our life, we are all still experiencing this spiritual journey, however we may not recognise the choices that are open to us and the full extent of the opportunity to learn and enjoy that life offers. Instead, we will be limited by our own self, because it is our own thought-patterns we are identifying with rather than something far greater.

God

God is the all-knowing and all-loving creator of our universe and it is the energy that radiates from Him that sustains all of creation and everything within it.

Our physical forms, the extent of our ability to think, feel and create, all exist because His creation made it possible and it is the energy that radiates from Him that sustains all. Because His consciousness is the whole of existence, He has full knowledge of everything within it. Whatever preconceptions we have of God, as our Creator and Guardian His is the ultimate perspective and far wider than we can comprehend. Because His consciousness encompasses all that we are, we are only able to see Him from our narrow viewpoint, like a grain of sand comprehending the entire beach, sky, sea and all around it. He is the reason for our being, because without His life force we would not exist and being part of His creation allowed our human form to develop. We are made in God's image, yet on the physical pathway of the human race, we have existed within His blueprint for only a small portion of our journey. Our minds have not yet developed to comprehend Him or the true extent of the energies within His existence, so that we cannot yet see and accept Creation for what it is.

If we put our minds to God and his energy, the role that we are able to see Him fulfilling for us is that of our very best friend and parent who knows us better than we know ourselves. Yet he is still more than this.

Only He has an all-encompassing insight and knowledge that is greater than anything we can imagine. Like a Guardian watching over us, he sees what is best for us and however we regard Him, His kindness and compassion for us is all-forgiving. He lets us take our journey of life, watching over us as we learn and play, sharing the experience while we are offered chances to improve ourselves.

God's voice is the voice of everything and it is our choice in life whether we look outside of ourselves or are only prepared to look within our own knowledge for answers. God offers us the opportunity to have all our questions acknowledged and for our life to make sense. If we seek to hear His voice then we have opened ourselves to His understanding. Yet if instead we choose to close our minds to His voice then our window to the world is far more limited.

God watches us develop as we find ourselves here in what can be a lonely place of frustrations, anger, violence and pain. His wish is for us to open ourselves to Him so we can let Him in and in doing so we can recognise the signs that show us the way. We are here on our journey and our Father has not forgotten us, we could instead say that we have forgotten Him.

It is our choice as to where we direct our lives and some of us will have a need to find freedom and explore our own boundaries. Yet if we go too far, this experimentation can take us in wild and reckless directions, beyond what is good for us.

We may be trying to find ourselves, identify our role in life and even feel lost and alone, looking, searching, seeking a place of solidity and belonging. The fulfilment of our ultimate journey comes through seeking the compassion, love and examples that God sets for us. If we seek the perfection that is embodied by Him, it can seem impossible, yet we can lead ourselves towards the completion He offers. We do this by doing unto others as we would have them do unto us and this is our pathway to happiness.

Our journey is one of self-development and each of us is looking for success within it. Yet we do not always meet with the feelings of happiness we hope our efforts will bring. If we seek to find and be part of His example, we can be enlightened to His presence and become true to ourselves, others and our own conscience. We are all equal in God's eyes and He has given us the best opportunity to succeed in our choices, providing everything we need to exercise our free-will to live, grow, expand our knowledge and develop.

We have regret for many reasons. We can regret because we did not try hard enough or because we feel we did not get enough chances in life and therefore got less than we deserve. With a spiritual attitude we can look at each of these instances in a different way. This may then liberate us from negativity and point us towards a more positive outlook. Even if we think we are too old to change, we can find that change is still available to us.

The choice of where we direct our thoughts and our lives is ours, for some it is enough to know that God is there for them and that is a source of reassurance, whereas for others it opens a pathway to follow.

If we choose to exercise our freedom of choice, to love one another, live honestly and recognise how wide the universe is compared to our one existence, we can appreciate the beauty of our planet and nature and all of creation in its fullest sense because we see it all has a higher purpose. This, in turn, allows us to recognise how truly alive we are.

Expanding ourselves in this way helps us to be more conscious and to recognise that absolute perfection can only exist in a spiritual sense with God, whereas here on Earth our perfection comes through finding peace of mind and by doing something positive with our lives so that we leave a valuable legacy of good feeling. Our human family can then learn from one another to follow His example and learn in turn how it is we can truly love one another.

The greater understanding we achieve by living in this way builds the foundation to let God into our lives.

Prayer

A true prayer issues with total surrender, bringing forth our inner most thoughts and feelings from the depths of our heart, from our very core. True prayer comes when we know that God hears us and we can hear Him, so that we may work together in a union of oneness.

There are many reasons that we seek to pray. It may be that we have a need to seek help, guidance or comfort. If this is the case, and especially if we have no belief in a higher source, prayer can often be our last port of call, that we resort to because we have exhausted what we see as all the other possibilities open to us. If this is the case, then prayer can serve to open the doorway and let God into our lives. Alternatively, we may pray because we enjoy joining with like-minded people in a community or group and therefore uniting with those around us in putting forward good feelings in an act of good will, linked though a common purpose and joining with a higher source. Or it may be that we pray because we find it delivers peace of mind and enables us to share our inner thoughts, worries, doubts and troubles so that we can benefit from the feeling of letting go. Prayer can also be our way of helping those in need or near or dear to us, extending our feelings to them by asking for help from above.

The privacy that prayer offers, means that we are able to voice in our minds more than we would dare or perhaps be able to say elsewhere, where our inhibitions or circumstances may prevent us. Prayer also serves as a way of enabling us to find our true feelings because we are giving ourselves time to express our inner self.

Because prayer is a way of putting forward sincere and focused good wishes, we are also encouraging our mind to pursue a positive train of thought. This, in turn, serves to open us to a positive outcome.

Doubts can also be addressed through prayer, where we are seeking an insight into the right choice to make or to allay our fears over a direction we have chosen.

Another function of prayer is that it allows us to truly investigate and ask forgiveness for those things we wish we hadn't done. Asking for forgiveness in this way helps us to understand that we are accountable for our actions in a very real and immediate way, because when we do something harmful it troubles our conscience. Praying means that we are able to give ourselves the time we need to find this openness within and to bring it into our lives when our prayer time is over.

There are also many different times at which we can pray. We can choose to pray at any minute of the day or we can make it a special time for ourselves, perhaps with a ceremony that is special to us. We may also pray at times of special significance such as weddings, funerals, christenings or at times of death and birth. We can pray in any situation, but true prayer is that which comes from the depth of our being, joining our hearts and minds with one voice.

However we pray, it is an act of communication with something bigger than ourselves. Searching beyond the physical, we may pray to God, to the universal energy or according to our preference, religion, or belief, we direct our prayers to a higher source.

We may pray to angels, guides or even to the world of spirit where the souls of our departed loved-ones reside, so that they may intercede on our behalf. Joining in prayer in this way, through beings we can visualise, or that once shared life with us, can help because we are better able to relate to them and we can understand that they have our best interests at heart. It may be that we feel more comfortable with this than praying to a higher source that we do not understand. It could also be that by praying for help on this level we feel less pressure to expose the very depths of our beings, or are more comfortable when we do so. Where we direct our prayers is up to us, yet the most benefit comes from directing them to the ultimate source or God, however we perceive Him.

The act of praying teaches us to recognise and separate the physical and the emotional elements of our lives by tuning into the inner self. By praying, we can become aware of how deep our emotions are and relate to the feelings we each hold at our very core. This helps us to both reach into and express the truth within.

Wherever we are directing our prayers, it is not a superficial act, it is our way of talking from the heart and sending our hopes needs and aspirations to a higher source. Through prayer, we are releasing expressing and sharing and it is a way of exploring and finding belief in something more than ourselves.

Through prayer, we are addressing ourselves to something pure. By establishing this communication we can learn to experience all the things around us from the perspective of our higher self. We are touching the truth within, free of outside pressures, free of the influences of society and life and with this freedom can come far greater inner peace.

By praying we make ourselves fertile ground for the right things to happen and we become receptive and open to positive change. When the time is right, the very act of being truthful to our self will provide answers.

Prayer is therefore the opening of a doorway that allows positive spiritual energy to flow. However, it does not put us in control, nor if we do not immediately get the answer we ask for, does it mean that the prayer is of no benefit. Prayer at its deepest level is a request and submission to the will of God and even prayers that are answered can be seemingly ignored because we do not know His purpose, nor what outcome is for the greatest good in the long run.

Reading or recalling written prayers from memory can help, but while it can be useful, it is the emotional depths of our self we are seeking to express. However, if we are praying without true depth, or we are not clear what it is we are really asking for, then we should not worry. God knows us better than we know ourselves and the very act of praying helps us search for and connect with what we truly need.

Prayer is so important, because it is our way of asking God to help us and to answer the needs of our inner self. It is our way of expressing those needs and the very act of praying helps us to tune into them, so that we can find our true essence and look to where fulfilment lies. In other words, we get in touch with the truth within our hearts and speak from there. What is absolutely true for us comes out through prayer. This is why prayer is not about satisfying physical desires. Although physical needs may be answered through prayer, it is not there to address our wants, nor the frivolous, nor the superficial, for none of these are our inner truths. What is most important is to pray sincerely from the heart. If we voice our prayers from there, then we can encounter God.

Many of us when we connect with Him experience deeply positive emotions and an understanding that He is the ultimate compassionate and caring figure. Our conditioning may be such that we have an expectation that God is male and this is a result of our upbringing and commonly accepted Christian lore. There are many views as to His form and ultimately we can identify with God as we wish. Yet, he is neither one thing nor another; God is a form of energy for us to experience and our labelling Him as being male is purely a reflection of how we are feeling and interpreting that energy. After all, He does not have a physical existence here on Earth and therefore it is not relevant to Him to assume a male or female identity, because He already embodies and understands both and everything in between.

God is bigger than our boundaries and if we look at the extremes and limits of the ideals and ideas that God embodies, we can see how far he is beyond our experience and abilities. If our perception of Him is that He is a Father figure, or a Mother, then equally in either instance, what is most important is not His gender but recognising that our relationship to Him is that we are His children.

If we seek God, He can appear in many forms, His energy can be very subtle and it often comes with feelings of love and compassion. Equally, if we sense God to be a female energy with all these divine attributes, then this is right for us. It is what God is that is most important and it is that to which we pray.

Astrology, the planets and their effect upon us

Astrology is the study of the stars, planets, the heavenly bodies and their effect upon our lives. The physical universe is overlaid by a vast network, a grid of energies and lines, all of which are interconnected. The planets are part of this network and our life's journey is part of this cosmic web. Consequently, the alignment and movement of the planets has an effect on each and every one of us.

We are born into our physical body as a singular individual and for us to be this unique person, with all of our distinctive characteristics, our birth coincides with the appropriate alignment of the planets and associated zodiac sign. In other words, we are born at the right time and place for us to pursue our life journey, with the astrological sign that will provide the right characteristics for us to do so. As the planets move and the energies move with them, each within a cosmic pattern of potentialities, so the influences of that pattern will be felt by each and every one of us. Our zodiac sign is merely shorthand for the situation, influences and timing of our birth, while in reality, every birth will be represented by a complex astrological chart which calculates, or reflects the influences of the minute, hour, month and year of our birth. Each of us will feel aspects of that clock in different ways, according to our own internal energies and where we fit in with the movement of the universe. These energies can be very subtle, pulling gently at our moods and the way we feel at any given time, but they do not dictate what we do nor how we do it, that choice is always ours alone. Likewise our horoscope is a description of the influences that are potentially affecting us and also recognises what we are likely to be affected by, because we are each born into a pattern that expresses our journey with the basis for a personality that is equipped and open to what we need to learn.

For each life's journey we are born into the appropriate zodiac sign for that life and because each sign has a particular emphasis of personality and outlook, so our spiritual journey is to work with our own unique characteristics and to grow and develop as individuals. It is a chicken and egg situation, our moment and timing of birth means we manifest physically with distinct traits and influences, while our soul chooses the moment of birth for us so that we may experience these influences and feed our own development.

Our star sign can enhance us so that its positive traits provide us with the possibilities and strengths we need in this life. Yet, we may need to work through particular aspects of our spiritual development and have to wait for the right circumstance and sign to be available so that we may be born into the right life at the right time. With the vastness of time open to us in the spirit world, we may have to wait centuries or even thousands of years for the right circumstance. Whichever way we look at it, this means that whenever and wherever we are born is the right time and place, because it provides us with the right personality traits and opportunities to approach our journey and learn the lessons we have chosen. What happens here on Earth is then subject to free-will. What is certain, is that if we develop clear vision and work with that Spiritual Energy, rather than opposing our purpose, we will have a far more satisfying life because our soul's journey will be fulfilled.

As our zodiac sign and the circumstance of our birth is determined individually for each life, so we can be born as any star sign in past and future lives; even if we are a Virgo in this life, in our previous lives we may have been any number of different signs; Aquarius, Gemini, Capricorn; there is no limit to what we can be when we are down here. The journey for each lifetime is unique and therefore in each one we experience various planetary alignments that help us to fulfil that journey.

Through our clear vision we can become increasingly aware of these astrological energies, but we need not study them, because clear vision can bestow the ability to look forward each day, and across our life's journey, so that we are aware of the situations that are upon us and those that are coming toward us.

In the spirit world we do not have a star sign, we are not a Leo, or an Aquarius, or a Taurus, our star sign is a trait we have in the physical universe only. Because we learn through our physical existence on the Earth plane, we need a distinct personality as it is our vehicle to learning and experience. This is not needed in the world of spirit, because there we are soul-energy which is formless and learns through choice, but does not have the benefit of physical experience. The personality is a vehicle for learning, in the same way that the physical body is a vehicle for us to experience and interact with physical existence. The personality differs in that it is shaped by experience and whether we take ourselves in positive or negative directions. Yet the soul has no need for either of these in spirit world. There our soul has the benefit of all the lives we have lived, each one of which will have been assisted by its personality and star sign in that life. While each soul is created with a similar energy form, it will be unique, having developed its own characteristics through learning from each physical life's experience.

When we have joined with our developing bodies in our mother's womb, we have incarnated with a particular time and date of birth in mind. We must remember that the year and month of our birth are influential, but that the astrological clock is moving all the time; nothing is set in concrete. Once we are in the womb, that time of birth can, like all things in this life, be altered by circumstance and outside influences. If it is and we are born prematurely or overdue, then we are still the same soul incarnating here on Earth but we may be born with a slightly different set of characteristics than was originally intended. A good point to remember is that though the medical professionals estimate the due birth date, they do not know our spiritually allotted time of birth. So it may be intended that we are born at a time that the Doctor determines to be premature, but for us was chosen as part of our original blueprint and therefore exactly the right time for us to arrive. Come what may, if you were born under the influence of a particular sign, then that influence will continue throughout your life. So for instance, if you were born between 23 July and 22 August as a Leo, it would not matter if you were due to be born on 22 July or 23rd August, if you are born in the Leo period you will have a Leo's personality traits and be under the influence of that sign. Whether you work positively or negatively with your sign's traits is up to you.

Once we are in the womb as a growing foetus, we sense the outside world and listen through the skin and water sack. This is just like our communication with the spirit world when we are a fully grown adult. Here on Earth we are in a plane of physical matter which is dense and real to us and to receive communication from the spirit world through this dense matter is like a baby trying to hear the spoken word through the amniotic fluid. It is like we are at the bottom of the deep end of a swimming pool and trying to hear someone above us on the poolside as they try and speak or shout to us. Locked into this dense matter, it is through our minds that we can connect, using our clear vision, to the energies around us and the spirit world beyond.

In the same way that when we pass over we are received into the light of enlightenment, so when we travel down the birth canal, we emerge into a new life in a physical plane. Either journey can be a very traumatic experience. Both in birth and death we are on a journey into the unknown and the process itself can be physically painful. In each instance, we are leaving a situation of comfort and familiarity to put ourselves in a place where our future is unknown to us. When we pass over, our friends in spirit world celebrate our return to our home, while our Earthly relatives and friends mourn their loss. When we are born into this world, so our friends and relatives in spirit world will mourn our departure, while our Earthly parents celebrate our arrival and birth as a child.

Death

It has been said that death is something that typically the young do not imagine, the middle age avoid as a subject and the older amongst us sometimes dwell upon as the inevitable date draws nearer. For some of us, death may already have made its mark through the passing over of a loved one, friend or family member. For others, we may never have had to consider death and it may seem a distant and unlikely event, perhaps even not worthy of thinking about.

If we take time to consider it, many of us may be afraid of dying or the manner in which we die. It is a daunting prospect to face, to think that some time we will be fighting for our final breath or in a situation when our life finally slips away from us. Yet instead of accepting that this is the inevitable destination of all physical life (and yes it is in case you hadn't thought it through!) and acting accordingly, all of us to varying degrees act as though our time here on Earth is unlimited, as if we can act in any way and without fear of ultimate consequences. If we truly realised that at some point all of this life will come to an end and we will be looking back on life and questioning it, then would that change the way we conduct ourselves?

Of course, we know that each and every one of us will sometime die and when we think about it, it may affect us in any number of ways. There are those of us that recognising it has a limited span, choose to live life to the full, by grasping at every opportunity for experience, perhaps earning and gathering as much material wealth around us as we can. There is absolutely nothing wrong with seeking physical comfort and enjoying life, being joyful and learning through our life experiences is what our journey here on Earth is all about. There is too much doom and gloom in our modern lives and at the same time, especially for those who have experienced wealth, we can recognise that it is not as important as good health, love, contentment and respect both for ourselves and others. No one thinks well of another just because they own a fast car, but we may respect someone who has worked hard to become successful. So we must recognise the place in life that success and excess occupy. Success is the fruit of our labour, while excess may do nothing positive for us as people, other than show us our boundaries and what happens if we exceed them. If we choose to open our minds and our hearts to the spiritual we will find everything we need to make our lives meaningful. Being full of this meaning, having absolute proof that there is something beyond the physical, gives us the opportunity to see everything in perspective.

Knowledge, even when it is knowledge that there is more to life than we can understand, lets us change and soften our attitudes. Eventually when we look at death, we can understand that it is going to happen, that our physical bodies will die. We may also recognise that our soul will continue and our spiritual journey here on Earth will inform that soul with all of the life experiences we have had and the lessons we have learned. When we have this knowledge, then aside from acting out of habit and perhaps succumbing to our weaknesses, we may choose to realise that our soul journey is the most important part of our life and that to further that journey we can guide ourselves spiritually through our connection with the Universal Energy and God.

Why do we face so many problems in life?

If we look deeply, we can see that each and every one of us is potentially lost and alone here. We are born into the world with a body that will eventually die and throughout our lives we will all have experiences of loss, pain and separation that can sometimes make the feelings that come with being human almost too much to bear. The flip side of this coin is that we have so much potential for good feelings in our lives. Life can be full of love, loyalty, lightness and laughter. To allow these feelings into our hearts, we need to have a connection with those around us, then that can give us an appreciation of community and provide us with a sense of bonding. We can find these feelings from loved-ones in our family and if we are lucky enough to have caring, loving people around us, we can enjoy fond relationships and memories that comfort us when times aren't so easy. As we grow, seeking out those with a common interest or focus provides us with opportunities to bond. The feeling of working together as a group can be wonderful in itself and yet for many of us, the occasions where we truly work with a shared sense of team spirit may feel few and far between. Yet, our loneliness may only be held at bay by the presence of other people and our good relationships with them.

Ironically, it is sometimes the toughest times that give us the potential for the greatest growth, fulfilment and bonding. Wars and natural disasters are sources of pain and yet they can actually have the side effect of drawing people together and bringing out the best in them. Sadly, camaraderie, friendship and bonding often only come in their strongest forms when we are facing a common adversity or foe. They come when life is reduced to the basics, when we are forced to focus on our own survival, rather than on our petty differences. It is of course sad that something that threatens us with suffering is needed before we choose to form these bonds. It is a great shame that we often need pressures and times of trial to help us recognise the good solid things that can be achieved through working together. Often, we fight each other instead of fighting for each other and we only truly appreciate something when we lack it, or there is a threat of losing it. Merely living together happily can be fulfilling in itself. We form clubs and groups and associations to express and fulfil our common interests and to pursue good causes, or further pastimes and find that in common purpose and camaraderie, we can achieve what is most valuable, yet costs us nothing. The best things in life are free.

It may be that we can recognise only the full extent of our opportunity to develop personally through interacting with each other, once we have found our true purpose in life. Spirituality helps us to identify the lessons we are here to learn on Earth and it can help us begin to let go of our fears and how they make us act. Spirituality gives us a framework for relating to each other because we can let go of the distracting thoughts that sometimes fill and even overwhelm us. Our negativities can lead us to extremes, so that we work in competition, or even give up totally on our life. Clear vision lets us discover that, if we instead focus on the positive, we can experience what is right for us and others. This, in turn, allows us to discover our common bonds. It therefore gives us an opportunity to learn our lessons the first time they are presented to us. If we have this positive attitude we can overcome situations that might otherwise threaten to overwhelm us, or that we avoid and might otherwise constantly repeat until we are ready to learn.

Each of us has an existence in the spirit world between our lives here on Earth, where we are all of like mind and everything is glorious. Our experience there is vibrant and full, with none of the threats that we feel here in our physical bodies, bodies that are subject to ailments, physical threats and old age. In spirit world the soul knows life to be everlasting. By comparison, the reality of living here on Earth can be terrible; many of us walk around estranged, cynical and suspicious of each other's intentions. We do, after all, need to feed, clothe and protect our physical bodies and that means we are all seeking to use the finite resources available to us. The temptation is to work against each other rather than consider each other's needs. With so many of us now working with disregard for one another, mindlessly or selfishly feeding our own agenda without taking heed of how our actions affect others, we may have very good reason for keeping people at arm's length.

If we develop ourselves so that we connect with the bigger more beautiful picture, we can develop our own wisdom and understand ourselves better. This, in turn, gives us the key to our own emotions and reactions and to appreciate why we feel and act the way we do. This is the pathway to understanding why so many of us, who have not opened our eyes to spiritual life, continue to live in ignorance and how our actions can cause problems for other people and ourselves. On the spiritual pathway, if we are to widen our vision and understand ourselves and be free from uncomfortable negative feelings, then we need to understand what motivates our fellow man and woman.

Knowing that these problems don't exist in the spirit world, may make us think that that is the preferable place to be, but we should bear in mind that in general we need difficulties so that we can learn through experience. This is not advocating a philosophy of 'no pain-no gain', nor does it mean we should foolishly put ourselves in bad positions so that we develop quicker. Quite the reverse in fact; if we develop a spiritual perspective, we can see our opportunities to develop all the more clearly and we can choose to react in a way that means we don't need to learn all our lessons the hard way. Spotting a person that isn't going to work for us in a relationship, understanding what is going to help us and what is going to harm us, learning what we should have a healthy respect for and identifying which of our fears are groundless, all of these are things that come to us with our clear vision. Even with this knowledge and attitude, life may not instantly become easy and full of happiness; we may need to learn patience, while life works itself out for us. However, regardless of what we face, we can say that life becomes more productive because we are learning from it and that the fruits and rewards are far more personal and fulfilling. Spirituality isn't necessarily about having an easy life, it is recognising, achieving and enjoying the true fruits of our journey here on Earth and these are worth working for.

Karma

Karma is the natural law of the universe, the law of cause and effect and of balance. The laws of karma are not prescribed, nor are they man made. In reality, the law of karma is an observation of how things are, a recognition that what comes around goes around and what we put into life we get back, be it in this life or the next. Another way of looking at it is that our karma is a reflection of who we are and what we do and who we were and what we did. It also offers us the option to be now what we wish to become. In this way, our journey is both to work through our past karma and create positive karma for our future, by experiencing all that life has to offer, both the negative and the positive and contributing only that which is positive.

Understanding the principle of karma helps us to recognise the value of working with life's negativities without adding to them, or becoming negative ourselves. Approaching our karmic lessons from a spiritual perspective means we can accelerate this process of moving through our karma, so we can progress on our spiritual journey.

Part of the karmic law is that like attracts like. So, being positive attracts positivity and repels negativity and the more positivity we generate, the more positivity comes back to us.

In each life we may have a karmic challenge, something to learn. Yet if we are born into this life to learn something such as the acceptance of others and we do not make progress, then we will have to go through the same karmic journey in a future life. This repetition can occur in life after life and will continue until we have worked through that particular lesson. Learning enables us to progress spiritually, so that we are ready for our next life lesson. It may be that we have just one lesson we are capable of learning in any one life, or we may have many, but learning spiritually is not easy and usually, even though we can improve our soul in many ways, each of us will have one predominant karmic journey we are making in this lifetime.

Like a curriculum, life presents one karmic lesson after another as we gain in knowledge. While we in these physical bodies see our human life-span as the be all and end all of life, the karma of one lifetime can be inconsequential when viewed against the journey of our soul, a soul which may manifest through countless physical lifetimes.

This is why a spiritual perspective can help us to work through our karma so much more quickly. If we saw our challenges as barriers to our achieving what we want from life, we could become absorbed by negativity, resentful at how tough life can be. If instead we see our challenges as learning periods, we can recognise them for the karmic lessons they contain and approach them as the next step upwards in our spiritual ascent.

So, every life offers us the opportunity to learn and develop, but it is not our brain here on this Earth that remembers our lessons. Rather our life is a journey of the soul and it is our soul that carries on the memories and lessons of each lifetime.

Yet our awareness of this soul journey is limited. We do not necessarily see how our current actions; what we are doing right now, affects our character for the future, nor does our viewpoint recognise how inconsequential one small moment of our life can be in comparison to the whole of that life, or indeed to other lives. This is all part of our limited human viewpoint; those things that appear momentous at the time may seem inconsequential once we have them in perspective, while those moments we overlooked might be some of the most important to us in retrospect. In the same way that our dreams may be difficult to recall, so it is rare to spontaneously remember the experiences of past lives and be conscious of what they are. If we have developed our clear vision, or are born with heightened psychic abilities, we may have some access to the memories of previous lives. Generally, we do not remember them because each life is held like a bubble, as an imprint on our souls. However, our soul is the common element of these lives and if we develop ourselves and learn to experience that soul, then we can gain glimpses of these past existences and by practising specific exercises, can learn to explore them. If in this way we gain knowledge and faith of our past lives, then we can learn to treat each moment of this life with the respect it deserves and the light heartedness that life often demands, in the knowledge that each moment is an infinitesimal and essential part of the bigger picture.

Chapter Eleven - Why Do We Believe it is God Who Allows Us to Suffer?

One of the most common questions asked is, "How can God allow all of these bad things to happen?" Why, when we experience and feel God as a loving parent, do we see so much suffering and pain in the world? How can our loving God allow this? Why do people die before their lifespan is complete and why are we exposed to malice and violence? How can God allow all these things to happen, when as an all-powerful entity, it could instead be his will for us to experience nothing but paradise or heaven?

The answer to these questions lies both in our wish to have free-will and our need to experience. When our souls chose to incarnate, they did so out of a desire to experience the sensations of life, to feel the wind on a physical face and the exhilaration of the unpredictable. We also chose to be here so that we could learn and embody our spiritual nature, bringing the experience of patience, compassion and love to our souls. To do this we need free will, for without it there is no chance to develop. We exist on Earth with total freedom to choose how we act and react, to create whatever we wish within our abilities and circumstances and none of this would be possible without free will.

Therefore many problems here are of our own making, while others serve the purpose of shaping us so that we can learn positive lessons from them and bring that learning back to our soul.

Here we look at some of the most common and perennial problems that plague our planet, alongside the forces that are outside our control and why each exists.

Natural disasters

We have no control over the laws of nature, rather they follow their own flow of cause and effect. Some things are constants such as gravity, night and day, the sun and the moon and all the things we accept as enduring, yet even today much remains largely unpredictable. We can find evidence of this changeability in all of nature, in the weather, storms, through the movement of the Earth in earthquakes and volcanic eruptions or in the influence of planets, such as the moon, when tides combine with other influences to create floods. Although we have methods for detecting their imminent presence, we do not control the ebb and flow of these immense natural forces.

Even with its volatility, nature has its own natural cycle of birth, life and death and everything on Earth exists within this. Dependent on our viewpoint, or its effect on us, nature itself can seem either soft and beautiful or hard and ugly and it has the potential for both creation and destruction within it, as do we. But without unpredictability and the potential for suffering that comes with it, we would have far fewer opportunities to learn, grow and care for other people. Those who suffer because they are caught up in nature's movements and in the worst case are victims of natural disasters.

There is no way that we can predict everything that we will encounter in life and that is why our free-will is so important. Free-will allows us to choose how we act and how we react. If everything were predictable and there were no natural disasters or unforeseen circumstances, free-will would have little use, because we would have no choices to make, nothing 'unknown' to face. With no danger of loss, we would have far less need for developing positive traits such as patience, fortitude and creativity to deal with the unforeseen.

Our souls chose to come to this planet to live within natural laws, so that we could exercise our free-will and embody the positive traits we desired. So without the unknown and the unforeseeable, life would serve far less purpose for our spiritual journey.

Disabilities

There are many forms and degrees of disability, from those that are most severe and affect our ability to move and function fully, through to the minor, such as colour blindness.

Disability can be chosen by our soul to provide us with a challenge in this life, to bring the best out of those who care for us, or to provide an example of strength of spirit to those around us. Likewise, we can become disabled by chance or genetic trait, which is not a choice of our soul necessarily, but a reflection of the unpredictability of life.

None of us can know the true extent of God's purpose. Each of us has limitations and we are beings that exist within His Creation, therefore we cannot hope to fully comprehend or understand the purpose behind all of life. To know and understand this we would have to have the same intelligence and creativity as Him. In other words, we would have to have the power both to understand and to create life as He has.

Yet, none of us has anywhere near the abilities and attributes we could even imagine God to possess. We are like grains of sand on the beach of life. However, we can choose to be aware and guided by His will. If we seek to feel God and his presence through prayer or through our everyday life, we will naturally become more aware of ourselves and of His presence.

While obviously our general well-being is important, it is primarily our soul that God is concerned with. Therefore a spiritual approach can help us be happy within life, despite its difficulties, because it offers us a refuge for our feelings no matter what life throws at us and the chance to develop fortitude and contentment. True happiness is our goal.

The choices we make in life

We are not alone, for each and every one of us is born into this world with gifts that can help us in every element of our lives. One gift that we are all born with is the ability to heal and we also have the gift of clear vision, which can provide the insight we need before we cross life's busy roads. Most of all, we have our feelings and learning to trust our feelings is the most powerful gift of all. So we are not abandoned and left here to fend for ourselves, but rather we have the spiritual gifts of love and compassion, alongside help and aid from above to assist us on our journey and physical gifts to help us create a life for ourselves.

To enable us to understand the importance of how we feel, how we react and how that guides our life, we can take just about anyone's life as an example. Let us now look at the example of a young girl, one who is born to parents that move from place to place throughout her youth. At an early age she is abandoned to live with relatives in a new and unfamiliar town, without friends. There is no love or compassion shown to her, no feelings of warmth from her kin. This kind of situation could lead her to a fear of rejection in her life. Likewise therefore, this person could react to this fear by overcompensating, trying too hard to win the approval and love of others. If this is the case, then, as she grows older, we can see her developing as a person who cannot relate to bonding within relationships, because she has not experienced it. Without the ability to bond, we can experience feelings of loneliness and isolation. If this is the case with us, our insecurities can run wild; because we have not been loved, we have not learnt to trust others and we do not know ourselves. Nor do we know what we are looking for because we have never experienced it and we do not know that it lies in the simple act of loving. A person working with these particular problems has a journey to make, a journey towards loving themselves, trusting their own feelings and being freed to love others. The true sadness for someone locked in this situation is that because they have not experienced the positive feelings of love, bonding and security, they do not know how to recognise what it is they are seeking. Clear vision provides us with a way of ensuring these kind of problems are overcome, recognising our self, our soul energy and identifying where fulfilment lies for us. In this way, it offers a way of structuring a life that provides substance. Knowing who we are, we can then make the right choices for ourselves.

Choosing peace

Many choices are thrust upon us through circumstance and one of the most difficult choices we make, and that which often causes us problems, is how to react when we feel we are threatened. Be it physical threat or a verbal attack, often the choice we make for ourselves is between some level of fight or flight. The question that confronts us is whether it is better to be a pacifist and turn the other cheek, or to defend ourselves and risk harm to us or another person. Should we go one step further and take flight and avoid confrontation, perhaps sacrificing our pride or some material thing we would otherwise seek to protect? This kind of choice, when our spiritual aspiration meets with the constraints of our physical life here on Earth, can often seem the hardest and the truth is that there are no rules to follow.

Choosing to harm another person can have an immediate and profound negative effect on their state-of-mind and on ours. They become fearful or experience hurt, while we become the type of person able to harm another. The reason we should not harm other people is that in doing so we become a vehicle for harm and the cumulative effect is that it can make us perhaps callous or violent. The law of karma means that whatever we do in our life, we will need to experience the effect for ourselves. Therefore, whenever we are able, we should choose to act as peacefully as we can, both verbally and physically, in thought and in deed. Perhaps the most extreme example of a negative act is murder, the ultimate form of violence. If we end another person's life, we have made a choice to devalue their existence to the point where we see them as of no or little importance. We see them being of such little consequence that we seek to destroy them. However, karmic law dictates that because we made a choice and acted upon it, therefore we are subject to experiencing it for ourselves. The consequence of killing is that we will experience violence upon ourselves in this life or another. There are deeper effects too, if we are able to kill another we may experience remorse and therefore life is constantly painful as we struggle with our conscience. Alternatively, we may have switched off our emotions so that we are distanced from our humanity and because of this we become an automaton, with no emotional link with life or those around us. When someone who has no regard for human life and is unrepentant passes over, their soul will feel the results of their actions as remorse and pain, while they will meet the consequences of their actions in this life, or the next.

Yet, we are sometimes thrown into conflict either by circumstance or choice, rather than acting out of malice. We might find ourselves conscripted into an army to defend our nation or protecting our family against physical attack. So what happens to the person who kills because he, or she, has been ordered to do so, perhaps in defence of his country or other people's lives? What then? Many would say they have at best a very limited choice, or no choice at all. It is not an act of protection that creates heavy negative karma, but rather harming a person's life without reason, or without thought to the damage we are doing to them and to our soul.

As human beings we cannot control everything that happens with us and we can only do the best we can. The most we can hope to control is how we act and how we react to life and this can often be a challenge in itself!

The choices we are presented with are not always clear, even to the point that we are not always aware there is a choice to be made. To disclose our options in life, we first need to be honest with ourselves about our emotions and then have the courage to act upon them, for love can come from honesty, while compassion can come from acceptance. It is our motivation that is the true key and to truly know our motivation, we must be as honest with ourselves as we are with God, for ultimately it is to Him and our own conscience that we are truly accountable.

There is, however, a distinct difference between the positive acceptance of life for what it is, that allows us the freedom to get the most from it and the opposite, an apathetic viewpoint that life is something we cannot influence, so that we make no effort. The former acknowledges that we cannot control life, yet that we should make the best of it, that we are all in it together, that we have choices (at the very least in how we act) and even how we feel and react. The latter, while it accepts life, takes the viewpoint that it is fixed and does not change, negating any possibility of growth.

At a fundamental level, we have chosen to come here, because our soul chose to manifest in a human form and create a conscious human life and while we are here, we should never forget to do our best for others and for ourselves. Yet many people find it difficult to accept that we firstly chose to come here, because if we did, why do we not recall our previous existence or our existence in soul form in the world of spirit. One of the reasons why we do not remember where we came from is that we might not try our hardest if we knew that we can come here again and again. If we knew this physical existence were just one of many and that we have innumerable opportunities it, would be so easy to give up and just avoid all the things we need to confront. Yet taking a spiritual journey opens up our perspective and if we continue that journey through prayer and meditation, we can come to know that our existence is far wider than just this one life. Each of us is capable of developing and finding the knowledge that lies inherent within. If we expand our awareness spiritually, then we naturally begin to appreciate the value of each journey for the opportunities it affords.

If we look at the seed of a tree in the ground, it serves many purposes in its growth and yet how many of us recognise these? In maturity, a tree's falling leaves in autumn will nurture the soil, while its branches provide shelter for animals and perhaps bears fruit they can eat. The growing tree will breathe and provide us with oxygen, while its presence is naturally beautiful. If we looked at the tree without considering the bigger picture, then we might only see potential firewood or leaves that make the ground slippery underfoot, or the exposed roots set to trip us up. So it is with life; the wider we cast our vision, the more of its beauty we can appreciate. Beyond this, with eyes truly open, we can begin to see the wider purpose life serves.

There are many reasons for seeking, it may be the life we had previously mapped out or the pathway we were following no longer felt right for us, or situations that we once calmly accepted now feel wrong.

The spiritual pathway is about internal change and if we embrace it, we become aware of our own innermost feelings, bringing them to the surface of our consciousness. So if we choose to tread a spiritual pathway, using our clear vision, we will recognise those feelings, appreciate more of life and be aware of so much more around us.

If we recognise what we feel inside and work with those feelings, then we will achieve clarity, which in turn enables us to recognise those same traits in others. An increasing awareness demands patience from us, because we become more conscious of both the good and the bad in those we love and those we encounter. We need also to recognise that we are not all here to pursue the same journey, nor concentrate on the same development. That means that we cannot dictate how people act, nor force them to change, merely because we 'know' what is best. On the other side of the coin, we do not have to stay silent when confronted with bad behaviour if it hurts us beyond our capacity to take it. The spiritual pathway doesn't give us the right to tell others how to live their lives, nor does it mean we should be doormats. If we look at it another way, then it is no good holding spiritual views and values and then acting badly towards other people or judging them. Yet if we feel that we have to act to put forward our views, we should do so. We can always check whether we are doing the right thing and ask ourselves whether we are acting out of pride or out of a spiritual motivation; 'are we building ourselves or are we building our spirituality?'

Through opening ourselves, we bring light to our emotions, so that we learn the role they play. As a result, we also expose ourselves to the emotionally painful things in life, yet the ultimate solution to this pain can be found in embracing and acting with love and the more open we are, the more love we may receive. No matter what faces or confronts you, love can overcome in the long run, because it demands that we act with patience. This is why we say that love can bring pain with it, because conversely it demands we open up and in so doing become vulnerable. Yet being open to both pain and joy proves we are truly alive. By contrast, shutting down the emotions may feel like we are protecting ourselves from the hurt we might otherwise experience, but what it truly does is to limit us as human beings. By armouring ourselves or numbing ourselves to the painful emotions in life, we also limit our capacity for joy, making ourselves less alive. By refusing to recognise the emotions, we shut off feelings that might otherwise overwhelm us or throw us into despair, when in fact the true journey is to become navigators, so that we travel through these emotions and learn from them. If we do this well, we need only do it once, because we become a teacher to ourselves and develop the capacity to set examples and help those experiencing these challenges themselves.

Yet even if we see things clearly, it is up to the individual to change; our ability to help anyone in this life is limited to the extent that they, in turn, are able to help themselves. If we are in dire straits and drowning in our emotions, we either need to strike out for ourselves or ask for help spiritually. The first step is to signal that we feel we deserve more from life than that which we are enduring.

So life can be either a wasted journey, or if we recognise its wider spiritual context, it can be a voyage of wonder and splendour. Even so, only a few of us want to succeed in overcoming the spiritual challenges we have in life. Amongst those who choose to develop spiritually, enduring all that is sent to them, are the older souls. Because of their experiences they are much more able to recognise the spiritual nature within themselves and through their actions provide an example to those younger souls, who are also learning.

Young soul or old, when we reach the stage of our development where we have recognised ourselves on our pathway, we are ready to embrace life as it should be, knowing that life is not to be challenged, but rather to be embraced. But some souls are not ready, or refuse to hear and go on to rebel against the natural order of karma, refusing to develop their own wisdom, or benefit from the wisdom of others. There are many reasons for this, it may be that they are not yet strong enough, have not yet matured enough, or that they have not learnt to be able to fully relate to existing in a physical body. While this physical existence with its natural order is there for us to follow and improve ourselves, our journey doesn't come easily for it tests and tries us as we learn our strengths and weaknesses.

Our ultimate potential here on Earth is to live in the beauty, harmony and happiness that come from life itself. Many of us seem to have forgotten that we are living in a world that offers everything we could possibly want or need, yet we think that life owes us more than we are prepared to put into it. If we did not exert effort to earn our rewards, then we could not pay our bills or live the life we would hope to, so we earn our way towards the things we want to comfort our individual world. Yet this, as we know, doesn't always fulfil our needs. If we put our energy into life, loving for loving's sake with no thoughts of rewards, we will eventually get back more than we ever thought possible. It is so sad that we choose to think that 'this is it!' If we see the world as a negative place to be that brings no reward then we can turn to our own sadness, needs and pain, as our point of reference, because we have decided "this is just the way things are". If we are seeing life from this perspective, where the uncomfortable and unpleasant are uppermost in our thoughts, then this can lead us to seek solace and find a means of escape from the emotional pain. If, instead, we recognise life and hold ourselves open to it, then a better existence is available to us, merely through the experience of life itself.

We get from life only as much as we put into it and that we can take from the lessons that are put before us. If we look at our mistakes as things to be learnt from, we will gain a better understanding, so as not to make the same mistakes again. If we find ourselves in the same situation time and time again, then we are metaphorically speaking going back to the same bus stop, without having moved on to the next stage in our journey. If we are in this situation, then life may be telling us that there is something we should learn to enable us to move on.

Even if we recognise that we have karmic lessons to learn, we should not assume that this is a linear journey. Whoever we are, we don't always learn from a lesson the first time it presents itself. If we are young souls or learning things for the first time, we could continually repeat mistakes before we 'get the message' and this cycle can repeat until our lessons truly change us from within.

Although we have spoken about lessons and tests, life is really an experience that, if we listen, can tell us what is right and what is wrong for us. Because none of us are perfect, finding and experiencing what is right means that we will feel particular situations as challenges, while in others we are entirely comfortable. We are each unique to ourselves and one person's tough lesson is another person's ideal place to be, therefore sometimes we can find help or guidance in the examples set by others.

We are here for much more than we think or know. Life is precious and we come to this physical existence to introduce ourselves to all worldly things, exploring our personal needs, testing and stretching ourselves against the rights or wrongs that we find ourselves caught in. And when we arrive, we find ourselves living with strangers, learning to accept and co-exist with them. By learning how to tolerate others, we can recognise their mistakes and our own and how we need to change to move on, gaining knowledge and understanding. With a spiritual approach, we can be an example to others and learn from them at the same time.

Our development is about experiencing life itself, for this experience is what we take with us when we go home. If we have lived and loved and given our best, then when we come to the end of our life's journey we can find ourselves in the most glorious place in the spiritual universe.

The soul

The soul comes here to learn through us, so that we can take this learning home when the physical body dies. The goal is for our soul and body to act as a team striving towards the same goals, the same recognition and what is best for us as a whole. One way of looking at it is that the soul has a contract with the body that it will not leave while we still exist in this life form. It is only when our physical journey is over that our soul departs. This is why we should go with the flow of things and trust our inner voice.

Each of us is affected by how we are brought up, the life we have lived and the life we are living now and these experiences can condition us to act in any number of ways. We can learn through reacting to life instinctively, responding automatically, governed solely by our limited viewpoint and perspective or we can choose to look deeper.

If we look at the body as a microcosm, a spiritual universe in miniature, then we can see that the brain is the higher energy of the body; in that it has abilities to think and function that the body does not possess. However, obviously the brain needs the body to enable it to function fully in this world. Therefore, if we visualise our body as a contained universe, the brain fulfils the function of creator of reality and of higher life form, providing the motivation, reasoning and abilities that the body alone does not possess. It is creator because it processes our sensory input and enables us to recognise touch, sight, smell, taste and feeling; all the functions that enable us to relate to and interact with reality. Therefore, the brain creates our physical reality for us because without it, we would not recognise contact with the outside world and instead of vehicles of experience, our bodies would be prisons to our minds. We are a smaller version of the Universe and God made us in this way in His image.

Outside of the body we have the universe and all of the planets and also the non-physical universe of spirit world where our souls come from. Our brains also serve a purpose in connecting us with our psychic abilities and if we choose a spiritual purpose for our lives, the brain can serve to bring our body and actions in line with that purpose, as well as providing us with all we need to develop our clear vision and to connect with spirit world.

We have a reason for existing and a reason for occupying these bodies. We are water based so that we may live on this Earth. God sent down the soul that will live forever, so that it might experience and learn. Therefore, we are immensely important to the spirit world; without us they would not be able to experience, to learn, to reproduce and have laughter, human interaction and the pain that goes with life. We are each of us a duplicate of

God's Heaven. The difference is that we have a skin on us, but God's Heaven does not. Heaven is a mass of energy, while we are miniscule representations of God's realm with our brain in charge and our soul seeking to connect with that wider picture.

This may seem complicated but the actuality is quite simple, it is our inability or unwillingness to accept it that holds us back.
Therefore our soul is inseparable from us, from our identity and from our life journey. But our soul encompasses everything we are in this life, because it is the deepest part of us and is learning from our life journey here and now. Our soul is within us and collects information from every life and each life sits within the soul as an imprint.

We come into this life with the ability to tune into our soul and to learn about it, so that we can understand the journeys our soul has taken in past lives. Feelings of fulfilment and completeness tell us we are fulfilling this life's purpose and therefore our soul's journey. So, to learn what will be the most fulfilling pathway for us and therefore what direction we should steer our life, we need to understand ourselves and in this way we achieve peace.

For our soul will have countless lifetimes of experiences and interaction in its spiritual universe and is therefore a wonderful potential source of wisdom. Where we dwell as a soul, between lives, in spirit world, our desires are realised through the manifestation of our wishes, so if we dream for a big house, or an idyllic holiday, then our soul can experience that wish's fulfilment by manifesting it. Our soul does not have a physical existence other than when it is connected with a human body here on Earth, so when it dwells in spirit world it can experience all the manifestations of thought of which it is capable, such as manifesting a beach or a garden, but the physical experiences elude it. Therefore life in spirit world is a reality through which we progress, but without the ultimate solidity of physical touch, or the solid feedback of our five senses. Instead, life there is lived through the energy of direct manifestation. Our existence here on Earth joins us with a physical reality that feeds the learning of our soul, so that it is able to test in reality its every action.

Positivity is food for the soul because it recognises that no matter what we are facing, we are moving forwards with our intention. If we become negative in our thoughts and attitudes then we do not move forwards, instead we hinder life, obstruct the development of our soul and even become stuck.

In the extreme, if we become really embedded in a pattern of behaviour, fears or negativity, then when we die and the time comes for our soul to pass over, we can instead become stuck to Earth. Rather than return to the dwelling place of our soul we remain in a form of consciousness on the Earth. There are many reasons for this happening. Earthbound spirits may be stuck because they had a fondness for a particular place, person or situation, or our grief can hold back the soul from returning on its journey upwards to its existence in spirit world and so can the soul's attachment to a loving family home, or a place that has given us great joy in our lives. In this way, what we love here on Earth can delay us from moving on. This shouldn't be a cause for worry or concern; you are not going to spend the rest of your existence after death on a park bench just because you happen to like your local park, but once you have passed over you may wish to visit that area because it holds fond memories. Likewise, just because you happen to love your partner, if you pass over before them it does not mean you will be stuck in an Earthbound existence, you can still visit or see them from spirit world.

It is very important to realise that our soul does not forget the living or its wish to help those that were loved in this life. Usually those who have passed over manifest at special events or on memorable occasions or when they feel they are particularly needed by loved-ones who remain.

However, our soul, once we have passed over, is existing in a much wider reality, free from the worries, constraints and pain, of this physical existence. This means that we do not spend all our time in spirit world focusing on the Earth plane, instead we have a journey to continue; we cannot spend all of our time looking back.

Here on Earth we are limited by a clock and the passing of time. Yet one life here is merely a moment taken from the eternity of our existence. Also, time does not exist in the dimension of spirit world and so conversely a lifetime spent here on Earth may seem a fleeting instant for a soul viewing from spirit world. This is partly why our viewpoints are so vastly different.

We should not think of the soul as being a separate entity, with separate thoughts from our own. Rather, it is a deeper level of our being, the deepest level. The soul is part of us and we are part of it and the more we get in contact with our soul by living a life in accordance with its needs, then the more we will experience our lives in a way that is fulfilling.

If we take a step back and look at the soul's journey in another way, we can see that learning through a life lived positively helps the soul to develop greater clarity. The soul lightens and becomes independent of that which would otherwise weigh it down so that it can travel upwards and achieve its purpose through positive spiritual development. However, negative imprints from a life lived against the principles of this positive spiritual journey can burden a soul, weighing it downs so that it descends. Positive learning and actions, like expressing love, clear the soul making it lighter and more responsive to change and to its journey. The lighter the soul, the more lifetimes lived positively, the more it is able to ascend in its upward journey.

We may not understand why others live in ways that are negative or harmful to themselves and those around them. However we look at it, our challenge is to stay positive, not by ignoring our feelings and what is going on around us, or the thoughts in our own minds, but by acknowledging what is there and ensuring that we act in a way that is best for us and those around us. In that way our soul progresses as it should.

One thing we should remember is that all of life has a purpose and while we can condemn an action, we cannot judge others. We are on our own development and a spiritual journey is lived within. There may be a reason for a soul experiencing a life here on Earth where they act negatively. For instance, that soul may be on a journey to work its way through negativity so that it can feel and understand it from the inside, or it may be in a position where it has been offered the chance to take a negative start in its physical life, so that through understanding it may transform.

We are here to learn and develop unconditional love so that we live in harmony with ourselves and others. Those who are acting against what we feel is the positive flow of things are giving us the biggest challenge and test for our ability to do so. That is not to say that we cannot condemn an action and each of us should be held accountable for what we do. However, we are not spiritual judge and jury and should be mindful before we condemn someone in their totality. One of the beauties of life is that there is hope for all of us if only we are willing to learn.

Soul mates

Our purpose of life here on Earth is to learn, to develop our ability to love unconditionally and to progress to the point where we are at one with ourselves. Achieving this state means we are then able to continue our existence solely in our spiritual form, with no need to be reborn into a physical existence. This state is achievable only when we have learnt all that life has to teach us and all the spiritual lessons we are able to take on board.

Just as in spirit world there are levels of progression, here in our physical world we progress in understanding and knowledge.

Having learned our lessons as an individual, we then share it with someone so we may learn the value of joining in this union.

The function of a soul mate is to allow us to experience a unity of oneness on our physical journey and meeting our soul mate is, for the majority of us, an essential part of our spiritual journey.

A soul mate is a person who has worked through their negative karma, completing enough of their journey that they are ready to meet with their soul mate here on Earth and join in a positive loving relationship that feeds both. True love is the foundation by which a soul mate can join an energy that is identical to their own. Like a twin, a soul mate is completely in tune with us emotionally and even if you have differences in life, the bonding, once it is achieved, is so great that you will want to be with that person forever. Having met a soul mate in one life, we will encounter them in life after life thereafter without end. In the same way that we must learn our lessons here on the physical plane for our soul to truly embody them, likewise we meet our soul mate here on Earth so that we may completely experience a union based on unconditional love in its totality.

A soul mate is a person with whom we experience a unification of emotions and with whom we bond physically and emotionally in a union of love that never dies. We are a match, a perfect complement and free from negative emotions and insecurities such as jealousy and possessiveness, free to love for loving's sake. So this union is one of the most profound expressions of love to be found here on Earth, an extension of the unconditional love God seeks for us all.

We can still love a partner with all our heart here on Earth and find a devoted and fulfilling love and yet this person may not be our soul mate. A soul mate is the most perfect partner we could wish for each other and comes with the potential for a relationship where all of our existences are shared. So to be ready to meet

158

your soul mate and for the union to last, you must both be at that stage where you are ready for the relationship to bloom and flourish. If you are not ready to meet in this life, then you will come down in life after life seeking each other.

When you first meet your soul mate you may not necessarily stay with them. You may, for instance, meet and part early in your life, or you may meet them at the end of your life. The reason for this is that the first meeting may just be there for you to make the connection. Thereafter, in every life for all eternity and until you are both ready to complete your existence in spirit world, you will have a relationship in life after life that is a complete union of togetherness.

Relationships between soul mates are so rare, partly because to find your soul mate you need to have developed to a point where you are equal to each other. Once the union has been made here on Earth, a link is formed and from that point forwards you will always have a connection.

To join with your soul mate, you must both be ready. If you meet at a time when either you or they have not developed sufficiently, then the relationship will not develop or last. You may then wait for life after life until the opportunity arises and you have another chance to meet with them. Ultimately, it is our destiny to meet and develop with our soul mate, so in one life or another we will meet and begin the part of our journey that continues on with them forever.

Soul mates should not be confused with people whom we have merely met in past lives. For instance, a friend who helps us in this life may have been a sister, brother, mother or lover who we assisted in a previous life and is now returning the favour. If they are of the opposite sex, we may feel a connection with this kindred soul and imagine it to be our soul mate.

A soul mate is an extension of our thoughts, feelings and emotions. They give and receive love in equal measure, so that there is a harmony and an understanding that is full of growth and possibilities. Working as a team, you share responsibilities with each other.

Children who are raised by soul mates are very fortunate, because they make very good parents, providing an environment of unconditional love. They benefit from their parents relationship and the positive nurturing and security provided by two people who are able to take a long-term view, having learned many of life's lessons, such as respect, compassion, loyalty, self-discipline and the value of nurturing, and are able to pass these traits on to their offspring.

The reason that soul mates are part of our journey here on Earth is because we need to become familiar with sharing and unity. Our ultimate goal is to pass on to spirit world and there we continue our existence within a far greater unity. Therefore, to embody and be ready for this, we must first earn and experience unconditional love in a physical union.

Once we have worked through our fears over the course of many lives, we progress beyond the limits of our negativities and become whole. We are then in a position to fully appreciate and receive the unconditional love that God offers us. By practising this love here on Earth we become familiar with it and can embody it as a way of life, so that it changes us within. This enables us to recognise it when we pass over to our spiritual existence. Practising love in this way, we progress to a higher level of spirituality, part of our journey towards understanding the oneness we are seeking to become part of on the other side. Therefore, a soul mate relationship is always a very spiritual encounter fuelled by unconditional love that enables us to progress without looking back.

Progress and compatibility allows us to achieve a level where we can have a soul mate because we are capable of this union of oneness. A relationship with a soul mate is one where you have no challenges to overcome, instead you are entirely compatible and give one another respect, understanding and forgiveness so that the relationship is nurturing and entirely wholesome. This is the way that all relationships should be. However, to reach this level of learning we will have had to have learnt the ultimate of all things that we are down here to learn, which can take hundreds of lives over thousands of years to complete. Our soul mate does not complete us, we have to be complete to meet our soul mate and when we meet them we have the potential to build a union with friendship and family. The offspring of the relationship is a flourishing of positivity that extends far beyond the two.

Each of us is looking to experience unconditional love so that we have it for ourselves and are able to pass it on to others. To reach this state we must address our shortcomings and failings as individuals and learn love and patience. To reach this state of grace we need to be able to provide the unconditional love and acceptance that we are seeking from our partner. What you give out you get back, which is why a relationship between soul mates is so remarkable and only goodness can come from a union like this. It can also serve as an example to others that all this is possible.

We should remember that all relationships are capable of developing unconditional love between the two partners, regardless of whether they are soul mates. By trying to understand and accept one another, any relationship can become part of the journey that we are all here to make, so that we are developing and bringing ourselves nearer to our own spiritual pathway. This does not mean that we accept the unacceptable, but rather that we can recognise what is beneficial to our development and what we can work with, so that our lives get better. Doing this means we develop ourselves and our relationships in a way that prepares us for a soul mate relationship now or in the future.

A union with a soul mate is our physical expression of spiritual progression and while it is a milestone, it is also the beginning of the next stage of our journey.

Through prayer and developing our connection with God, we can find the unconditional love and acceptance that each of us are ultimately seeking in our relationships here on Earth. A soul mate relationship embodies love in physical union, while our connection with God is a spiritual union that enables us to develop and embody love as an individual.

The spirit

The spirit is our energy, our life force, the conscious manifestation of a soul that exists to sustain soul and body for the duration of each physical life.

Each life has many treasures of knowledge within it. By choosing to develop our spirituality, we choose to unearth hidden or already obvious treasures within our spirit. Life experiences either yield up direct treasure, such as when one has achieved pleasure through a spiritual practice, or at the more extreme level, bad situations when viewed in hindsight or from a spiritual perspective can actually yield up the greatest wealth, because they show us the benefits of facing adversity. We will each have bigger or smaller challenges to face and these will be in areas that we have chosen to experience. Like hair-triggers, our souls respond quickly to the developmental needs we dictate in each life. The accuser may need to experience the life of an accused, in the same way that the murderer may come back as a victim so that they may both experience what they created and overcome the negative aspects of past actions.

A spiritual practitioner may need courage and understanding as well as diligence to pursue their path and the areas we learn in may be emotional and physical, as well as in the area of relationships and love. All of these can prove problematic and our problems can highlight areas where we would most benefit from development. While we may find relationships with others easy, another person may not. Yet another may find love, but may have problems finding a reliable source of income. If we have a problem that recurs, then often it will be associated with the area in which we most need to develop.

If our minds and hearts are like a palace with many rooms, then spiritual practice can gradually open the doors to these rooms, clearing obstructions and airing negativities which would otherwise remain hidden and blocked. An open palace gives us more room for others, more depth of personality and because our creativity has room, everything is open and bright and accessible. Because we have let more light in and developed ourselves, we can become a warm inviting person.

Unexamined areas within our consciousness are the dark rooms we most need to recognise. If we do not, then we cannot recognise them in others and we cannot help them to develop themselves in these areas. When our palace is open, our spiritual practice can help fill us and our many rooms with the beautiful rewards of experience.

We can now turn our attention outward, to put others first, and in this way, our palace gardens become beautiful and inviting. We have created something wider than the original house of our personalities. With fewer negativities to divert us from life, our ability to stave off negativity is now more naturally embedded within us. We have less fear and our emotions become more robust, meaning we have less need for self-protection. Taken far enough along our pathway, we can become fertile ground where only positivity can gain hold. As we develop and we are open to meeting others of like nature, we will find not only more spiritual things in our life but more spiritual people too.

The benefits of a spiritual pathway do not come in palaces in the material world, but through the construction of palaces of feeling within. While we may like to have the nice things in life and they can serve to make us grateful or as a reward for our hard work, yet if we idolise our material possessions, then they will have a hold over us. If we value them above our friendship with ourselves and with God, then we are at risk. By contrast, the less solid and fixed the object of our worship, the less it is subject to threat or being taken from us. So if we put our faith in God and the universal energy, then we know that these things can never be taken away, because they are as much a part of us as we are of them. God permeates all things, He is immutable and unchangeable and if we take care to nurture our spirits then ultimately we grow closer to God's love, the only truly everlasting thing in the universe.

War

We are not born to go into conflict and kill other human beings. We are born here to live and associate with other people, to live and learn and develop ourselves. In the past, there have been times when we all had to pull together to face a common undertaking. This could have been a foe, such as a neighbouring state or nation or the natural world and the challenge of survival. Nowadays, it often takes tragedies to bring people together so that we are all pulling in the same direction and facing a common goal with like minds. This is sad; we could all be much closer if we could simply befriend our closest neighbours without the need for a common enemy.

Many parts of the world are experiencing war and conflict. For many people, the daily reality is of living in fear with the threat of losing friends and family or their own lives and livelihoods.

On Earth we have full command of our own actions and freedom of choice and yet despite knowing the awful consequences, we fight violence with violence and fuel hatred with yet more hatred. Many question how God can allow the atrocities of war to take place, yet how can we blame God for allowing us to wage war, when all these acts are the result of what we humans do?

Often, as a way of justifying it, we make war in God's name, explaining that this particular bout of maiming and killing is to further God's wishes. Is it right, as some believe, that God licenses 'His people' to take the lives of others? There have been periods in the history of all nations when each has fought for their perception of what is right and to further the common good. There are even fanatical extremists that believe God will reward us for taking the lives of others. There is no reward for killing someone; what kind of God would reward us for killing our fellow man? If that were our purpose here on Earth, or how we dealt with those we disliked, then there would be far fewer of us around!

That is not to say that we should not fight to defend our own lives or those of others, but we should always seek the alternative where it is available and recognise the awfulness of war, rather than attempt to licence it to God as his will. How can God's will be that there is more suffering? If we are faced with violence, we can question whether we have an option other than responding with yet more violence. But no matter how we justify war, if we see killing as an option, as justifiable, or even of little consequence, then we are perpetuating the cycle and we should recognise that waging war brings war and violence upon ourselves. If, instead, we choose to allow compassion and kindness into our lives and concentrate on bringing a loving attitude into everything we do, we will put a higher value on human life and we are less likely to be in a situation where we choose violence over peace. Good or bad, we all have a right to live here on Earth and the more we are able to reject aggression, the less of it we will have in our lives.

We may question what we do when our country is attacked and conflict seems inevitable, unless we are to give up our homes to the violence of others. Sometimes it is true that in our physical lives, self-defence is the only option. But we should recognise that at best, war is atrocity. However and wherever we can, we should always look for the alternative, seek to find a compromise and search for peace. Ultimately, very little good comes to us while we are engaged in fighting.

However, if we are born into a world full of conflict, then it may be there is a higher purpose being served. It may be we are here to learn how terrible war is. Having experienced it, we are far less likely to choose it for ourselves and far more likely to choose peace instead. If we have witnessed war, we can also understand what it can do to people, how it can turn us into monsters, how the innocent can suffer and how we can become twisted by thirst for revenge. It is our choice what we do with this knowledge; whether we become angry and seek to harm those who harm us, or whether we learn the lesson of peace. In every case, it is not God who wages war, it is human beings. Therefore, war isn't something God chose or brought to this planet, it is something we choose for ourselves out of our own free will.

War and religion

If people of different faiths embroil themselves in conflict over their religious beliefs, then where is God's purpose served and how does this further our understanding and friendship? God's love isn't manufactured in a factory where weapons are made so we should not imagine that war and religion have anything in common. If two children argued in the playground and came to blows, would we choose a side? If fighting is wrong for schoolchildren, then what does this say about people who choose aggression so that violence is committed in God's name?

Solutions lie within the teachings of each religion wherever they steer us towards love and forgiveness, they do not lie in finding an

166

excuse for war. Where there is killing and death, throughout history man has sought to put God on one side or the other. Yet God's burden does not lie in picking sides, but rather in witnessing the folly of human aggression and for followers of religion, the burden is to understand and forgive.

It may be that we have to pick up arms in self-defence, such as when we are defending our country. But this is not justification; we must look to ourselves before we enter any conflict. Violence is the last resort. If we are drawn into conflict we must seek not to commit our hearts to hatred. Instead, there is still the hope of conducting war with nobility and respect. Anger destroys character, whilst respect, determination, courage and fearlessness help build it.

There is no ultimate answer to these situations, no ultimate right or wrong. People are not ultimately Muslims or Catholics, Christians or Buddhists. People are not collective groups with generic traits, rather we are all individuals. We should seek to find the good within each other, whatever the religion, whether we are a priest or a cleric, or whatever title we bear, we are merely men and women. Spirituality and our clear vision can help us root out our own prejudices and, if we are willing, pay heed to our insights. If we have illuminated ourselves within and, as a consequence, are better able to act peacefully and with humility, we can be an example to ourselves and to others. The more of us that are able to take this attitude, the more we will gain the respect of others and the world can be a better place for it.

God and Jesus

Jesus can be the most important figure for us in our spiritual development, because he is a gateway to our Heavenly Father, God.

Jesus made it possible for us to recognise a spiritual pathway and that we are all part of God's creation. At the same time, he was born a mortal man, just like each and every one of us. He was a very special person, destined to bring about the religion of Christianity, nurturing the seeds that God had sown so that the people could develop spiritually in what was a very difficult time, when killing and violence were part of everyday life. Yet he was born a man, and because he then developed spiritually, humanity recognised him as the son of God, as are each of us. Because we are able to identify with him as ultimate living proof of love and compassion at a time when fear and aggression were the norm, in this way he became a gateway to God. Before his time, God was seen as an angry vengeful figure, but Jesus introduced us to this compassionate nature and by recognising the capacity for goodness we all have within us, enabled us to mature spiritually.

In the same way, each and every one of us has the opportunity to follow his example, setting love as our goal and using forgiveness and compassion as our vehicles. There are many that awaken to the presence of a spiritual universal energy and when they do they are able to perceive a far greater opportunity for inner happiness and peace. In his lifetime, Jesus became spiritually awakened and achieved just this and with his awakening came great knowledge.

Each of us is able to awaken to the divine universal energy that is God and receive the knowledge, as did Jesus. By following the example of Jesus, we can come closer to the presence of God. Whether we choose to develop and awaken to Him is our choice.

Spirituality is an open doorway and it is up to us whether we step through it. Not all of us are here to develop in a spiritual direction in this lifetime. Each of us can only learn through experience and it may be that we have goals to pursue or a journey to make before we can take a spiritual path, now or in this lifetime and feel comfortable with it. Whatever direction we take in life, each of us has a right to live here and all of us are accountable for our actions. We can be introduced to spirituality in many ways. We may be introduced by spiritual friends, or it may be that we are at a point in life where suddenly or gradually spirituality becomes relevant to us and we seek it out. It is then up to the individual whether they follow the pathway that opens up to them.

In the same way, while each of us are on our journey, awakening only comes when we are ready for it and some take longer to discover the spiritual pathway that is right for them. Some of us miss the opportunity to find our spiritual pathway when it presents itself, while others will recognise it and start to work with it and in doing so, their opportunity for greater happiness is revealed.

Following the example of Jesus and God

Currently, there is no way of providing categorical proof of God's existence. There is no laboratory test, nor chemical reaction that demonstrates His presence. Rather, because we are part of his Creation, to prove his existence, we must attune ourselves to Him through prayer. This therefore demands we change ourselves so that we can find Him through our connection with our soul. To do this most effectively, we can follow the example of those who have the strongest connection with Him. Jesus is one such man.

While there is much debate over the nature of Jesus, whether he was or was not the Son of God, whatever you choose to believe, Jesus exists in spirit form. He was also one of the first people to prove the reality of a life in God's name and to bring this belief of God into our world in such a way that it could not be ignored. Jesus holds a very special position; he lived and breathed a spiritual life and yet sacrificed it for the sake of humanity. Knowing the true value of his existence, still he allowed it to end for all our sakes. Because of this sacrifice, the total commitment that he showed and the widespread recognition of it, billions of us know of Jesus. He was an education to everyone during his time on Earth, showing them an alternative to the barbarism and suffering they endured. His teaching was one of non-violence guided by Love and living by that example showed us a way to a more perfect spiritual life.

God spoke to Jesus and gave him an insight into a life lived under His guidance, so that Jesus developed faith and understanding. Because Jesus had this ability to communicate, to listen to the ultimate source of higher insight and was prepared to act upon it, he is still thought of by many as being the ultimate example of a life well lived.

Jesus has become a clear window and a conduit to God for the rest of humanity. If we pray to Jesus, we are connecting with a higher energy that allows us to look through a doorway to the Creator and to gain a spiritual connection through Jesus.

However, there are some who have a belief in Jesus and refer to him as their example and guiding light and yet still struggle with the idea of a loving God. There are a number of reasons for this and predominant is the fact that life can prove to be harsh and even cruel. Yet Jesus himself, who loved God, experienced the harshness of physical torture as part of his spiritual journey. His journey to God included forgiveness, even for those who persecuted him. Even if we wish to believe, it takes time to develop faith in any kind of spiritual existence, because true faith can only be built on experience and Jesus's journey included some of the harshest lessons about human nature and suffering that we can imagine. Think what strength of spirit and determination it takes to love your fellow human beings if they torture and kill you. Think what compassion must drive a man like Jesus to act out of concern for the well-being of all, knowing his own life was therefore at risk. Imagine how progressed a soul must be to make the choice of being born into a life of such challenges.

Even on the spiritual pathway that is revealed through our clear vision, we may initially have no faith in spirituality or the existence of a higher intelligence outside of ourselves. However, as we progress, we can find our own spiritual beginning and learn to understand the spiritual universe, its structure and the nature of those who belong within it. It takes time to get used to these ideas, some of which may be new to us. That is where an open mind is our greatest strength, because it allows us to suspend judgement while we increase our understanding.

However, our belief and connection with Jesus, although it is a doorway, may not alone take us through to God. Jesus is a man we can relate to, a man of his times who brought a religion to us that has endured in many forms throughout the ages. Because his purpose in life was to help and guide others to wholeness, the very idea of a man who endured so much in human form, can connect us with one another and with God. So, His example has created a pathway to a collective thought and singular mind and even as each of us functions individually, yet we can be of one purpose if we channel ourselves through prayer to Jesus. If, in this way, we are learning through Jesus to become of one thought, one mind and one spirit, then ultimately that leads us to a pathway of love. While in this way, as a man, Jesus has made the pathway to God still more recognisable, still God is the Creator whose light shines around us to make all of this possible.

Jesus is not the only window to God, but as a human being who embodied devotion in Him, he is for us in this place and in this time, the clearest gateway. Other spiritual teachers and doorways exist and in our day-to-day lives they can be windows to God's love that are open every moment of every day. For each society and culture, there are ways to access these openings, through belief and the development of understanding that leads to faith and ultimately love; and faith in Jesus can create an opening to our Father.

By directing our aspiration towards the Creator, we can learn to recognise the ways in which we can reach Him, both through our prayers and the way in which we live our lives. Whatever the nature of our faith or the name of our religion, it can serve to connect us to the greater cause which is all around us. Working with love can make our lives complete, so that we are whole and at one with God's purpose. Spiritual development, whatever name we give it, can lift us out of our ignorance, so that we have a better understanding of ourselves, life and others.

All of us are learning and progressing on our individual journeys. The very fact that we are here on Earth shows that we still have lessons to learn and elements of life to experience. Those who have progressed and exist at the higher levels in spirit world have already gone through this journey in human form and learned understanding and compassion. From their position, we who are on Earth are like children who are still testing life and making mistakes as we progress, learning as we go along.

For many of us, spirituality is a new experience and we may feel the need to reserve our judgement as we learn this unfamiliar territory, our boundaries within it and how to incorporate it within life. However, as we develop our experience, we may be surprised to discover that there is more to life than we at first suspected. This realisation can lead us to want to know more and to seek out answers to life's bigger questions. To get the answers we seek and experience them for ourselves, we need to find a way of being open-minded and receptive to the higher levels where this knowledge lies.

Often our ingrained emotional and intellectual barriers are what hinder us from finding the best way forward, yet if we can recognise all the positive things in our life, then this in turn helps us overcome our inner conflicts. A positive perspective teaches us to identify with what we are learning, rather than what we are going through and even the most trying situations offer us the opportunity to learn from them. If we are grateful for what we have in our lives, it can be hugely beneficial to our development because gratitude is like a beacon both for human and spiritual beings alike.

This receptive attitude allows us to recognise that we are here for a reason and sows the seeds for us to open to a greater belief. Spiritual practice allows us to find a way to the source, to God and the spiritual universe rather than just our own singular mind. Gratitude therefore is a gateway. Jesus gave us the words and the way to find our Heavenly Father and if we can be grateful for that, then we are open to both and our life can become one of immense spiritual discovery.

What is the purpose of life?

God works in mysterious ways. In our physical bodies on the Earth plane, it is as though we are attending a school; this is a school of life where we have every opportunity to learn and progress through our experiences. God has provided us with a physical existence, so that each of us can attend and learn all of the lessons that life has to offer, to choose what perspective we take, to choose what direction and path we follow. This life is an opportunity for us to become increasingly whole. Everyone in the world is learning in this way and the act of learning builds us, so that we become whole in our own right. Ideally, our journey is one that allows us to go with the flow and to react positively to the challenges we are presented with; not so that we achieve material success or power over others, but so that we can be proud of the characteristics we develop, such as patience, compassion and a giving nature. Naturally, we gain the ability to recognise and apologise for our mistakes and at the same time to stand up and be accountable for our actions, to recognise that we are not the centre of the universe and to help others, giving us a worthwhile sense of humility. The whole time we are in this spiritual school of life, we are not alone, we have the presence of the universal energy that flows from God available to us, so that we can find direction and purpose in our lives.

While there is the potential for sadness in human life that can sometimes threaten our sense of well-being, the Creator is not overcome by loss in the same way that we are. Rather we can understand that God is like a father, a loving parent to us all and that our time here in our physical body is time spent away from the union of our souls with God. If we put our minds to God's position, and imagine we had effectively sent our offspring to boarding school, wouldn't we want to hear from them and receive their communications, to hear how they are and to offer advice and support? The opening is there for us to gain His advice and spiritual support through prayer. So, His sense of loss comes when we do not communicate with Him and share and thank Him for the opportunity that life provides. While our Earthly fathers may place conditions on their affection for us, our Father in Heaven has no limitations upon his love, yet so many of us are unsure how to make that connection and benefit from all it can offer.

Why did we choose a physical form?

There is no substance on the other side, there we have no body, only energy. This means that to build ourselves, to develop and create a mature character, we have to come to the physical Earth to learn. Therefore the human body is the vehicle that allows the soul to create this more mature character and to develop. Our body is a precious gift that allows us to express ourselves through touch, voice and to see the beauty around us. The physical sensations of love, eating, drinking, the act of creativity and of making friendships are only ours in physical form. Only here can we touch and feel through our five senses. Imagining what it is like to be deprived of these simple pleasures tells us why we choose to manifest here on Earth, even with the prospect of the trials and tribulations that accompany a human life. This incredible chance we have to experience directly through our physical form gives us a vehicle to address our lessons and create memories and feelings that we can take back with us to the idyllic world of spirit. In this way, each life here on Earth will build our souls with knowledge and experience and we should never forget that we are here on a unique spiritual journey in a physical body.

All of us are destined to depart life with nothing of our material wealth to accompany us. Thanks to advances in medicine, technology and nutrition, many of us are living longer lives than in recent centuries. Therefore we have more time to reap what we sow while in our physical bodies and work through our karma, so that we can fulfil life's purpose and live out the journey we came to make. This is our chance to be good to our fellow human beings so that we make the most of our visit down here and feel the sheer joy of living with sharing, caring, friendship, laughter and loyalty.

How we view life and how we view God

When we put our mind to God, each of us may receive a different image of Him for us to work with and interpret. How we perceive Him is less important than what we are able to give and receive in that relationship with Him. For instance, one of us may be aware of the power for relaxation and healing we feel in communion with Him and another may see the colour that is missing or present in their lives. Still others yet may see God in a familiar form, either male or female and experience the warmth of a caring friend who is able to bring completion to our lives. As the Father of all us children here on Earth, we may feel His authority and with it recognise how small we are in comparison. Each of us is shown and experiences what is right for us, as in our human form we are only able to perceive a tiny amount of His totality.

With this understanding, we can see the bigger picture. Each of us is present within God's energy, we are like grains of sand on the beach, recognising ourselves within him. We can also see that each and every one of us is destined to be a complete whole being, because we already share an inner completeness. Our journey is to bring that completeness into every aspect of our lives, so that we become whole. When we have achieved this through learning our lessons here, we are ready to be received in the spiritual sense by the other side. Having succeeded in our endeavours down here, we can then know that we have secured a place for ourselves in the spiritual plane when we pass over. There we can be empowered again with all the learning we have gained here. There is a place for all of us and we choose and become what we have rightfully earned.

God doesn't make it difficult for us down here on Earth, we make it difficult for ourselves. We think and question more than is healthy, we pursue Earthly ambitions and material goals to the detriment of our spiritual selves and we allow our minds to be negative when positivity is the solution. As human beings we carry the potential both for positive and negative within ourselves and it is humanity who introduces the negatives in our life. God wants us to enjoy our lives and all He is asking is for us to treat our friends and neighbours as we would like to be treated ourselves. Nowadays there is pressure on everyone, in many countries there is a lack of spirituality and a greater chance that our neighbours might be angry and bitter. Therefore, it is harder to love and turn the other cheek. For many of us, we are no longer in an age of total barbarism, fighting external wars. Rather, our struggle is within ourselves and yet this inner struggle is generating conflicts that spill over and impact on our fellow human beings.

Many find it easier to be at war than attempt the task of loving unconditionally. To love unconditionally is no easy task. How can we love when we know that the people and situations we are in have the potential to harm us? In this day and age we may feel we constantly meet situations where it is necessary to be on our guard. There are many of us, perhaps even the majority, who would rather not be in conflict with other human beings, perhaps preferring peace and putting our energy into something that fulfils us. However, if we do not stand up for our rights, the real and great danger is that other people will ride roughshod over us. This is the conundrum that faces us. We cannot avoid life and its situations, nor should we choose to be a source of conflict to others, so steering a peaceful pathway through this world means we need an inner strength that helps us focus on the long-term goals of our life. We need to let go of the things that seemingly hold us back. If we find this strength through God, then we are better able to remain focused on our life's true purpose.

Chapter Twelve - Spiritual Beings

God oversees the entire spiritual universe, while below him are many layers inhabited by angels and souls who have progressed in varying degrees in their journey towards union with the energy that emanates from Him.

At the uppermost levels there are the angels and below them the souls gathered into groups in one collective thought, each with their own purpose. Below these are those who collect in family and other groupings relevant to what they have shared together in their physical life on Earth.

Angels

Angels are a true representation of unconditional love. While God is the highest authority, existing at the peak of the pyramid of spiritual development, the angels are on the next level below. They are beings of God that exist solely to work in accordance with His will. Angels are pure uncontaminated beings that consist of Spiritual Energy as part of the Divine and they bring their perfection to our lives in order to help us.

Angels are higher beings because they already exist within the Divine. Whereas a human being can choose whether to encompass a spiritual path into his or her life, an angel is only ever on that pathway and progress their spiritual development by working with us here on Earth. Whereas a human being learns through his or her mistakes, an angel is already pure and perfect and therefore does not learn through their lives as we do; rather an angel learns by working with human beings and furthering their own development and understanding by doing so.

Angels are neither masculine nor feminine, rather they are a divine energy that is capable of encompassing and assuming either gender according to our needs; therefore they are perceived in the form they choose to project. When we use the masculine or the feminine here to describe an angel, it is merely for convenience or to reflect how they present themselves.

This is not a book on angels and for the purpose of this book we wish to give you just a general feel and an indication of the purposes and powers of angels and what they are there to do for us. Every angel has a purpose that is potentially beneficial to humanity. All angels are healers and there are angels for every emotional need.

The archangels of the highest order are well-known to many of us, archangels such as Gabriel, Raphael, Michael and Uriel work on a large scale to improve the bigger picture. Having learned to comprehend the pain of human development and how best to respond to our emotional suffering, these angels have developed to a stage where they are wise enough to work with the whole of humanity.

There are thousands of angels, on many levels, with different degrees of learning and we do not necessarily work with the higher levels of angel, but rather with those that respond directly to our emotional needs. The multitude of angels who are below the archangels will work over the aeons with many humans, healing with their unconditional angelic love. An angel's role is solely to respond to our emotional needs by offering healing. Angels are not here to administer to our wants for everyday comforts, such as parking spaces or material things we may feel we need. Rather the purpose of an angel is to elevate the energy within us, not to increase our material wealth. Angels respond when innocent souls cry out for salvation from their emotional pain and they will identify, help and heal those of us in the direst need.

Every angel can work with us in this way and eventually they become powerful enough to ascend to the next level. The higher levels occupied by the likes of Michael, Gabriel and Raphael operate on a far wider perspective and may work with whole countries to offer what they need, be it tolerance, guidance, love, forgiveness or compassion. In this way the angel will help large groups or countries to develop the positive traits that are most appropriate to the situation and suited to the angel that is called upon.

Over the centuries an angel can develop to a point where it has achieved the ultimate level and angels who have achieved this are the masters. They have reached the uppermost level for an angel, which is a position of supreme spiritual attainment.

The seniority of an angel is defined by its degree of learning and not by its age. However, an older angel will have a more mature feeling associated with it because it has achieved advanced knowledge. Human beings age in years while angels ascend like our souls, through experience. For an angel to progress this far he will need to be able to develop by coming down and doing his job, which is to respond to the cries for help we utter.

An angel that responds to our initial cry for help will usually be the same one that works with us from that point onwards. This is because that angel will relate to us and understand us as individuals. Angels may come when we least expect it. They respond to our prayers to God, or to the despair of a person trapped in a situation not of their own making. They will then help us and stay until that situation is resolved. When an angel comes they embrace us with love, which is of a pure nature in every way, a divine healing energy. This is the unconditional love of God, brought to us by an angelic being.

Words cannot adequately express the depth, nor the enormity of angelic love, nor the extent of the forgiveness these Heavenly entities feel for us through their understanding of our human frailties.

An angel may not be able to take all our emotional distress from us, because they cannot remove the situation we are in; rather, they may lighten the burden enough, so that we are able to carry on with our lives. It is important that we are able to let angelic healing come naturally and that we are open and receptive to it.

When we call upon angels for their help, it may be that the angel does not necessarily come to us in person. Rather, the angel may recognise the need and send their energy to us, so that we work within the light of that angel. Sometimes, just sitting quietly and allowing the feel of love and energy to arrive and surround you, can enable your angel to embrace you and help heal your emotional pain. Whether they visit with their presence or merely send their light to us, angels respond to the truth within us with unconditional love.

Meditation aids the process of connecting, because it relaxes and heals the mind and body. Sitting in meditation gives the angel the opening to arrive and to let their energy flow into you, so that their divine energy joins with the physical, becoming one with you. Work with an angel and your life will be enhanced and the burdens will be less stressful until such time as their support is no longer needed.

Healing Meditation with an angel

Preparation
Put yourself in a place where you feel at ease. Sitting comfortably or lying down, put on some relaxing music. Take some nice deep breaths and close your eyes. Move your mind-energy to the backs of your eyelids and, keeping your eyelids closed, look through them into the darkness beyond. Letting your shoulders relax, listen to the music and breathe peacefully. Let go of your Earthly vision and any distracting sounds around you. Focus your attention outward into the darkness and allow your mind to clear of all thoughts and worries.

Meditation

In your mind, simply ask an angel to come forward. Stretch your mind outwards into the far distance and become aware of a pinpoint of light far above. The light is barely visible as it manifests in your mind's eye.

Knowing that this is an angel coming towards you, see the light as it nears you coalesce into the form of a beautiful white cloud. The light that comes from this cloud is so brilliantly white that it almost dazzles you and emerging from the cloud is the form of an angel that gradually takes shape. You feel drawn towards this angel and await its arrival.

The angel comes nearer and nearer to you with outstretched arms. Feel the angel arrive and its wings fold around you until you are totally encircled. With this envelopment comes unconditional love and you experience the most angelic glorious feeling you can possibly imagine. Let the divine energy come through. Feel how safe and secure you are. Allow your body to relax and know you are loved unconditionally now and always; and that you are being warmed by a greater compassion than you could ever imagine.

Open your heart and voice to the angel's love. From your inner self, let the beauty within you come out. In truth and honesty, in your mind, communicate how you feel. Ask the angel for help and for love.

Remain within the angel's embrace, allowing the feelings of security and warmth to continue until you are ready to feel either the angel's wings begin to unfold or you feel the time is right for you to let go.

Now the angel begins to move away from you, rising up and receding into the distance until it becomes white light once more that dwindles to a pinpoint.
In your own time, rise from your angel meditation.

Joining with this angel can enhance your life and help you through your most difficult times. We should always remember that with an angel comes love, freedom and compassion, so we must never feel restricted in calling out for an angel's love and support for ourselves or for others.

We should never be afraid to talk to our angel or to call and ask them to ease our burdens. Your angel is on its own spiritual pathway and because it embodies love, will be there until such time as you are able to move on. When this happens, your angel will know that everything is alright and is then free to help another soul.

Exercise for asking an angel to help with rescuing the soul of someone who is crying out for help

Preparation
Put yourself in a place where you feel at ease. Sitting comfortably or lying down, put on some relaxing music. Take some nice deep breaths and close your eyes. Move your mind-energy to the backs of your eyelids and, keeping your eyelids closed, look through them into the darkness beyond. Letting your shoulders relax, listen to the music and breathe peacefully. Let go of your Earthly vision and any distracting sounds around you. Focus your attention outward into the darkness and allow your mind to clear of all thoughts and worries.

Exercise
In your mind's eye visualise elevator doors in front of you.

The doors slide open and you step forward into the elevator. Once inside you see a panel of buttons and in your mind you reach out with your finger to press the topmost one.

You feel the elevator begin to ascend. Be aware of this upward motion and sense it within your mind, allowing yourself to travel with the motion of the lift.

After a short while, the elevator arrives at its destination. The doors open and you emerge.

All around you is open formless, colourless, space and just ahead of you is an escalator that rises up into the distance. You step onto the escalator and feel yourself rise as it begins to carry you upwards.

After a while you reach the very top and find yourself on a solid platform surrounded by blue sky. Here you ask for an angel to come forward to show you how they interact and heal us in our physical life.

Above you a pinpoint of light forms that moves towards you, becoming brighter and brighter until it develops gradually into the form of an angel. In your mind's eye you see this angel descend and reach out to hold your hand.

The angel that has come for you then takes you down through the blue sky and clouds. Feel yourself descend until you can make out a town below, with streets, houses and trees. Continue Earthward until your feet touch the ground and you find yourself in a busy shopping centre.

When you arrive, the angel may retain its spiritual form or it may change to the form of a person of its choice. This can be one that you recognise or not, of any age, race or disposition.

Become aware of the noise and the people around you. Watch as they move about and interact with one another. Be aware of the hustle and bustle from where you stand with your angel. Now that you have recognised the scene around you, tune into the thoughts of everyone you see. You are now hearing the thoughts of each and every person. These will take many forms. Thoughts of happiness, good thoughts, thoughts of longing, of being away from home, of wanting to be somewhere else, thoughts of urgency and of watching the time, feelings of frustration, of being hungry, every kind of thought is there.

Now that you are here and aware, ask the angel to lead you to a person whose soul is in need. The angel will respond to the cry of a person's soul and you are led by the angel to that person.

The angel connects with the person, the cacophony of sound around you dies away and from that point onward there is silence. Once this connection has been made, focus your attention on these two alone. All around things have become still and quiet and we are with that one person and the angel. They are our sole focus. In communion together, the person's soul then talks to the angel directly. The angel has recognised the need, responded to it and having answered the call, is healing with unconditional love.

This healing connects directly with the area of need and we should feel and be aware of how this person's emotional needs are met. We observe until it is complete. When we reach this point, we will naturally feel the sound return and our awareness expand once more back into the precinct along with the noise and sensation of busy people moving around.

The link between the two naturally falls away and the angel is now ready to depart.

The angel takes our hand and we rise up once more together. We return to the top of the escalator and watch the angel ascend, moving away from us into the distance until it becomes a small pinpoint of light that finally disappears from view. You depart, now returning and descending on the escalator. Upon reaching the bottom, enter the elevator once more. Pressing the bottom button on the panel, the doors close and you descend again to where your journey began. Stepping out of the escalator, your journey is now over.

In your own time, allow yourself to come back with your awareness to where you are and close your meditation.

This exercise helps us to tune into the call of a soul crying out for help and to know that that plea can be answered. It also shows us that an angel's purpose is to help people on a soul level and not the physical level that we might normally look to.

The soul is the meeting point between Heaven and Earth. By learning from our journey on Earth, the soul progresses. If the journey here on Earth is too painful, it can be blocked by circumstances beyond our control, such as illness, grieving, or emotional pain. There are varying degrees of need, but when our pain becomes too much for us and our soul needs help, it will cry out. It is then that an angel can respond and for the person that the angel touches, life will become less stressful and less painful.

We can go wrong in life by imagining that the physical is all there is, but if we want to have a truly fulfilling life, we are far better off recognising the deeper sources of happiness that come from a spiritual pathway. The soul, if it is allowed to express itself by influencing or being part of our thinking pattern, can find the rewards it is seeking. However, if there is too much pain or anger or negativity in someone's life, their soul can become stifled. This happens when there is too much selfishness, a focus on the material, or on controlling situations. If this happens, the soul can become subjugated to that person's will so that it is ignored or ultimately even crushed. If we do not recognise or value our inner needs and, out of ignorance, we carry on putting our wants before our needs for self-development, a soul can become frustrated. Where our inner self has no satisfaction or priority, this lack of fulfilment will, in all likelihood, express itself as a feeling of barrenness or hunger. Feeding our soul with its natural diet of good, positive feelings and actions is what makes us truly happy.

The soul can only manifest itself through our feelings and, unless it is recognised and we act upon what our soul is feeling, it has no outlet. If it is not connecting to life through the bodily actions or being allowed expression through our thoughts, it cannot achieve what it truly needs, which is harmony with our outward life. Fulfilled souls shine out, while those that remain unfulfilled will be frustrated and, in extreme circumstances, cry out for help.

Therefore, one way of looking at a spiritual pathway is that it enables the actions of the soul and the body to be joined. If this is achieved by acting in positive ways that enrich ourselves and others, resisting the temptation to retaliate or put ourselves ahead of all else, then we have a union with the potential to defuse the negatives that we meet during the course of our lives. A life lived through our connection with our soul can have only a positive effect on our spiritual development and vice versa.

If this soul connection is not acted upon and a person has lived selfishly, or wittingly behaved badly to others, then when they pass over, their soul experiences a wider spiritual perspective. The opportunity to reap the rewards or make amends for our life takes place. Because of its union with the human body, the soul is accountable for the actions of that body and will need to feel the remorse and regret over the actions of that life. The soul will then need to experience the effect of that life's actions be they pleasant or unpleasant. If our conscience is clear and at peace and we have acted positively and generously, then we will experience the rewards both during life for the wonderful feelings that brings, after death and in lives to come. If we have acted maliciously, then we will need to experience what it is like to be part of similar suffering and selfishness to that which we have caused. This experience is negative karma and will be part of a future life. After death, when we arrive on the other side, we will experience remorse but no guilt, and will reap what we have sowed. Therefore, our pathway is not within our control, but how we choose to act upon it is.

If we are innocent or ignorant we can be pardoned for our sins, but the more self-knowledge we have, the greater our responsibility to our soul when we pass over. This is why it is so important to react as positively as possible to everything we encounter in life. The more we live through our karma right here and now, then the easier it will be on our soul now, on the other side and in future lives.

Souls are created by God and develop by being born on Earth into a human life. Just as we age in years, our soul grows and develops through experience and we can have life after life in which to create those experiences. When a young soul comes into this world, born into a body for the first time, everything it tries will be new to it. Without innate wisdom from past lives, it will experiment, learn by trial and error and will need discipline and guidance if it is to progress. Ideally this discipline will come from the parents, teaching the child good habits that become ingrained and allowing the soul within to learn by adopting a positive position. For young souls especially, there may be a temptation to rebel and fight with life, going into every situation with a competitive attitude. It may be a parent's soul's journey to aid and develop someone younger and in that way, good parents will aid the development of a new soul.

By comparison, parents who are providing the wrong kind of guidance will potentially block the soul's natural spiritual progression. Nowadays, with so many of us seeking happiness, the more we can seek to bond with our fellow human beings, be they family, friends or like-minded people, the more we have to build upon.

The soul is a totally different identity to the body but at the same time works within it and by the same token is happiest when it is allowed a role and a voice in guiding the actions of the body. This voice takes the form of our conscience and we feel it as a sense of rightness and wrongness about any given situation. It is our sense of misgiving, or our sense of liberation, that is the voice of the soul, depending upon whether we are letting it guide us or not. If we lead a good life our soul will be more at peace with itself and so we feel more at peace.

When a life ends, we pass over into the world of spirit and our soul is then given the opportunity to account for that life, to absorb what it is we have learnt and to address how we have lived. If we have wasted our life or acted maliciously or badly, we will be given our opportunity for remorse. Just as in our everyday lives, at some stage, we may be called to account and we will be given our opportunity to address those things we have not yet learned. Our soul can feel remorse which may feel like punishment in itself. At some stage, every negative action will need to be balanced, normally by feeling the consequences of that action for ourselves in a future life. The vast majority of us are merely learning here according to our ability. Our souls will benefit from all the good things we do, feeling the great liberating joy that comes from helping others and being a positive influence. This means that those who have passed over and whom mediums connect are expressing the learnings of this life and remorse and happiness will be expressed according to their actions.

The implication for us here in our lives is that it is far better to live in awareness of the consequences of our actions and to recognise our soul, so that we are living in a way that meets its needs. If we do not and we are guided by the conditioned brain alone then, in the most extreme cases, we have no feeling of what we call right and wrong. Therefore, what we experience here on Earth becomes our guide for what we do with our life. So we see situations where instead of learning from what it feels like to be treated badly and ensuring we do not do the same, instead we adopt that behaviour ourselves. So we see situations where those who are abused pass that abuse on "My father beat me and it didn't do me any harm, therefore I beat my kids." The soul does not rationalise in this way. Instead, it feels its own inner right and wrong because its inner compass points it to do things that are fulfilling and abhors things that are negative or destructive. That is why when a soldier is reluctantly called to war and has no choice, the soul will not rationalise the horror of war but will manifest feelings of revulsion and reject the killing. Whereas those who have tucked their souls away out of sight and out of mind may come to relish the violence for the feeling of power and control it brings.

Therefore, if we allow ourselves only to listen to the experience that we possess from our conditioning and close our minds to other sources of input, we will remain limited. The trick on a spiritual pathway, especially when developing our clear vision, is to suspend our judgement until we know with certainty and in the meantime, to ignore our own opinions until they are based on experience. But we cannot know until we have tried something, experienced it and have enough knowledge to allow us to decide what we feel is right for us. The more we are open to experience, the more we can learn. If we allow our soul to guide us, we will learn what is right for us to learn and importantly, to live without judgement.

Learning to be at one with our soul is a life long journey and we cannot learn what is in accordance with our soul from others, only from how we feel within.

The spiritual overseers
In the world of spirit, there are many levels. If you were to visualise a pyramid to represent the hierarchy, then at the top of the spiritual pyramid is God and directly below him are his messengers, the angels.

The next level is occupied by spiritual beings who act as overseers, helping and guiding the spiritual beings below them.

These overseers are supreme beings, perfect in every way and there are relatively few of them compared to the billions of human beings here on Earth. These spiritually perfect life forms have progressed far enough to oversee the activity of the entire universe on every level of reality. With positions of advanced spiritual authority, they make themselves available to manage all of the levels below them.

All of these beings have had physical bodies in previous Earthly lives and have acted as guides here on Earth. Yet they have progressed spiritually to a point where they no longer need to incarnate. With all their lessons learned on the physical plane, this ultimate level of being act as guides to the levels of spiritual beings below them in the pyramid.

The teachers

The next spiritual level down from the overseers is populated by the teachers. These are a level of being who are able to instruct the spirit guides (the next level down in the hierarchy). Teachers are also able to connect with human beings, however at this level, they will normally only connect with those human beings who are fulfilling some higher purpose or pursuing a spiritual journey and need a higher level of spiritual development. Like our guides and the other beings in spirit world, Teachers can provide instruction to those of us able to link psychically, as well as those who are open enough to receive guidance through their intuition, whether they realise it or not! However, teachers are always acting for the widest greater good and will usually only contact those Earthly beings who have a wider spiritual path to pursue and therefore need a higher level of tuition.

Spirit guides

The level below the teachers is populated by spirit guides and they are spirits who have themselves progressed but not so far that they have achieved the same status as the teachers or overseers.

Spirit guides act as guides to those of us here on Earth and in the world of spirit. These beings are able to appear in seemingly physical bodies because they have progressed to a level where their spiritual incarnation is complete. They are sufficiently conscious of themselves that they can manifest in the shape of a body. The same is true for teachers and overseers, who are also incarnated completely in Spirit World.

Tuning into the spirit guides can be difficult and yet they are easier to reach than the teachers and overseers who are on a far higher level.

For each of us, did we but know it, there is a guide we can connect with, or who may be looking out for our needs. Guides may be linked with us throughout our entire lives, appear at the times of our greatest need, or where physical or emotional changes are taking place. Our level of awareness of these guides depends on our ability to directly perceive them and our openness to their influence. With training, we can learn how to recognise our guides and make contact and even communicate with them. In all instances, our guides will only come to us when we are ready to receive them and we can therefore benefit from their positive influence.

Guides bring harmony and stability and if we work with the guidance they offer, it can help us develop. Our guide is there to put balance and structure in our lives, enabling us to access a spiritual viewpoint when we may most need it. Therefore working with our guide can aid us on our spiritual journey and help us attain our spiritual goals. Guides help us gain the freedom of knowing who and what we are, and what we want from life.

If we are lucky enough to see our guide either physically or in our mind's eye, the appearance, nature and type of guide we receive will be a reflection of the type of support being offered to us at that time, which will always be what is most needed. So for instance, an American Indian guide is associated with nature, taking what they need rather than too much, operating in total harmony with the motion of life and never challenging the Earth but working with it. If we see this type of guide therefore, it will be because either emotionally or physically we have become lost, or we need the balancing guidance the presence of this guide provides simply through the act of being. The American Indian guide will help a person to look at their own priorities. This is because an Indian is all about bringing the priorities back to where you really belong; this means to the home, to respect of nature and to an appreciation of the things you have in your existence. American Indians, when their civilisation flourished, were at one with the land and therefore they understand and embody simplicity. An Indian as a guide is therefore all about bringing you into harmony with yourself and finding a spiritual awakening through this simplicity which can in turn give us an uncomplicated ability to express ourselves.

If, for comparison, we see a Nun as a guide, she will be providing us with help in building our faith and establishing inner peace. A nun is there to help us find strength within, to pursue a deep inner journey for our soul's sake. A nun can help us in our spiritual search, because the purpose of a nun's life is to understand and develop their own faith. A person with a nun as a guide, therefore, is finding themselves by building an inner sanctuary of faith. Nuns are usually with people at a time when they have discovered their spirituality and are now establishing their own likes and dislikes, their strengths and weaknesses so that they can build upon their spiritual strengths. In short, a nun provides a route to self-help through inner strength.

Another common example of a guide would be a Zulu warrior. Typically, a Zulu warrior guide will be there to provide strength and the ability to unite with people that will help and protect the person. For instance, if someone were facing a legal case, a Zulu warrior might come to help them bond with like minds and provide the ability to fight a battle. This warlike challenging nature is there not to help us fight physically, but to provide us with the will and perseverance we need in times of struggle.

Child guides are all about putting simplicity into one's life. Children live life as free spirits and therefore, as guides, help us let go of the stress, strains and worries that plague us. They can remove complication with their innocence and bring with them a playful light heartedness, as well as an uncomplicated curiosity in all that life has to offer.

There are many different types of guide and we have used only a few as examples. We don't necessarily have to change what we are to live down here and neither are our guides here to change us. Spirituality is all about being complete and being one with our beliefs and the convictions by which we live. It is this living in accord that is the important part and when we are ready, and only then, a guide will come forward to help us on our journey of self-development, influencing us as we most need it.

Whereas angels can be evoked to visit with us and heal our needs, offering love, a guide will appear only when the time is right. Therefore, when we reach a stage where we have developed far enough and yet are in need of further progress, invariably this is when our guide will become apparent.

To recognise and see our guide, we will need to have reached a stage where our guides are both present with us and ready to show themselves. If we are at this point, we may be able to meet with our guide with our mind-energy and therefore form an impression of them in our mind. Alternatively, we may just be aware of the presence of our guides by feeling them near to us, or it may be that we feel a separate type of thought pattern in our mind. For instance, when we are seeking inspiration, or looking for an alternative way of building our life. Whatever way our guide comes in, they are there to help.

Progressing to be a spiritual guide is part of a spiritual journey and sometimes our guides are young themselves. Whatever their age our guides will also be learning through us.

Eventually, having experienced enough lives on Earth, we will pass permanently to Spirit World. So when we have learned all of our lessons here, we reach this point of no return. Having earned a permanent place for ourselves in spirit form, from that point on we are re-born into our own souls, rather than into a physical body. If we have developed enough self-understanding, we will have wisdom of our own that we are able to pass on and we now have the choice of whether we ourselves become guides.

Chapter Thirteen – Our Spiritual Journey

Each of us has a unique personal perspective on our life and the world around us. Whatever our outlook, we learn and grow from our smallest physical beginnings as children, developing into adulthood and old age. The feelings we experience as we grow both create and influence our developing perspective and determine our attitudes in later life. When we are young, we initially see life from our own singular viewpoint and as we grow older we have opportunities to see many other points of view from people with experiences different to our own. If we have an open mind, this will benefit us because we have the flexibility needed to allow learning and accept what feels right for us. The widest opportunity we can create for ourselves is to adopt a spiritual perspective. That is because spirituality is able to help us to step back and use our intuition and our feelings to guide us through life. This approach helps us to perceive an ever widening panorama, because from a spiritual viewpoint we have the chance to see ourselves and the world more clearly.

Clear vision is a gift in the truest sense of the word, because with it we are able to look at life without the interference of conflicting emotions and see it for what it is, an essential ingredient for our spiritual development. By developing this clarity, we are able to step back and perceive the ebb and flow of humanity.

If we are able to take in the whole picture of billions of people throughout the ages living and dying, we can see just how small one life is in comparison. The lives we have here on Earth, the births and the deaths are all part of our natural progression. We are here, right now, experiencing just one of our many lives, as is each and every person around us. There is no physical thing that can ultimately reassure or protect us from the hardships of living, life's threats and challenges and ultimately even death. In each life, each of us is on a journey, making our own choices and taking our own chances within it. There is no hope to survive life and yet we can make this journey the best thing that has ever happened to us, if only we choose to learn.

All of us are seeking happiness and perhaps the fulfilment of our needs for comfort and security. However, we do not always receive what we want, nor are we all totally fulfilled. Here on Earth we are granted moments within which we experience sheer joy, but to experience these feelings consistently, we cannot hope to do so through the physical alone, instead we need to understand how the physical and the spiritual work together.

Our soul's journey is similar to the development of physical life here on Earth. We begin with a young, vibrant and immature soul that is initially like a new born child. That soul typically will learn through centuries of experiences gained in each physical life.

Being spiritual leads us on a pathway of understanding and the more we progress, the more we can appreciate the benefits of experiencing both the positive and the negative on our pathway. By growing and becoming one with ourselves, we gain a better understanding of life and those around us and can learn to appreciate that challenges help us grow. In developing this understanding, we can not only find joy in the things that bring us pleasure, but also find pleasure in the things that bring joy to others.

Love

Taking a spiritual journey involves relaxing, letting go and broadening our thinking to encompass the spiritual. Being at one with ourselves can be achieved in this way and if we choose, we can pursue a pathway of becoming one with everything, joining with the universal energy that emanates from God. In embarking on this journey of becoming one, we recognise that our physical lives, if lived spiritually, can have a meaning that never ceases to increase so that we achieve fulfilment. If we are living in this way, we can recognise the responsibility we have for ourselves and the way in which we act. There will always be an option for us in how we choose to direct our thoughts and our actions. On a spiritual pathway we can become more flexible, choosing to involve our minds with the universal energy and beyond.

Whether we realise it or not, the universal energy radiates from God and permeates us all and we may be working with this loving energy in the actions we take. It is up to each and every one of us whether we choose to look for this energy and bring it into our lives. Regardless of our viewpoint, simply helping and loving others or being a source of good will can enhance how we feel and change our perspective. Treating others as we would wish to be treated can pave the way for love.

Experiencing love can be one of the highlights of our life and many of us have an idea of what love can mean for us. We may wish to share love with a partner, our family or children, or we may have a need to receive the reassurance that being loved can bring.

Yet there is no way of knowing if what we think of as love means the same to others, nor may we be aware of just how essential love is to our lives, or how deeply it can change them. The love we give and receive here on Earth pales in comparison to that expressed by those in the spirit world, who are free of our thoughts and distractions and do not have to devote time to their physical survival. Their love and the love contained in the universal energy is far greater than that which we are able to experience here, because there, love is the driving force, whereas here on Earth it can be a privilege we experience only briefly. Here on Earth, we are limited by the very fact that we are on our physical journey, perceiving and giving only a small part of what we are ultimately capable of. We are able to experience a greater love and to do that we can focus our thoughts on the higher planes, to the spirit world and to God's universal energy because ultimately, God is the greatest expression of love that there is.

So when we examine it, love is a topic that fills our lives and if we fill our lives with it, then we can be fulfilled. Yet when we talk of love, do we have a full understanding of what love can truly mean?

There are many types of love. There is the emotional love experienced between partners in a relationship, there is the love between family members, there is erotic lovemaking, the 'love' of infatuation and there is the bond of love in friendship. The most selfless love we see here is the love of a mother for her child and it is this love that is the closest we have to unconditional love or the Love of God. This kind of love means accepting someone with all their faults and frailties, understanding that each and every one of us is fallible, but loving them nonetheless without judgement. For all of us, this unconditional love is the hardest to achieve. Why, after all, should we love the people we dislike or those who we think are acting against us, or even try to love people we have barely met or may not even know?

The reason it is so important to love is that love is a reflection of who we are. If we are able to open ourselves to Spiritual Energy, then what we get back is the love of spirit world and if we are able to open ourselves to the universal energy, we are open to the love that emanates from God.

Another reason it is so important to be open to love is that it can make us feel so good. Even the love of one person can make us feel happy and secure and it can change how we feel to a huge degree. Love shared in a relationship can bring feelings of warmth and loyalty that bond us together, love between families can make us feel part of a bigger picture, a partnership that has bonded.

We are distinguishing between the different types of love because it is important to understand the conditions and circumstances surrounding our Earthly love so that we might imagine a greater love, one that transcends and yet encompasses all these different types. If we realise how loved we are by the spirit world and God, and choose to let that love into our lives, we can encounter feelings of fulfilment beyond measure.

Starting a spiritual journey

In today's hectic societies, where many of us are crowded together in towns and cities, there are many times where we are brought into contact with people and situations that cause us stress or even anxiety. Travelling, working, shopping, even socialising, we find ourselves in circumstances where we are side by side, much of the time with people we have no acquaintance with, alongside those we may know.

With the mass of humanity expanding, it can become stressful just to journey to work. Often, we can find ourselves with people whom we simply wish weren't there because they are slowing us down. People may inconvenience us just by being in our way, let alone the ones who are deliberately impeding our progress! Cramped on the bus, tube or train with people who inadvertently bump into us, or stuck in traffic with cars all around us, it can be very difficult to keep our minds open and recognise that we are all just trying to get along with our lives. These are just the very simple examples. The more complex areas, such as our relationships, money matters and love lives can sometimes contain what seem like insurmountable challenges. It can be difficult even to just be indifferent to the people around us, let alone experience feelings of love!

We have all been in at least one situation like this where we get frustrated with our progress in life and life's constraints. Even if we are simply queuing at the supermarket or waiting in line for a train, we can have our plans frustrated and become impatient.

While not everyone in the queue is feeling this way, we may be late for an appointment or picking up the kids from school and all these little things can make us eager to get on. Typically, at some point, we will start to feel frustration and anger, or even a dull resignation that seems to deaden us to the situation. This is just an example of the smallest frustration, yet countless times a day we can find ourselves seemingly pitted against life's obstacles. If we looked at the whole planet at any given time, zooming out to a satellite view of the Earth, how many people are there experiencing these feelings in their day-to-day lives? It is millions, if not billions of us.

Whatever the situation we find ourselves in that is leading to these feelings of frustration, disappointment and even anger, the irony is that none of us want to feel this way.

In reality, no matter how big they seem at the time, many of the daily irritations we experience can be seen as just that, small things that niggle us but aren't spoiling our whole lives. We may already have a good perspective on this and not let the little things annoy us too much, yet each of us has a limit to our tolerance. The important thing is that we keep life's irritations in perspective, so that we can instead concentrate on the important and positive things in our lives. Practising clear vision can help us by giving the overall life perspective we need to stay calm and centred, not because we are holding on tightly to our reactions, but rather because we know our life's purpose and that being held up in traffic will not alter it. Clear vision can give us a wider viewpoint on life and this, in turn, can increase our ability to relax, accept and let go.

'God,' we are told, is Love. Even hypothetically, if any one of us were in a relationship with someone who loved us unconditionally and only wanted the best for us as a person, then that would feel good. If it were someone who would forgive us any weakness and want us to feel good about ourselves and life and to fulfil our potential, imagine what that would be like. If that person could radiate these feelings to us, so that whenever we tuned in we could be filled with it, then that is close to what we can receive from God's Love.

Imagine if by using our clear vision we were to discover our life's purpose. It may be that it is to have the feeling of loving a family or to experience many types of relationship. Whatever our purpose, allowing ourselves to feel surrounded by this type of love, the day-to-day irritations can become less intrusive.

How long would our frustrations last if we knew that we were loved totally and unconditionally, come what may? That kind of feeling is possible within this life if we discover and acknowledge our connection with the universal energy. It is up to each of us to decide whether we wish to incorporate this connection into our lives

The first step towards achieving this unconditional love is to allow ourselves to imagine what that kind of love is like. If we take this step, then instantly we are opening ourselves to wider possibilities. If we make some space in our mind to ask for that kind of loving feeling to enter our lives every day, then we have taken the first step towards an experience of that love. The only barrier is our own mind and if we are prepared to start working positively with our thoughts and emotions, we have already allowed ourselves the flexibility to be open. If we are able to open in this way, we may find that this love comes into our lives far more quickly than we expect.

If the warmth and fulfilment that comes with this love is in our lives, we begin naturally to see things in perspective. We don't have to consciously decide to take a wider view; we don't have to do anything other than open ourselves to love from the universe and a more relaxed attitude is the natural result. The wider a perspective we take, the less the negative things in our day-to-day lives can affect us and the more we can enjoy every minute.

But is it possible? Can we truly achieve that state where everything is in total perspective where we receive love and give it freely? We might think it is attainable or we may feel that there are too many barriers in our way. Often our feelings can run unchecked and despite our best efforts to direct them in positive directions, our emotions can run riot and work against us. For instance, if a relationship ends, do we still feel the same about our ex-partner? We may have negative feelings of hurt, rejection and even anger or resentment towards them. Even if we desperately want our heads to be clear, it may seem as though we have no option as to how we feel. However, the more we can think positively towards everyone in our lives, even those where we find it most difficult, the more we can begin to get the feel of this Unconditional Love. Clear vision offers us an insight into ourselves and those around us, so that we can unravel what may initially seem like a tangle of emotions and pursue the strands that take us towards a happier life. In this way, clear vision teaches us how to express our free-will in positive ways.

We are each a grain of sand on the beach of life and it is the universal energy that delivers each grain of sand into this life. In today's society, many of us are packed tightly together, each grain of sand resting directly against the other. Whether we are packed together, or whether we are living in an area with more space around us, as we progress in life we have a need to interact with those around us and a great need to get on with our fellow humanity. There is always the danger that our rough edges will catch and grate against each other. Often it is our family, friends, neighbours and work colleagues who are seemingly the source of many of life's frustrations because they are the closest to us. Yet each grain of sand is unique, each of us having different thoughts opinions and viewpoints. So why should we expect everyone to share the same thought pattern as our own? By recognising these differences and choosing to accept situations and people for what they are, eventually we will find a niche that is perfect for us; because we are acknowledging life, we can focus on where we want to be, and not on what is holding us back. The fewer issues, baggage and hang-ups we have about people and ourselves, the less our lives will seem stuck. With no chip on our shoulder we are better balanced and in a better place.

So why is life not perfect? Why the daily frustrations? Why can't we each just be happy? To be happy all the time, life would have to be perfect for each and every one of us and if that were the case, we would not be in a position to learn anything and we would have no need to change or consider our own role in the situations around us. So life here on Earth cannot be totally perfect. To find true happiness within, we need to look at the way in which we approach and deal with life. By tuning into the universal energy, we will become more positive within ourselves and we will grow and develop, increasingly in tune with what is happening around us. If we experience feelings of being out of kilter, of being frustrated, or not feeling that we are getting what we want from life, then clear vision lets us see the bigger picture and how to tune into it so that we can accept and go with the flow.

The doorway is always open for us to experience the feeling of the spiritual, allowing healing into our lives, using clear vision and, if we choose, to act upon what we find. The more we can develop and apply a positive outlook, the more we progress on our spiritual path.

Because we are choosing to step outside the narrow track of our automatic reactions, turning to sources of wisdom other than our own conditioning and thinking of viewpoints other than our own, we are making choices that are far more positive and well considered. The habit of making these positive choices makes us more rounded and better weathered as individuals.

Because we are taking a seasoned approach rather than seeking to impose our will upon life, we become a rounder grain of sand, less likely to get stuck in one spot because of our rough edges and more able to go with the flow, naturally finding situations that are 'right for us.

Once we have found our niche, we can understand our position within the bigger plan and appreciate just how small each of us is. This, alongside a realisation of our significance and our purpose, means we can recognise how each of our lives are interconnected, ultimately originating from the same source both spiritually and physically. In this way we are able to maintain our individuality while recognising how we all fit together, and this helps us to develop greater love and understanding for ourselves and others. Knowing that we have tried and tested the choices we have made, and acted upon what has brought the best results, our journey brings us to a place where we can feel good about ourselves, take pride in our wholesome achievements and continue to develop our positive traits more fully.

Spiritual freedom

Many of us in the west live in a society where we have at least a basic level of material comfort. We live in countries that enjoy freedom without war on our home soil and with opportunities to access a wide range of educational prospects well as media and entertainment. In short, many of us enjoy a level of personal freedom that allows us, perhaps with some effort, to point our lives in whatever direction we wish.

And yet, in this society we see increasing levels of stress, of feelings of lack and lonely people without true happiness in their lives, even amongst those who have achieved fame and fortune. Why, with so much around us and available to us, do we see so many people using anti-depressants or turning to drugs, alcohol, even anger or violence to numb or vent their frustrations with life?

Many of us have what is really a narrow viewpoint on life and our focus is on what we want to achieve for ourselves, either in relationships where we put our own feelings first or materially, where what we want is of paramount importance. This acquisitive striving for fulfilment can blind us to what we already possess and can blind us to the feelings of fulfilment we can have right now, regardless of how far we have progressed in our search for a fulfilling relationship or the satisfaction of our material desires. The danger in striving for an outside source of fulfilment is that we are inevitably concentrating on what we feel is lacking in our lives and what we need before we can start feeling happy. By thinking in this way, we can end up cutting ourselves off from our ability to enjoy what is around us and recognising how far we have come on our journey. Spiritual freedom is available to each and every one of us. To gain it, we need to see what is holding us back in our lives, whether it be our thoughts or physical restrictions. In talking about progress, we are not talking about becoming a millionaire or driving a fast car, having a huge house beyond our needs, or a partner who fulfils our every wish. Rather, we are talking about progression in our personal happiness and an increase in our ability to deal with life, regardless of situations and their consequences.

Whatever our viewpoint, if we continually feel the stresses and strains of life, we can begin to feel under pressure and frustrated with our problems. Eventually, feelings of frustration can disorientate us and we may begin to feel lost.

For each of us, there is the alternative of looking with a wider perspective to truly understand the meaning of life. If our focus is on the whole journey, then perspective is easier to find. If we trust that life will continue, we are less likely to be panicked into acting upon our own negative emotions. We can then differentiate between getting what we think we want out of a situation and what is right for us.

To overcome the stresses that cause us so many problems we need to take a regular holiday from our day-to-day pressures, so that we can regain peace and calm and give ourselves the space to deepen our spiritual perspective.

Meditation is a way of regaining this perspective on a regular basis. Dependent on our viewpoint, we can meditate so that we gain this from within ourselves or, if we choose, look wider and access far deeper and greater peace from a universal source. We can choose to develop to whatever level we are comfortable with. We may be content in finding solitude and comfort from being with our own thoughts or we may choose to encounter and even to absorb ourselves into the universal energy, through the narrow chink of our mind's eye.

If you are able to meditate or can learn to relax in this way, then the doorway to self-development is open to you. If you are not yet at a stage where you can meditate and feel this is not currently possible, then you need to start somewhere, with something positive that brings these feelings of calmness.

Many of us find it hard to unwind. We may have become conditioned by the pressures upon us and perhaps blocked the emotions that alert us to the possibilities for change, or would allow us to do things in a different way. It may be that we have in small ways become solidified, either in the way we think or the way we do things, or so stuck that we find ourselves in the same unpalatable situations over and over again. If this is the case, it is time for us to break the mould and start again.

It is our busy minds that are continuously in overdrive that bar us from relaxing and our minds are often busy because of the circumstances around us. This is our 'catch 22', our conundrum to solve. There may be too many burdens at home that we feel we cannot let go of, our jobs might be stressful or we may feel overwhelmed by our own or others problems. By being able to see another side to a problem and have at least an option of seeing how a different approach might work, we can begin to work our way out of these cycles and rigid patterns.

Regrettably, many of us do not recognise our own stress until it is too late and we have already fallen out of harmony with ourselves, developing diseases or discomforts. That is not to say that everything that is wrong with us physically is a product of the way we are thinking (we are all subject to old age and to life's physical and emotional knocks). Rather, it means that we have a way of choosing the best way forward and one that avoids unnecessary stresses and strains.

Many things can stop us making changes; we could be afraid of the outcome of change, afraid of letting go or even afraid that we might let slip our rigid attempts to control life. Yet, if all we have ever had has been hardship and a tough life, this could drive us towards spirituality as a way of understanding and improving our lot. Alternatively, we could seek to cushion ourselves against life's vagaries by becoming materialistic and pursuing wealth. It doesn't matter how rich or poor, self-sufficient or needy we are, a spiritual road offers us a way forward, whatever our situation.

Even if we accept that spirituality has a role to play, we may question its importance in our life. After all, God cannot pay the mortgage, can He? If He did, we wouldn't have any challenges or stake in our own achievements and we would not learn from our mistakes. God's role is to care for and look after us, but He does not control our everyday lives. The guidance and love is there for us, come what may, but as a Father, he cannot pay for our mistakes, otherwise we would never learn from them. In Heaven, God pays the mortgage and we can exist without the striving and challenges we experience on Earth. Heaven is God's realm and so, once we are in Heaven, we no longer have suffering and pain. Hardship comes with our Earthly existence and exists so that we can develop character through experience.

Our role here is to get on with our spiritual journey. If, instead, we choose to fight against a way that is guided by stability and giving – the harder our lessons will become, not because we are being punished but because we are going against the flow.

Spirituality offers us a way of overcoming all these barriers and shows us that there is so much more to life than just 'this'. There is a huge difference between the exciting expansive feeling of spiritual exploration and the more limited feelings we experience in our day-to-day lives.

Letting go of ourselves, we are able to realise the greater knowledge and true self-development of the spiritual path and here we gain our feelings of freedom and release. With this development comes the knowledge that whatever our current situation, a positive outcome is possible. By letting go, we create a spiritual dawn for ourselves and can balance everyday life and the journey of life itself.

On this pathway, we will naturally develop a better nature and an increasing interest in others, because our own negativities have been cleared and we don't have to spend so much of our time thinking of ourselves and our problems. By replacing "I can't take any more" with "what can I learn from this?" and "what changes can I make?" we can gain a greater understanding of our own limitations and capabilities and further our own development.

If we trust in the flow of the Universal energy, we can live a life that best realises love.

When we read for others using our clear vision, we will seek to look at their emotions to help us identify with where they are and how they are feeling. Sometimes it is difficult to read the emotions, for instance if they are being suppressed. We can overcome this kind of difficulty by looking at the inner child of the person we are reading for and learn how negative feelings in childhood can build into the problems of adulthood. Knowing that people who are acting negatively are perhaps suffering or living a life of limited emotional well-being gives us perspective. This insight can teach us to be unconditional in our relationships and if we combine this attitude with trust in the flow of the universal energy, we can live a life that best realises love.

Letting go of control

Once we are on the road to seeking and developing an understanding of the much bigger picture we can awaken to our own importance and the fact that we do count. Overcoming the feeling of being an isolated singular "I", or someone who is out for just what they can get, opens us to a universe of teachings, far more than we might otherwise comprehend. There are some lessons in our lives that we very much need to learn and thinking of only ourselves can bring problems and difficulties which are the result of our own selfishness.

Depending upon how we grow in childhood, we can develop a selfish outlook or become a 'giving' person. If we have a selfish outlook because we aim to have things our way, we look for power and control over others. If we are frustrated in our relationships, we may become angry at life for not meeting our needs, or even if those needs are met, we may guard them jealously while still feeling something is missing. If, instead of seeking to understand other people and learning from them, we are driven by our insecurities and unprepared to compromise, then this outlook, in turn, makes us afraid to let go and trust in people and life. Ego, stubbornness, lack of respect for others and things that aren't ours are the result of this attitude. We feel we have to hold on and make sure that everything goes the way 'we' want it to. If it doesn't, we feel threatened and exposed. Our own fear of change and of losing control makes us selfish. If there is no wider spiritual life, all we have to reassure us is our power, possessions and the respect we seek to command in others. Respect should come as a consequence of who we are and what we represent; we cannot force others to respect us. If we crave that acknowledgement it can be a sign of our own insecurity and can lead us to seek to command it through force and fear. Self-respect and self-confidence on the other hand, need no outside approval.

So where does a selfish attitude take us? None of the blinkered blinded viewpoints it gives us will attract friendship or love. This attitude of selfishness may give us material rewards and respect for our achievements, but does not directly promote a feeling of love for who we are, either inside or from others; and yet it is this feeling of self-respect and love that offers us the greatest fulfilment and basis for happiness.

With a viewpoint that puts ourselves ahead of all else we develop a warped view of the world. We may even see kindness as weakness and, lacking an understanding of selflessness and generosity, question the motivation of anyone who acts kindly towards us. We can see this attitude develop amongst people in big cities where we are pressured and stressed and a kindly person may be seen as strange, or viewed with suspicion. This may be for many valid reasons, but it shows that we are suspicious, or suspect that many people are acting with their own selfish motivations at heart. We do not trust that a stranger could naturally be concerned for us.

A selfish attitude doesn't take others into consideration; if we are not careful, this mind-set can take us over so that all we do is focus on satisfying our own desires. In the extreme, this outlook becomes obsessive, leading to greed or a preoccupation with increasing our own power. Yet, greed is a foolish attitude because it can never be satisfied and we therefore live in a constant state of dissatisfaction, possessive of what we have and craving that which we do not. Therefore, with greed in our hearts we cannot be truly happy because we cannot hope to be fulfilled. We don't have to be wealthy to be greedy; it affects rich and poor alike. Yet greed can be compensating for an underlying lack of fulfilment, masking an emptiness we do not know how to deal with, so instead we fill our lives with material things.

Wanting to improve in our lives is not a bad thing as long as it is balanced. 'Scrooge' provides a classic example of the difference between hoarding and sharing. There is nothing wrong with wanting to improve our situation for ourselves and others; we may for instance like a special holiday with our family to share it with them, or for our children to be happy in a bigger, safer vehicle. If, however, we are seeking results purely for the status they provide, so that we can feel superior or because we would otherwise feel inferior, we are allowing ourselves to be driven by our insecurities. If we are stable in ourselves then we can look to receive our feelings of fulfilment, not just from what we get from life, but from the satisfaction of being able to share with others and enjoying the act of giving. If, on the other hand, we are hoarding above and beyond what we truly need, we are being driven by fear. By allowing life to flow through us instead, we are better able to relax and share.

Putting our spiritual journey into practice

By embarking on our spiritual journey, making just a few simple changes, we can begin to gain positive results and validate what we have learnt. In this way our positivity builds, the way we feel about ourselves improves and we have a greater sense of freedom within.

Meditation can relax us and liberate our minds and as we begin to learn the symbolic language of the universal energy, we develop our intuition. In turn, the natural order of life reveals itself to us and we can naturally flow within it. Our own clearer vision gives us proof in the form of affirmations from those for whom we read. Developing insight allows us to see our own situation more clearly and from this we grow. Our clear vision improves our spiritual journey and vice versa. Both are there to allow us to access help for ourselves and others.

The soul's journey

We are here to achieve a goal that clears the pathway for us to progress our true happiness here on Earth and on the other side. As we develop our spirituality, we can realise that our soul gives us more wisdom than our brain can ever possibly provide, that there is a pathway that is right for us and listening to our inner voice can help us to stay on the right track.

The purpose of our spiritual being is to bond with the physical, to gain knowledge and understanding of what we are here to learn. We all have something in mind that we are here for and we all have a starting point, but may stray from the path our soul has invited us to follow. Our initial start in life is given to us and allows us to develop in the best way. Our birth does not dictate where we end up; we have choice in how we proceed. Inner guidance points us towards the best direction and the best result.

If we are advanced enough to mentally let go of our body through meditation, then we can become aware that the soul joins the body for a reason. While we are on this Earth, our physical body should learn from our soul and be guided by our spiritual side. It is the interaction between our spiritual and physical that is our journey.

Therefore, to get the best results from life, the physical body must work in with spiritual guidance. The more we are informed and work from our own intuition and spiritual perspective, the smoother our lives become.
If we work the other way round there is a danger of losing the plot because we are choosing a selfish and not a spiritual path.

We are still human so we needn't cut off the physical nor ignore our own needs; we need to recognise the spiritual side of our nature and ensure it is working well with our physical life. We just need to be ourselves, open to the bigger plan and finding the lessons we are here to learn.

Our soul possesses the greater knowledge of what we have learnt here on Earth, while in our physical life here we possess the knowledge only of what is directly relevant to it. The physical body is just a grain of sand, while our soul when it is in spirit world unencumbered by our body (existing as pure energy) is part of the wider picture because our soul contains all of our lives and all of our existence and as energy is directly linked with that of God.

To accept logically that all this is so, we are forced to confront our own conditioning, opinions and current understanding. For many of us, it is easier to use exercises to join with this other world and feel these energies, than it is then to incorporate these feelings into our logical view of life. In short, there is no complication in spirit world, we are loved and not alone and the spiritual answers in life are simplicity itself.

We don't need to struggle, our spiritual experiences come naturally and we learn to trust the answers we receive. Clear vision shows us how to interpret these answers, because it teaches us how we can both know and feel what is right, experiencing the results of a spiritual approach to life and of knowing oneself.

In other words, we increasingly recognise our bias, conditioning and predispositions for what they are and by contrast gain a feeling for the inner self that exists eternally. Knowing oneself allows us to differentiate between the energy of the soul and that from our own brain. Getting used to the different feeling from each allows us to distinguish between logic and intuition. Our feelings and what we see clearly are then differentiated.

With each new life our brains are born anew to this world, while the soul is constant and retains the memory of each and every life it has experienced. This is a wider truth than many of us accept.

Brains, however, are obviously needed to help us control our bodies, to think logically and enable us to function and survive in this world, connecting all the functions of the body and enabling us to access reality through our physical senses. The soul is the goodness and beauty within us and the soul is God's child, so that on a spiritual level we connect to the source of all things through our soul.

Chapter Fourteen - The Purpose of Our Life Here on Earth

The purpose of our life here on Earth is to take a spiritual journey in a physical body.

The body is a vessel that facilitates all of our lives here on Earth, helping us to move, eat, sleep and enjoy the tastes, feelings, sights and sounds around us. Of themselves, these provide us with pleasure and a way of availing ourselves of the possibilities that life has to offer. With so many options open to us, each of us need to identify for ourselves where our true fulfilment comes from.

If we are looking for true happiness in life, our sources of security and comfort come ultimately from our connection with ourselves and with those around us. Our relationship with life is dependent on how true we can be to ourselves. A lack of the clarity this truth brings can throw our thoughts and emotions out of balance. It can even create an inner turmoil between what our soul wants from life and what we are bringing to it. Having a clear conscience, good relationships, a sense of our place, purpose and aspirations for self-development all enable our spiritual progress. Without the balance of caring, both for ourselves and others, our lives can deliver much less than their true potential. Therefore the spiritual side of our nature is of the utmost importance and if we are looking for true happiness within, this spirituality must be acknowledged and acted upon.

In this search for purpose, finding a reliable guide is perhaps one of the most difficult steps. However, no matter where we receive our guidance from, we will ultimately be pointed deep within ourselves for our answers. All we can gain from others is instructions on how to direct our inner journey; it is our soul that can show us where to take our lives from our most inner needs. When these needs are met, we are at our most fulfilled and it is therefore our soul that is best placed to be our guiding force.

In these modern times, looking to our own soul for direction and focus may seem like an archaic concept. Yet it is not our brain or our ego that should advise us. The brain is a facilitator and whatever direction we choose to take, our brain is the vehicle for acting on those directions. Therefore, if we rely on our brain or the intellect alone, we are ultimately relying only on what we know from past experience, what we 'think' is right for us to be our guide.

Of course, thinking isn't wrong, we all need to think, to figure out situations in life for ourselves so that we can learn through experience. Yet relying on thought and logic can lead us to rationalise putting ourselves in a situation where we only accept those opinions we have formulated for ourselves and not able to accept that there may be a bigger picture than the one we are able to perceive. This can lead to us becoming opinionated, rigid or even stubborn and many fall into this trap. It may be that there are many ways of doing something, but from our seemingly logical and rationalised singular viewpoint there is only one option to take – the one that we rationally see to be right! Because logic ignores our emotions, it can ride roughshod over them and we can end up in a situation that might logically seem 'perfect' but does nothing to fulfil our true needs, nor have a positive effect on the way we feel. Logically, none of us should ever make a donation to charity because it takes away money that could help us now and in the future. It is only when we begin to factor in our feelings that we can see the true benefit of doing things that are perhaps illogical. If we put our reasoning aside and allow ourselves to experience, then the information we reason with can increase and, therefore, so can our perception and awareness of life. Like taking a swim in ice cold water, abandoning logic can actually wake us up far quicker than we imagine. Therefore, we are not putting forward a doctrine of abandoning common-sense, rather putting logic on hold can be a stepping-stone to clear vision.

Each of us operates to a greater or lesser degree with a balance of our emotions and intellect, both of which will be flavoured by our view of life, which is a product of everything that has happened to us and everything that is happening to us now. Most of us will have functioned this way for our whole lives, yet clear vision is extremely subtle, we attain it not by abandoning logic and making less of ourselves, but rather by developing through meditations and exercises that can help us become completely whole. Without a spiritual aspiration to guide this process, we have nothing to ultimately rely on, yet with it we can open ourselves to guidance from the universe itself.

One thing we should remember is that clear vision is a positive force and never does it work against people; it is there for us to work things out for the best. It will always guide us in ways that may require personal effort but always for the greater good.

If we look to live out our selfish desires alone, we live a two dimensional life. Whereas the guidance we receive from our clear vision illuminates our lives and will direct us in beneficial ways, our own thought-patterns may be misguided, disjointed, ill-advised or incomplete. That is not to say that we need to become martyrs to our spirituality. We are here to enjoy life and it is essential that we point our lives towards long-term happiness. What we need to remember is that the short term pleasures we enjoy from life can consume us. These pleasures are not bad things per se. They can divert us and provide us with great experiences and memories; yet ultimately none of them are going to fulfil us. If we go to the extreme of abusing them, as many of us can be tempted to, we can become slaves to them and our lives lack meaning.

This is why it is so important to tune into the spiritual side of our nature, because it is this that brings all the higher feelings, aspirations and greater joys, such as love and caring. The soul brings into our lives all the good, enjoyable, long-lasting qualities that establish us as worthwhile, wholesome human beings; it is these qualities that give us our deepest awareness, happiness and joy.

If this all seems like too much to think about, then remember that for each of us, life can be both a learning zone and a balancing act. The more balance we achieve, the more we learn and vice versa. There are immediate pleasures to be had through meeting our superficial desires and there is the fulfilment of having our deeper soul needs met. We don't have to struggle against one and strive for the other; instead the more we relax and let go, the less reliant we are on short term pleasures to divert us from our lives. If each of us relaxes more because we know that ultimately we are looking to work for our own and other's good, just imagine how nice a place we can have inside our hearts.

We looked earlier at how the soul is our best source of guidance. The soul is a mediator for our body in that it can function to bring harmony into our lives, communicating with us through our conscience and our feelings. It is the soul that provides reasoning, understanding and through its very nature, gives us patience and balance. Therefore the soul provides the vehicle for having our deepest needs met while we enjoy life and the sensations within it for what they are. The soul can put all of our life into perspective.

If we look at it from another perspective, if we did not have souls, none of us would have a conscience. Without a soul, we would have no human nature and we would instead rely on our intellect alone to guide us.

If we want to prove the existence of our souls, currently it can only be done through personal experience. There is neither instrument nor machinery that can conclusively measure energy to the extent that it is scientifically proven, nor any form of apparatus that can look into our soul or the spirit world. Yet, working with our clear vision, we can tune into and be aware of something beyond our understanding. By connecting with our soul using our clear vision, we can feel the difference between our needs and our everyday wants. In this way, we can appreciate the difference between inner fulfilment and superficial desire and understand more deeply how the brain functioning without reference to the soul can steer us in directions that prejudice our spiritual growth.

Connecting with the soul opens the sensitive deeper side of our natures, where our feelings are joined with the actions we take. It is the soul that lends ultimate accountability to our lives and realises the higher elements of our nature such as compassion. If we were without souls we would have no conscience, sense of responsibility nor shared unity with others. If we have inner feelings of disquiet about how we are acting in life, then this is most likely our soul informing us through our conscience. If we listen to it, our soul keeps us on the pathway to inner happiness.

Our soul also gives us continuity. Without the soul, we could not grow as individuals, all we could learn would be the very basic disciplines of working for personal gain and looking after our own needs and without a soul we would have nothing to be reborn into the next life. The soul is the vehicle for our on-going development because it is the soul that takes on the experiences from living each life. This is an important point to remember; we are not here to punish ourselves for past mistakes. Each of us strays from the pathway at some time or another - if we did not, we would not learn. But that is not an excuse for ignoring our responsibilities or not making amends for whatever harm we have done. That is where the soul comes in as counterbalance. To live accountably to our soul we must live with our conscience.

Ultimately any of us can only fully meet our emotional needs by developing wholeness in ourselves. The quickest way for us to find the pathway to feeling this harmony and equilibrium is by recognising that the body is a vessel through which we achieve our soul's purpose. If our focus is on this soul fulfilment, then our lives will be lived along lines that deliver to us the potential for true inner happiness.

The soul is the guardian and originator of our most central self. In it we find our deepest purest thought-patterns. Our greatest heartfelt needs that underline who we are as human beings and individuals can be found there.

We experience the needs of our soul through our emotions. Emotions do not stop at expressing our pure needs however, or our lives would be clearer cut. If we are thwarted in our original desires, we can become impatient, embittered, jealous and even angry. All sorts of negative emotions can become confused with the underlying original purpose of the journey through which our soul is here to guide us. In this way, circumstances can drive our emotions out of control so that we lose sight of whom and what we truly are. We then seek the fulfilment of our emotions in ways that are not fulfilling, rather than weathering life's storms and staying true to our original purpose.

Emotional pain and our conscience tell us when we are going 'wrong' for ourselves. If we are going through life feeling superior, or inferior, with a chip on our shoulder, angered by what we feel life has done to us or experiencing any kind of emotional pain that we cannot seem to release, our quickest way to feeling better is to look to our own needs and find where our disharmony lies. If we base our lives upon our soul's journey the lessons we learn can offer us options to our emotional pain.

Being able to live with ourselves is one of the most important things in life. That is not to say that we should live blame free lives, or that we cannot experiment. After all, what is right for one person may be wrong for another, so much of life is about trial and error. It is fine for us to have human desires, be they sexual, material or otherwise. However, we should not let them take control of our lives. Life is for joy and loving and giving, not getting stuck on the gratification of our immediate desires.

Everyday life and the situations it presents can make us forget what the journey is about. The small things that happen to us can appear much larger than they are. Bad experiences can make us nervous if something similar reoccurs in our life - and the more we allow ourselves to worry about these everyday problems, the more they can take over. However, we are only human, so we should not blame ourselves if we let these everyday concerns get the better of us every now and then; this is understandable. The key, again, is balance; by developing harmony between the soul and the brain, our human life is a progression of the soul's wishes.

By developing our ability to see the bigger picture and look beyond our immediate environment, we can rid ourselves of the insecurities that can otherwise gain a foothold. Clear vision teaches us to see life and people for what they are, thereafter we gain a greater understanding of our natural spiritual development.

We need not get hung up on the material, it is only when our pursuit of our desires conflict with our spiritual progression that we need be concerned. The natural personal progression we experience from developing this spiritual perspective can be diverted if we use our advancement to further our own ends. Clear vision aids us in developing ourselves spiritually and material benefits are a bonus. For instance, if we have a chance of material advancement, knowing that to gain it will mean harming another, we know that there is potential conflict and we must examine our conscience to see if what we are doing is right for all concerned. That is not to say we do not put ourselves forward for a job promotion based on our merit or work for what we want. We do not have to deny our abilities, but rather show as much respect for others as we would like for ourselves.

With an open mind, we can learn to respect others and consider their feelings alongside our own. If we do this then we may better understand them and develop humility, in that we appreciate our place in life. Behaving in this way allows us to love ourselves more fully and in turn be loved for who we are. We can do none of these things if our mind is closed. Spirituality comes to us when we are ready for it, not when we want it necessarily. Therefore, a key part of our journey is having patience with ourselves as we develop.

The meek do inherit the Earth because they have learnt to love and respect other human beings and their experience of life is therefore enhanced. A meek person is not a doormat, rather it means they have learnt to put others first, to be what they are and no more than that. Therefore, the meek inherit a life free of the negativities that can otherwise plague us and they inherit the Earth because they are the ones that are making the most of their time here, not wasting it on thoughts that hinder their lives.

Threats to our emotional and physical well-being in this life can give rise to insecurities, but these insecurities are not necessary to our soul's development, rather they are a product of our own negativities and vice versa.

As we develop our clear vision, we will naturally begin to view life differently. Situations that we previously found stressful, or avoided, will either disappear or we will view them in a different way. Gradually, we will clear and deal with the emotions that trouble us and we may gain a much clearer understanding of why we develop our stress. This self-knowledge enables us to deal with life with a clearer mind.

We are given free choice in this life but that is not all that God gives us. He gives us an environment that we can find beautiful and that will meet our needs. In our life there is, of necessity, the opportunity both for pleasure and pain, for reward and disappointment. If God puts us onto the beach of life to swim and play, then that beach must have a natural order that governs what happens on it. In the same way that one cannot have water and the joy of swimming, without the threat or fear of drowning, we cannot have the good things in life, like the joy of developing a friendship, without the danger of falling out. If we had no free-will we could not learn and develop. How could we recognise pain if we had not experienced it? How can we be wise if we have never had a lesson? Those lessons we are told or learn from books can guide us, but are in no way as impactful as those we experience for ourselves. For our souls to develop, we must learn, to learn we must experience and to experience we must be truly involved, so that endeavour and action may show us the consequences and corresponding beneficial or negative results. Part of our journey of experience is to recognise the value of the things around us. We can learn to value the rewards we get from the effort we put into our lives and therefore what we achieve within them. If everything were to go our way all the time, how would we comprehend cause and effect? If we have our fingers burnt we can warn others of the danger, but only by being burnt do we truly respect the flame.

Life's journey is one that offers us enjoyment of every moment for itself. However, if we focus purely on instant gratification and fulfilment in the moment, we can rush headlong at life with no awareness of our inner needs. In this situation, the danger is that any of us can become totally wrapped up in our pleasure seeking, even to the extent that we only look to what we consume to fulfil us. Anyone with an addictive personality can attest to how destructive it can be to focus exclusively on outside substances and situations for our fulfilment and to the very real detriment of all else. What once was pleasurable instead becomes a source of pain.

Relationships, alcohol, drugs, food or even work can be used to distract us from a lonely inner void. Yet they can never fulfil us and if we develop an appetite for them it may never be satiated.

Looking at it another way, if there is no end to our desires, how can we ever hope to be satisfied or content with what we have?

Having needs or ambition is not a problem. Rather, it is the dependency on fulfilling those needs for their own ends, or the absolute dependence on meeting those needs where the problem lies. If we achieve a state where we are happy within ourselves, everything else that comes into our life can be a bonus to be enjoyed. We can then savour everything we have for what it is and not devalue it because it doesn't meet our vision of what we deserve or think we should be getting.

Needing material things in our life isn't wrong, nor is having them. Neither is it wrong to have high aspirations for what we achieve, or to wish for a happy life. What we should recognise is that the greatest enjoyment comes from inner fulfilment and this is made possible by a clear conscience, from holding love in our hearts and seeking to enjoy life regardless of what we receive from it.

Nor should we be seeking perfection; nothing is perfect in this world. Rather, spirituality can lead us towards the most giving life we are capable of so that we feel the best feelings within, come what may. The more in-tune we are with ourselves, the spiritual universe and the energy within it, the more of these things we are able to perceive and enjoy. Just as the good in life is where we find it, so developing our clear vision is invaluable because it allows us to see so much more of where this good lies. In this way, we can be proud of what we are, truly learn to love ourselves and come into our own.

How we choose to view life and people

Clear vision offers us the chance to look at our own situation, both spiritually and objectively. If we are seeking to learn from life, this allows us to see the lessons it offers us for what they are, allowing us to grow and progress. This attitude helps us to understand naturally why things and people around us are as they are.

Another way of looking at it is that if we are experiencing life and not learning from it, we are wasting that life. If we are rejecting what life offers us and not moving on, then this reduces life's meaning. Therefore, the ability to see what we can learn from a situation gives true meaning to our life of itself.

Each and every one of us is an individual in our own right, with many differences and when we meet someone new, we can very quickly form a first impression that is either benign, favourable or adverse, all based on their unique characteristics. Yet even though it is formed just on a few moments' observation or interaction, how we subsequently deal with that person will bear relation to the opinion we formed in those initial moments of meeting them.

For instance, each of us will have experienced the feeling of meeting someone that we are instantly unsure of or dislike. We may find ourselves on our guard, with our barriers up, thinking "I don't like this person! I can sense something about them." Yet, as we get to know them, we can then form a totally new opinion. So what feeling do we trust?

Clear vision gives us the opportunity to look deeper into our reactions. It can tell us whether we have a reason to be on our guard, or whether feelings of mistrust are based on our own bias, preconceptions or insecurities. It can even be that someone is perfectly nice, but is totally incompatible with us. Clear vision can give us the answer because it sees more deeply than do any of our physical senses.

We also have free-will and even if we are not compatible with someone, we are still able to get on with them if we make the effort. Making this effort expands our boundaries and opens our minds, overcoming our bias and negativities rather than feeding them with more of the same.

How we get stuck in life

At some point in our lives, any one of us can become stuck. Invariably it is because something has overcome us, something that is bigger than we can deal with that may stop dead in our tracks. We may have suffered a bereavement or loss of a relationship or find ourselves at our wits end. Where is the good in life then and how can we move on from the most devastating of circumstances?

When we are challenged by seemingly overwhelming events, we can become stuck, it can move us to question what faith we have, or it can drive us towards a search for meaningful answers. Spirituality can teach us both to understand why we get stuck and to put our circumstances in perspective. In this way, it can soften the burden. Whatever approach we take, time is a great healer and yet we may never truly overcome feelings of personal loss. Being human means we are subject to the pain of losing that which we love. Being spiritual means we always have an option, no matter what the circumstances, of pointing our minds to greater understanding.

Our clear vision helps us in all circumstances to see life free of our own negative judgements. It helps free us from our usual habit of evaluating and even judging based on our personal preconceptions. Rather than judging others from the outside to reinforce our bias and views, clear vision allows us to understand someone from within. This works to our benefit and theirs, and this is partly why it is key we keep a clear spiritual motivation to work for the benefit of ourselves and those around us. This means being honest with ourselves about what we are doing and why we are doing it. If we are able to maintain this kind of clarity, we are less vulnerable to our emotional insecurities and it guards against them ruling our actions. If, on the other hand, we are not clear in our own minds then we are more vulnerable to being guided by our clouded emotions. That is why it is key that we develop the ability to relax and focus so that we can see things clearly. Clear vision can then expose to what extent our emotions dictate how we react to other people and offers an opportunity to choose to be free from this clouded perspective.

We can all think of examples where our emotional response has surmised wrongly. For instance, the person who is blank faced and doesn't reply when we say 'good morning' may (we feel) be rude or ignorant. But if we look at them from a spiritual perspective, using our clear vision, we may find a different story. That person may be quite thick skinned or they may simply not have a problem with acting grumpy if they are grumpy. Or even (Heaven forefend!) they don't actually like us and they don't have a problem in showing it. Many may consider this rude, but we could choose to see that this person has no pretence or is self-confident enough to speak their mind and we can therefore trust what they say. If someone were actually deliberately rude to us, we could also choose to recognise how this reveals our own insecurities.

If things aren't actually hurting us, but they merely don't necessarily suit us, then we always have the option of letting them go, so that we can move on and preserve our equilibrium without creating negativity. Also, we should always bear in mind that we can look to see whether there is a reason behind what is happening around us, whether it is positive or negative. Sometimes it can take a great effort to understand why people act in some of the incredible ways they do, especially when it comes to the people around us! It is up to us how far we go with challenging our own reactions, however, as we develop understanding, we will naturally judge others less.

Each of us has different patterns, behaviours and outlooks on life. If we have negative opinions about people, it is always an enlightening exercise to ask ourselves why? Have we come to our conclusion because we truly believe that is how things are, or rather is it because we have been brought up to think a certain way, or perhaps we are limited by our own fears, or because we feel we should come first. Finding out why we think the way we do means inevitably, we understand ourselves better. Understanding helps us release negative attitudes, means we are less cynical, makes room for better things to come into our life and clears the way for us to progress on our journey.

By reserving our judgement we become less fixed in our opinions. This flexibility with ourselves and other people can then allow us to contemplate ways of acting that we might never have considered before. For instance, instead of dwelling on people and situations, we can more readily let them go. Rather than reacting to what we see, we can learn to understand, firstly that there are a whole host of reasons why things happen and secondly that those reasons may not be the ones we initially imagine.

As we learn to keep an open mind, so we develop acceptance and recognise the value of being positive. Within any situation we can seek to apply a spiritual viewpoint. Instead of looking for negativity and pigeon holing people and situations, we can look for a meaning; we can look for lessons and we can learn about ourselves and about the options open to us within life. We then naturally become more open and positive. Because like attracts like, we will find that we are attracting openness and positivity into our lives. All this comes because we choose to change our attitude.

As humans, we are always looking for a state of happiness and perhaps contentment. A spiritual pathway can provide just that. Yet we may find it difficult to see the value of spirituality when everything is going well with our life and we feel no need to have anything more within it. Alternatively, we can be in the middle of the road and our situation has never been so bad that we feel we need to look for an answer elsewhere. In either of these situations, we may lack any motivation to seek something more.

By comparison, those whose lives don't seem to be working out, or who have experienced a grievous loss in some form, are quite commonly amongst those who would come to a spiritual path seeking an alternative. What is certain is that, whoever we are, spirituality can enhance what we have, broaden our horizons, shift our attitudes and even provide us with greater goals to aim for.

Because clear vision is all about insight into ourselves and life, because the path is one of internal development, any of us in any situation can discover the purpose of our life. All we need do is keep an open mind as we engage with the exercises.

As adults, we have a choice in our actions but we are often blind to our own faults. Most people can relate to this thought in some way, yet many of us simply do not realise where our limitations lie. It is through the process of becoming more self-aware and self-realised, recognising and seeing how we act and also fulfilling our own inner happiness that we see the 'before and after differences.' However, we may not realise until the change has been made or is developing within us. Therefore, our focus should be on the process and not necessarily on analysing or looking for a desired result. Either way, clear vision will enable us to see our way through.

Along this road, not only do we gain insight, so that the more trivial matters are put into their perspective but learn to love ourselves and gain self-knowledge, which helps us to accept others for who and what they are. Self-awareness is a long-term journey that is part of life and if we become stuck at any point, our clear vision can show us a way out.

Forgiveness
Clear vision also gives us the insight to see whether we are acting badly towards others, perhaps being selfish, negative or deluded. Knowing ourselves better therefore shows us that such negative behaviours have a reason and knowing this we can understand

other people better. Because we realise that we are all human and fallible, forgiveness comes more easily and we can afford to be lighter about things.

However, should we forgive everyone everything? What if people are deliberately rude to us or nasty? What if people are clearly acting aggressively? What about those who murder, maim and destroy the innocent? As we develop, we can understand why people act in the ways they do and we can condemn an action without necessarily condemning the person. Yet just because we recognise their motivations, it does not mean that we have to forgive everyone everything. The important thing is to know that we are not like that ourselves and not to be influenced by those who act destructively. We owe it to ourselves and to those around us to be the best we can be and to live good lives. In this way we gain more freedom.

However, life is not necessarily easy and when it becomes tough, we are all prone to emotional responses or falling back on our conditioned opinions. Stressful situations can make it more difficult to take an independent view. Therefore, each time we choose a spiritual approach or react with forbearance, we will receive better long-term results, because developing a viewpoint that is independent of our obstructing emotional responses can be the greatest ally in finding what is right for us.

All of us are human and we should not forget that we are here to learn. So life is not about perfection but rather about our willingness to live it and help each other as much as our position allows. Without making, we will never be able to distinguish right from wrong. Instead of blaming ourselves when we make mistakes, we can endeavour to learn from them and take steps not to make the same ones in the future.

We should not need the love and approval of others to be happy. The more we are happy and solid within, the less we judge and the less we feel the need to justify ourselves. If we encounter someone who is disagreeable or aggressive, then they may be surprised if we are solid enough in ourselves to adopt an understanding and caring attitude in response.

While we must be careful to keep our feet on the ground, a spiritual attitude and approach will produce a better result in the long run. Time is always a big factor. It takes time to learn this way of looking at life. We may have elements of it already – or have mastered it entirely! But to learn clear vision and see ourselves and others clearly, generally takes a while.

Anger

Anger is a result of the feeling of frustration we get when things aren't going the way we want them to, or we meet a situation not to our liking. Behind this is our desire to find a life that meets our needs. However, the reason for our anger, the energy that drives it, is not necessarily a bad thing; it is our impetus to express our frustration. But this is not an excuse to get angry. Anger is an incredibly destructive force and therefore it is learning to channel that angry energy before we use it destructively that is of most benefit. If we can learn to understand why we feel angry, then we can learn to channel that anger into expression, let the angry emotional feeling go when we recognise it is not productive, or use it as a prompt to understand ourselves and our own reactions that much better, so that they do not control us in future.

When angry, we can often act without reason, yet once our anger has passed, we may then realise the error of our ways and feel remorse. So it is better not to react with anger, even if a person is being angry towards us. In some situations, anger can escalate. Yet in many cases, if we don't react, a situation can defuse itself. If we are able to walk away from the things we do not like, or learn to accept, then this is a step towards overcoming our frustrations before they develop into full blown anger.

If we understand that no one becomes angry without a seemingly (to them) valid reason, then we have a chance of relating better. At the very least, an understanding approach and attitude will allow us to develop not only our understanding but it will also help us in our clear vision, because we will be better able to relate to frustration and anger and advise on how to overcome it.

It is equally beneficial to learn to let go of situations. This isn't to say we can't have input or guide a situation, but if we are able to allow things to flow without controlling them, it lessens our need to have things go our way and our way alone. A golden rule is to recognise that none of us is God and we must therefore not seek to control or manipulate another person.

If we are prepared to see what outcome might come from another's point of view, then we are more alive to learning and appreciating different ways of doing things. The other element here is that, of course, it isn't always that disastrous if things do go wrong.

Irritations can arise because a situation isn't 'controlled' just the way we want it to be. But if we allow ourselves to 'let it flow and let it go' we are more responsive to the flow and influence of the universal energy and things don't get stuck with us mentally or emotionally.

The added bonus that a clear insight can bring with it is that we are able to tolerate situations and people that we would have previously found very difficult or unbearable and we can learn thereby to be kinder to others. At this point, we can recognise just how well this training works and we can see that we are less likely to take on board the rudeness or bad behaviour of others. This doesn't mean that we don't abhor bad behaviour or bad actions. However it does mean that we don't have to become emotionally involved.

If we are aware of our actions and the effects they have on ourselves and others, then perhaps we would be more mindful.

Escapism

If we are seeking a spiritual pathway, it's usually because we want a better life, we want to help others, or we just want the kind of happiness that fulfils us within and we haven't found it elsewhere.

Sharing life is one of the greatest joys available to us. It is a spiritual act, yet we live in a world where we may not even know our neighbours. Our culture is focused on individual needs, rather than working for the majority and there is an emphasis on competing, one against the other. For this reason, we learn to feel hemmed in and territorial, which can lead to bad feeling and in turn can make us feel alienated. All these factors can build within us so that we become hostile to our fellow human beings. This, in itself, deprives us of the opportunity to share, for how can we openly share with those who we feel indifferent or even antagonistic towards? Life can feel solitary and painful. Inside us we have needs, an idea for happiness and a desire to fulfil ourselves. Yet for many of us, we do not even know in what direction fulfilment lies and we have no experience of the happiness that a cohesive community can help to build. Therefore, we are aware of a need to find a place for ourselves, a position, or something that will deliver happiness. Yet the irony is we have shut ourselves away from the very community that could go a long way to help us feel both secure and fulfilled. Often, instead of looking to meet the needs of a community, we seek to solely meet our own and instead of having a refuge within to turn to, we turn outside to escape our own pain because we don't have somewhere within to fall back on. If it's a bad day for us, we might grab a coffee or a chocolate bar, or escape into wishful thinking about our holidays, going home or perhaps anticipating when we can next escape our burdens. By turning our mind inwards, to solitary thoughts, we become isolated and ignore the opportunity to connect with others, perhaps in part because of the effort involved and the responsibility this would bring. Escapism can be a part of our everyday lives and yet we may not recognise it for what it is. Were we in a community where our lives had a common purpose , we could bond, connect, share and have less need for diversion from our reality because we are connecting with other people, with like minds and even seeking to meet each other's needs.

If our need for escapism is short-lived, it is not necessarily a problem; we are here to enjoy life and everyone needs some way of letting-off steam or turning away from every day cares. The truth is that all of us seek ways to divert ourselves, even if it is just to relax and find some space. It is when our escapism hurts us or has a negative impact on others that we need to look at it again and understand what it means to us and why we need a release to the extent that it harms us.

If we go too far down the path of escapism, then it can seem impossible to return. Whether we escape into food, drink, smoking, sex, gambling or many of the other forms of escape, it can damage our lives so much that it is difficult to find normality again. We can even lose respect from others or for ourselves.

Taking drugs, for instance, is one way of experimenting. It projects our minds into another reality and is a way of escaping from emotional pain that can otherwise be overwhelming. If our need for escape is strong enough, we can continue so that this way of getting away from our problems continues throughout our lives.

Having a purpose in life provides us with the potential for fulfilment. This is where a spiritual journey can help us, by finding that purpose within. Spirituality is not about imposing a regime, rather it is learning about ourselves and moving towards greater understanding. Tools like meditation provide the good feelings we are seeking through our escapism in a far more beneficial manner.

Putting our worries to the side, we can gain perspective and allow positive thoughts to take their place.

Nowadays, many of us are in a boiling pot of pressure, not only to earn and progress in our own lives, but also to meet the images of perfection we are presented with in advertising and the media and even perhaps to impress those around us.

In this way, life's demands test us and divide the weak from the strong. Spiritual thought reveals our inner strength, meaning we can live our lives with an understanding of who and what we are and create something good for ourselves. Clear vision can help us to gain this self-knowledge and if we are lucky enough, show us a wider universal picture. If, instead, we wait for life to embrace us or for things to get better without any sense of our own purpose or without our own effort, we run the risk of being unfulfilled. This can, in turn, lead to a feeling of stagnation, which can lead us to become disillusioned and negative.

Even if we do put ourselves wholeheartedly into life and achieve our material goals, without gaining a clear perspective, we can still feel lost and very alone. We may have an attractive partner, a high level job and a successful career. We may have a happy healthy family and a lovely house and yet, without inner knowledge, there may still be a feeling that we should be looking for more from life.

If we stake our goals purely on materialistic things such as cars, partners or money and achievements, then we may never be satisfied because there is always something seemingly more attractive around the corner. Yet we may have no real idea of what we are looking for from this material security and knowing that it is how we feel that counts, rather than what we possess, is a good starting point on any spiritual journey.

If we decide to choose things for the feelings and importance they have for us, rather than the importance that others might attach to them, or how we feel it might improve others' view of us, it can give our lives a totally different meaning. If we take this approach, we can feel a sense of achievement for what we have learned about ourselves, what we have earned for ourselves and the fact that we are now living our lives consciously.

It isn't wrong or bad to want comfort, security, happiness and stability; having needs and striving to fulfil them isn't a bad thing. Indeed, once our needs are fulfilled, we can live our lives from a sound base and if we choose to pursue a spiritual path, it will be from a firm foundation. But knowing that spiritual attainments are of more importance than material rewards loosens the chords of the desires that bind or pull at us, allowing us to learn to prioritise our spiritual needs.

Spirituality is there to guide and enhance our lives, to make them wider and fuller so that we can truly enjoy everything that we have and not be wrapped up in the striving for material things to make us happy. It is not an either/or choice between spirituality and life. Rather, it is the case that spirituality can permeate our lives. Still it can appear that the materialist is the happier person. In fact, it is our method of thinking that makes us think that the person with the most money is going to be the happiest. However, while material comfort is pleasurable, in the long run it is the person with the greatest inner contentment and peace that gains the most from life.

Faith

No matter what pathway we choose, we can only live in our own flesh in a physical world and that is where we must make our lives. Our life is in the material world while we are in it, yet the spiritual world is part of that life, not separate. The more we develop our own spiritual view, the better life can feel. Spirituality can open our eyes to all of life and we become explorers, so that we discover the joys while we are better able to avoid the pitfalls and ruts that we could otherwise find ourselves in.

If our life is a rocky beach, our spirituality helps us to appreciate the soft sandy gaps between the rocks for what they are and also to appreciate that life's trials are often stepping-stones that enable us to be stronger. The ultimate gift is to be able to help others on their own journeys. We can also recognise that the toughest trials are those that strengthen us the most.

It isn't just hardship that can lead us to seek meaning in life. Even if we are living a life of privilege, we can look for something else within it. If we spent our time eating nothing but ice cream, we would in all probability learn that eventually it loses its appeal and in the long-term, it is likely to make an unappetising diet in itself. Very soon we might long for some more substantial food – anything but ice cream! Therefore we can see that fulfilling our desire for pleasure doesn't bring lasting happiness.

If all goes well, we will learn these kinds of lessons in childhood, that one can have too much of a good thing, that one can have too much pleasure and that it can, in fact, be harmful. With clear vision we can choose to access the limitless sources of knowledge available and learn that there is substance to life and it is enjoyable in itself.

There are many ways of gaining fulfilment and the pleasure we derive from helping others does not harm us. However, we are not here to ignore our own needs. We must be wise and look after ourselves as well as we look after others.

The meaning of all human life is to learn our lessons and to progress spiritually and emotionally, so that we embody the journey of our soul. To do this, it helps greatly if our minds are open to a wider reality than we may currently comprehend. We need to release ourselves from negative emotions and open ourselves to positive viewpoints that will enrich our lives and bring joy. To give our faith and viewpoint substance, we build it on the bedrock of experience.

Nothing on the path of clear vision is taken on faith, yet it can build our faith so that it is the most steadfast part of us. We may already have beliefs without necessarily having experienced proof, yet faith gained through experience is the strongest and most profound. On the path of clear vision we can find proof for ourselves. Conversely, while we are seeking our proof, we can see the logic within the structure, the evidence from others and the benefit of the teaching. However, the danger of developing faith without having experience is that it is based on our opinions and opinions change.

Developing faith without proof can actually make our minds narrower because we are programming ourselves to accept something for which we have no evidence. We can even be trapped by our own understanding of what we read in religious texts, accepting or rejecting on the basis of our own bias and experience and interpreting without understanding. If we blindly accept, then we could, in effect, choose to have faith in anything that makes us feel better or contains just a grain of truth. If we believe without proof, then we can falter because faith is not something we dictate; instead it is something that should be built on the foundation of experience. However to experience we must first put our judgement aside and allow our minds to open.

With clear vision, we see life with increasing clarity and therefore faith comes from direct evidence. That is not to say that we know everything just because we have some knowledge. At first, we may be like someone who is partially sighted. Yet as these glimmers of proof come to us, our preconceptions can fall away and allow us to feel the warmth of enlightenment within our lives. This proof gives us faith in the possibility of something bigger that we do not yet truly understand. What is important is that we remain open-minded. That allows us to develop for ourselves as we test what it feels like to bring this spirituality into our lives and recognise the good that is being achieved. Gradually, through integrating this spiritual life, we become living evidence of its benefits. In this way, building our faith on this indestructible foundation of awareness, we become enlightened. We may never know what revelation is coming next, but with an open mind, tuition and practice we can continue to improve and widen our experiences for the greater good.

Faith that is based on experience allows us to be flexible while at the same time, like a rock in our belief, not because we have all the answers, but because our clear vision gives us access to a spiritual universe full of knowledge and understanding. On a spiritual road, self-realisation comes through mediation and prayer because they are doorways to honest communication with ourselves and with the universal energy. So on a spiritual road, the truth will prevail because it enables us to access inner understanding.

That is not to say that we cannot learn through reasoning; intellectual understanding can be a huge assistance. It can help us to learn. It can help us in our search for answers and allow us to question and satisfy our curiosity, but of itself, it cannot provide us with experience. It can provide us with the tools to develop skills like mediation, prayer and analytical arguments for or against the importance, or even the existence, of spiritual development.

However, unless we use personal practise to develop, we have no point of reference to guide those who have no existing understanding or learning of spiritual development. If we are not purposefully pursuing a spiritual pathway, we can still be thoroughly nice people, perhaps with well-developed spiritual natures. The point here is that for us to embody spirituality, we need to have felt and emotionally engaged with it. Our spirituality can become a barrier of protection but it is far better for us to develop an inner light, as this will help us most. Knowledge gained from reading and intellectual understanding in this context serves to guide us towards correct practice. But intellectual knowledge should not become reinforcement for our opinions; it is there to help get us nearer to feeling and understanding so that we truly know.

Once we have experience of clear vision, we will find that information and answers can come from above that are far better-informed than our own. Outer knowledge, wider knowledge, spiritual knowledge, giving oneself up to the greater good, giving oneself up to God, the Tao or whatever is our path, all of these serve to widen our perspective and move us away from the narrow belief that we are greater than all that is around us. How can we, who are short-lived and fallible, truly believe that we have anything like the comprehension that resides within the universal energy? Whatever belief, spiritual or religious path takes us towards a faith in something greater than our own comprehension, it opens the doorway to self-development and discovery.

We have all seen the results of misunderstanding that a narrow perspective delivers. Someone may have the best of intentions, but overlay a spiritual message with their own bias. Such as the man or woman that interprets the word of God for their own selfish ends or even as a means towards violence. This is like a doctor who treats us with dirty hands; the intention is good, but the consequences are potentially dire, because his medical care may leave us infected. In the same way, a limited perspective will not deliver the wholesome results that might otherwise be achieved if we can abandon our own bias and preconceptions.

A spiritual pathway can involve what may seem like difficult choices. For instance, we may be called upon to understand why bad things happen to people, or to gain a perspective as to why people do bad things. We may invest in our development, look at our own behaviour and, through investigation, learn more about ourselves. The understanding we achieve can expand our minds and enable us to appreciate and accept others for who and what they are. If we overcome our inner barriers and insecurities, we can get to a wider perspective that much quicker.

Even if we believe that we are born time and time again, it is always our current life that should concern us most, for it is only this one we can affect. Life is one meal and so is every moment within it – a meal that we cannot send back to the kitchen. Therefore, if we practice and develop while relating our spiritual journey to our own life, we can appreciate what it has to offer us and learn as we savour every moment of our experience.

What is the true meaning of humility?

A common misconception is that to be spiritual we must be a doormat for others. Far from it. Being meek is good because we do not put out negativity, but we must still preserve ourselves, our beliefs and our faith while we forgive and forget the faults we perceive in others.

If we reach a stage when we are totally in tune with ourselves, the universal energy, the goodness and love in the universe, then we desire less and begin to take joy and pleasure through the pure act of living. Therefore, being humble is an outcome of being accountable. This means there are fewer challenges for us because we are happy and at peace, yet this is a difficult world in which to free ourselves of materialistic desires.

However, we can say that as our desires decrease and we begin to think of others more than ourselves, we become more in tune with the world around us. This is the beginning of the journey that leads us towards humility.

The true meaning of humility is kindness and love and understanding.

What does this journey towards humility look like in practice?

Our soul is the source of our most human attributes, it relates to love, compassion and understanding, and we can possess these spiritual attributes without being consciously spiritual. Our brain enables us to think, manage our body and survive. Yet, without the guidance of our soul, our brain would function only to put ourselves first and identify with our need for survival. At the same time, it is our brain that allows us to learn, evolve and develop the abilities that separate us from the animal kingdom.

Therefore we are seeking a balance between the fulfilment of our soul and the demands of life. This means life is lived walking the line between Heaven and Earth, or selfishness and self-fulfilment. The less of an agenda we have for ourselves, the more we can accept the world around us, because we are going with the flow and allowing ourselves to be guided by life. To do this we are aided greatly if we can learn to appreciate the beauty within the smaller, finer things in life. With compassion and understanding we develop the ability to look deeply into the world around us and understand why things are happening the way they are. Understanding ourselves means that we can be more aware of God and our role in life. Through this compassionate outlook, we can see why people respond to life the way they do.

Humility is not allowing others to walk all over you. It is not holding your opinions to yourself. Instead it is wishing well to everyone and not holding oneself back. It is having true self-confidence, feeling relaxed and happy so that we are less affected by the outside world. However, being humble demands we turn the other cheek and in this imperfect world that means the humble are open to abuse.

However, if we allow the universal energy to introduce itself into our lives and ask for it to guide us, we will be less likely to be guided by our own fears and negativities. We are then naturally drawn to like-minded people in the same way that they are drawn to us.

Competing with each other

Many of us will recognise the feeling comparing ourselves to others, perhaps wanting to be fitter, slimmer, richer or better looking.

Competition itself is not a bad thing, for instance, in sport, or in business, it may be a necessary part of that world. But we need to understand what alternatives are open to us and why true personal achievement means that we do not necessarily need to compete. If we compete, then we may be seeking our feelings of reward through feeling better than others and perhaps, as a consequence, hoping they do worse. How much more fulfilling is it to gain our rewards through knowing we have challenged ourselves to do our level best. If we truly know this then we cannot be made to feel threatened or insecure if others exceed our achievements. This is how the will to succeed can further our personal development, by fuelling our efforts in meeting our own goals and achieving the best we can. If through these efforts we do succeed and perhaps are viewed as being advanced in our field, then it is an opportunity to help others by passing on what we know. If we are not number one, then we still know that we have the personal rewards for our efforts. If we think about it, then in time, there will always be someone who can better us, but there is no one else who can live our life for us.

Competition within our daily lives is accepted in our society and even promoted as a good thing. If we look at it closely, feeling competitive with another person can also make us feel uncomfortable. It feels uncomfortable because it is difficult to compete with another person and at the same time feel warm towards them or even remain ambivalent; in fact the temptation is to develop antagonism.

If we see life as a journey where we want to be the winner, we will also fear being the loser. If we crave to succeed above others it may be our insecurities driving us and if we feel we have lost in life we can be devastated or angry. Likewise, if we see ourselves as winners, then we may feel continually threatened in that position and defend it at all costs. If we think and feel like this, then we are being competitive in the wrong way and wasting our energy.

There is a vast difference between wanting to improve ourselves and putting ourselves in competition against another. The former if pursued can deliver an inner feeling of satisfaction, while the latter can lead to a narrowing and a hardening of our attitude.

Many of us are seeking feelings of fulfilment in our lives. It is far better to focus on doing what is right for us and give every situation our best shot. If we see life as a competition, then we may never be satisfied and our determination to win leads us away from enjoying the sense of endeavour or participation for its own sake.

A neighbour with a desirable car, a bigger sofa or a nicer garden might make us want to have better versions for ourselves because we are insecure or want to have power over another person. If you are continually putting yourself into competition with another human being, then you will never be satisfied with who and what you are. Winning isn't about prestige from the outside, rather it comes as a feeling within and it is a result of having tried our best and given things our best shot – that is what makes us winners in life.

If we look at it simply, competition is a complete waste of energy when it is pointed at other people and can give rise to feelings of either inferiority or superiority, both of which keep us at a distance from those around us. Imagine what life would be like if we were self-motivated, content within ourselves and did not need to compete with others for our self-satisfaction.

The more we are able to let the universal energy guide us, the more we can relax, as everything is part of our picture of development. The more of our actions we can dedicate towards a greater goal the more we will learn. In reality the most anyone can ever do is their best.

If we choose to follow a spiritual path, we are open to learn from everything that happens in our lives. Eventually we may come to the point where we have no feelings of competitiveness and perhaps eventually we will be happy to do our best and enjoy the effort.

Materialism and spirituality

In this world we can better ourselves in many ways, both materially and spiritually, and it is natural to want to improve our personal situation. Whatever our focus, it is up to each of us to decide whether we are going to do our very best, or whether life's difficulties will overcome us and divert us from our purpose.

There are many people seeking to live good lives who may reject the idea of there being anything outside of our physical life here on Earth. Seeking to improve ourselves as a person, living our life well and being true to ourselves can naturally benefit us, whether we have a conscious spiritual outlook or not. However, if we are to achieve and benefit from the love, balance and good feelings that spirituality can bring, then we need to embrace it and be prepared to challenge our preconceptions and opinions.

There are many people here on Earth, seeking fulfilment in life in myriad ways. Life is an on-going lesson and we will not learn if we do not try; self-fulfilment can only come from honest effort. Yet if we look, our options for achieving true happiness are actually quite limited, as there are only so many areas where lasting feelings of fulfilment can come from and there is no guarantee that we will achieve our goals. Yes, there may be endless variety in what we can achieve, we can gain fulfilment from relationships, from family, from having achieved life's goals or we can get diverted from drink and drugs. Yet none of these things can be ultimately relied upon to fulfil us. The person who has houses and cars and wealth and all they need, may not have all they desire. There will still come a time when it is just us facing our life, when the children have moved on or age means we are no longer able to enjoy the physical aspects of our success as we would wish. It is only our inner feelings that tell us whether we have achieved all that we would want and that inner feeling comes from having achieved fulfilment independent of life's vagaries. For that reason, it is very true that outward success does not bring inner happiness, but that inner happiness is our greatest success.

A way of testing whether this is true is to look at an item we own that brings us happiness. It can be anything, our home, a state of the art television, a painting, our car, or an outfit that we feel suits us very well. What happiness does this item bring us and why? If we look deeply into where our pleasure comes from in ownership, this will also help us to develop our flexibility of thought. A rug may enhance the look of a room and therefore ownership can serve as a source of pleasure in sharing it with family and friends and guests. This kind of pleasure is limited but wholesome, in that we are delighting in the happiness of others, which is a selfless act that promotes bonding and correspondingly moves us away from selfishness. If, on the other hand, we find that part of our satisfaction is coming from a feeling of superiority in having a particular possession, or that we take pleasure in making others jealous, then we can see how childish and small minded this attitude is. If we are depending on others to envy us for our happiness, perhaps gaining a sense of euphoria from it, then we, in turn, may envy others who have more than us. This kind of thinking is a self-perpetuating cycle that only succeeds in making us feel that, no matter what we have, it is not good enough.

Therefore, ultimately, there is no satisfaction in objects in themselves and the more one feeds greed the more it rages, like a fire that needs continuous feeding. It is more wholesome to take personal satisfaction in the achievements that allow us material possessions rather than the possessions themselves. If we have tried our best and got a house and car, it may provide us with more personal satisfaction than if a better situation were handed to us on a plate, because we have made more of our situation and earned them ourselves. While there is no end to our desires, wholesome effort can be a reward of itself and if that effort is made, with knowledge of the bigger picture, then nothing can shake our feelings of contentment in having made it.

Chapter Fifteen - The Ten Points of Spiritual Direction. A Spiritual Perspective on the Natural Order of Progress and Development for Human Beings

The ten points of spiritual direction were distilled from conversations with Spirit World, to serve as guidelines in what is beneficial for our spiritual development. These are not rules to follow so that life becomes more complicated, rather they are a blueprint of behaviour patterns we all have the potential to fall into. If we recognise some of our own faults within these points, we can also appreciate the consequences of our actions for ourselves and others. It is up to us what changes we choose to make.

Imagine what life would be like were we all to follow these guidelines and imagine the freedom of mind we would each of us would gain were we to live by them. Here we present the ten points and their implications:

The natural order of development of human beings must not be interfered with.

Each and every one of us should be able to develop according to our personal needs. We should be allowed to grow and gain knowledge and strength without interference.

Each of us is an individual. Therefore the purpose of these laws is to allow us to grow in the way that is right for us. If we were to impose our views upon another, we would not necessarily be allowing them to grow and learn in a way that is beneficial for them. Likewise, if we are to envy or desire what another has, then we may be trying to take on what is wrong for us. We should seek to develop only what is right for us. In the same way, we should be mindful of our interference with other life-forms.

The soul must not be interfered with or denied the right to live free and develop within us.

1. Our will exists to express our purpose, not to impose on another human being to attain control, power, or personal gain.

By imposing our will on another human being we are creating a situation where their will is inhibited. We are, in effect, bullying them. This, in turn, can cause negative reactions; a person who is manipulated or controlled can become frustrated, confused, withdrawn, depressed or even angry. It is not wrong to seek to change another's point of view. It is the act of imposing our will forcibly, or in a manipulative way, that acts against love and bonding. The effects on the person who imposes their will are various. If we are successful in controlling a person in a relationship, we may become bored with them and lose the person we love. Outside of relationships, we may find that by imposing our will, we gradually lose friendship and respect and even become lonely. By imposing our will we are abusing our personal power. If we do this for material gain, we may find ourselves wishing for all the things we have lost, such as friendship and love. Ironically, it is often our own insecurities that drive us to seek control. The exception to this is where an individual is not seeking to gain personal control or power but rather is employed by society to enforce the laws of the land. **To rule another without consent brings destruction.**

2. We should recognise the power within ourselves and encourage it within others.

Life is about freedom of choice and it is harmful to take that choice away from others. To extend our influence, we may be tempted to repress others by manipulating them, undermining them or taking away their ability to think for themselves. Doing this can make them dependent upon us and put them under our influence. If we are doing this, we are taking away their independence and therefore their power over their own lives. For instance, we may find fault in everything that someone does, take credit for their achievements or give the impression that we are displeased with them or their efforts generally. Belittling someone is another example, although this differs from imposing our will and controlling someone as generally it is more subtle. It may be we do this to keep someone in a position where we can control their life. This may be someone we know or love or even work with. In this way, we can take away someone's will to live their life and express themselves. The person being suppressed can lose their own sense of identity. Suppressing someone else means keeping the situation under our own control so that the suppressed person cannot make their own decisions. In extreme situations, the repressed person loses their will to their suppressor. **Repression crushes another's will.**

3. We should use our strength to aid others.

If we are imposing our views on another, we are giving in to a temptation to dictate rather than lead by example. Dominating someone means we are seeking to feel more powerful at the expense of another human being. By domineering, you are setting yourself up in the superior role and this can apply to our relationships with fellow human beings, animals and children. If we place ourselves in a position of extreme power, controlling someone for our own gain through fear and intimidation, we benefit no one. Someone who is controlled in this way may have to spend their life thinking about how they can tailor every action to the needs of their dominator. Ultimately, someone who is domineered can lose their natural desire to live, having given up themselves to the will of another. The person who is domineering cannot be in tune with the other person's feelings. If they were empathising, they would not put another person in a situation where they cannot speak or act for themselves without permission. Domineering by nature is a defence born of insecurity. If we were not afraid of losing someone or what they might do without our supervision, we would not need to domineer.

Domineering keeps people in their place and often even the physical space they occupy, such as the home, can become a prison. **True power is self-mastery, not mastery of others.**

4. We should be honest with ourselves and allow others their beliefs.

There is a great difference between understanding what is right for us and making another adopt our opinion, or think our way. What we view as being right for us is not necessarily right for another. If we impose on another, this is an intrusion and an attempt to put our views above theirs. If we think that we are always right, we are driven to alter everything to suit exactly what we desire. We run the risk of looking at people as objects to fulfil our needs. If we apply this to our relationships, we will feel a desire to alter another to suit our needs, because we think 'I know better'. This can apply to cultural, religious or any other form of belief we hold. What we don't realise is that there is never a point at which changing someone will make us truly happy. Someone forced into beliefs not their own will chafe, or even rebel against what is imposed. There is a difference between wanting to help someone change for their own sake or for our own benefit. If we seek to change someone to conform to our views, either the way they look, what they do, or the opinions they hold then we are pursuing our agenda. Enforcing change depends on manipulation or force. If we pursue this path then eventually we will have to impose, manipulate or pressurise to achieve the change we want. We may impose our will or alternatively, seek to subvert another's by playing on their good nature or their fears, perhaps conveying a sense of dissatisfaction that makes them seek to please us. When they do what we want, we are pleased with them, but when they do not, we are unhappy with them and criticise, ignore or chastise. Eventually, the person we are trying to change will feel inferior or become so out of touch with their own needs that they will lose all sense of themselves. If their focus becomes meeting our demands, then they will be in a state of fear of not meeting our requirements. The relationship will be based on one person feeding off of another's good will and emotions, imposing punishment or reward, judgement and desire. Learning unconditional love is a remedy for this. Imposing your will causes emotional pain. **Self-betterment beats self-gratification at another's cost.**

5. You should have the confidence of your own convictions.

We must not deny a person the right to express themselves. This interferes with their ability to develop naturally. Controlling or denying another their freedom to speak or voice their opinions serves only to impose restriction or potentially make them fearful, rather than instilling within them the confidence to find their own path. That is not to say we cannot reason or discuss. Persuasion through reason is not a bad thing, nor is casting our vote, it is forcing someone to adopt our way of thinking that is wrong. Taking the will from another's life removes the precious meaning within it. Crushing another by fear develops an imitation of true power and our good feelings come from the delusion that we are powerful. Crushing another's will is a sign that we need to mask our own insecurities, by feeding off of others so that we deprive and create insecurities in them. **Crushing another's will reveals our own cowardice.**

6. Recognise your own value.

The fruit of our efforts is our reward alone and we should recognise our own worth and what we have achieved, just as we should allow others credit for their achievements. If, instead, we take the rewards from another's achievements as our own, or perhaps merely take credit for their hard work, we can undermine people and even make them resentful or angry. To take credit in this way makes frauds of those who do it. If we do this we are being false and the rewards we receive are the result of someone else's labour, creating loss. It may not be physical or mental work, but perhaps ideas that we steal. Either way we become vampires that feed off of others.

So how does this affect the person who falsely takes the credit? Taking unearned credit, in any walk of life or any shape or form, is not beneficial to anyone. If we take this credit without permission or consideration for it, we have stolen. If we are the person who steals we must question what we have truly gained. We have not learned nor had the emotional experience of having produced something from our own efforts. We have not challenged ourselves to commit effort and we may have an expectation of gaining future rewards falsely and easily. Taking this to the extreme, if we were to spend our lives stealing from others, we are cheating them of their earned inheritance. We may think of ourselves as opportunists that act on the spur of the moment, or we may plan in advance. **Both are degrees of theft without remorse.**

7. Recognise the worth of your word and fulfil it.

We gain confidence in ourselves and in others by acting on our promises and this, in turn, earns us respect. If, however, there is a gap between what we say and what we do, this confidence will reduce. There are many reasons that we are tempted to promise more than we can deliver; it may be to produce extra effort and hard work from someone or even to elevate ourselves in another's opinion. The promise of future reward that is proven to be lies or insubstantial can lead to resentment or anger. The person who is raising these expectations will be doing this only for their own personal gain and perhaps inflate their self-esteem. Raising false hopes can be used to keep someone near to us while they have an expectation of reward. It can also lead to a huge let down, taking away a person's trust in others and generating a sense of disillusionment. Disillusioned people lose interest in the person who has raised these false hopes. For instance, we may give a false impression to generate interest in an investment opportunity or a business venture. Alternatively, we may do it to keep our partner safe, in the hope that our ideas will become reality. The person who gives false hope is foolish, deceiving through illusion with no permission from their audience. If it is we who is creating the illusion, we must have need of something, be it the attention we achieve through a false impression or a salve for our own inadequacy. **In the short term, we receive the benefits of approval for this false impression. In the end, we create disillusionment and disappointment and must live with the knowledge that our word has no worth.**

8. Love your own life.

The experience of life itself is one of the most wonderful things we possess. We may want things in our life to provide for our needs, but if the desire for things is too strong, it may be a sign that we feel incomplete. This insecurity often comes from feelings that grow in our earlier years, a fear of rejection and a fear of losing what we have. These feelings of deprivation can lead to envy, a fertile ground for jealousy. Jealousy gives rise to an obsession with gain, creating a destructive form of competitiveness and with it comes a great fear of losing. Alternatively, we may covet another person's partner or possessions because we want the satisfaction of ownership, so that it enhances our view of ourselves and shows to the world that we can keep up with others. Taken to extremes, we can be envious even of those we love for what they have or who they are.

Being envious of another person's situation is never going to give us what we want. If we know who we are and what we are doing with our lives, we are far less likely to envy others because we know what is right for us. If, on the other hand we are motivated by greed to have more than we actually need, then we may never actually get to the point where we are satisfied. Instead, we will continually have this unpleasant feeling of wanting what we don't possess and we lose sight of ourselves, risking the loss of our individuality. Jealousy brings out the worst in us and makes us feel ugly inside, experiencing nasty and suspicious thoughts and if these thoughts show themselves we become unlikeable and unlovable. Jealousy can make us obsessive and we can be eaten up by thoughts of wanting more. This creates inner turmoil and can lead to destructive behaviour. Each of us has the opportunity to confront the jealousy within us; it is our choice. The remedy for jealousy is to recognise the good feelings others enjoy from their possessions, achievements or attributes and rejoice with them in what they have. Jealousy is, however, hard to eliminate. The reason is that our insecurities feed it and the more insecure we become, the greater our potential to be jealous. Jealousy exacerbates our own sense of insecurity. Focusing on what we think we lack will leave us with much less; we can become unhappy and stunted, suspicious of others, with a distorted ugly personality. If by contrast we live with our focus on loving our life then we are better able to go with the flow. This enables us to feel the joy of the moment and appreciate the beauty that surrounds us, such as nature, people, children and animals, alongside the joy of being physically alive. Appreciate what is yours and what you have achieved and the good things you can experience, a wave rolling in from the sea, a tree blowing in the wind, a flower growing, our achievements flourishing, acts of kindness, the love within our home or for those around us, cleanliness in our thoughts and our physical form, all of these are there for us to enjoy and relish. **Allow the half-empty cup to be half-full and it will runneth over.**

9. Choose life and do not regret nor reject it.

Life is full of polarities; we will be attracted towards things that we instinctively feel are right or move away from things that feel wrong. So it is natural to accept or reject the options we are presented with, according to how we feel about them. Freedom of choice helps us learn what is right for us and can help us grow emotionally and spiritually.

Within these choices come our relationships with people. Many of these relationships we can choose, while some, such as those within our family or in a work environment, are seemingly thrust upon us. We can choose whom we let into our lives but should be mindful of the feelings of those around us. Rejecting a person is an exclusion of them from our lives or from our friendship or from sharing our confidences, or even the act of giving and receiving. Rejection is the act of putting up a barrier at some level without considering the feelings of the person whom we are rejecting or pushing away.

If we cast our minds back, each of us has been rejected at some stage. It can be an uncomfortable feeling. If we are thick-skinned or complacent, we are less likely to be affected by being rejected. However, rejection has the potential to harm others, no matter how we do it.

If we do not want another person in our life, then we can tell them so, that is our prerogative. Yet we should not reject someone without considering their feelings and reactions. Therefore, we should think of both sides of the story whenever we are able.

Fear can often be a motivation for rejecting something or someone. The more we understand ourselves, the less we will react to unfounded fears about people or situations. However, none of us is perfect. That is to say, we have limitations and therefore predictable fears that motivate us to reject people who are beyond our ability to cope with. So for instance, aggressive, controlling, crass or seemingly unlikeable individuals may be beyond our ability to deal with at any given stage of our development. Therefore, by recognising our own limitations, we will know what legitimately to confront and what to avoid. Also, the clearer our vision becomes, the better we can identify and even anticipate these situations.

We should recognise also the times we have decided to reject another, before we are ourselves rejected. We may have a demeanour that keeps people at arm's length, because we have been hurt through rejection. Learning to open ourselves is a natural part of the spiritual pathway and will help to overcome the uncomfortable feeling of keeping ourselves closed off in this way.

We may reject someone on the basis of their personality, their perceived class, or the fact that we do not want to interact with them. There are many reasons; even our own shyness can play a part. The level of rejection can differ, dependent upon whether they are friends, colleagues, relations, strangers or even lovers. We may reject someone through hatred, anger, envy, disgust or as a product of our own insecurities. Whatever the reason, it is an act of pushing away.

In the extreme, rejection is an expression of ignorance and it can be either subtle or obvious. As soon as we have categorised someone in our mind, we can reject them verbally or physically. It could be as subtle as turning our backs and snubbing someone or as violent as a shove, or worse.

Rejection is not necessarily a one-off event, it can be a long standing thing where we reject another in a relationship. We can see many instances of couples where one rejects the other, but they stay together in a relationship that needs repair in some way.

We are, of course, each of us free to reject another's point of view or offer, or an attempt to overrule us, but we should seek to do so in consideration for the other person's feelings and look at both sides of the story.

The worst act of rejection for anyone to suffer is being rejected for who we are. At the other end of the spectrum, another form of rejection is that of rejecting an offer of help. The act of giving uplifts both those who give and those who receive. So we should also be mindful of how sometimes it can help others if they freely offer help or gifts and we accept them. By receiving, we teach the act of giving. By giving we are helping others to be open to receive. Giving and receiving openly without seeking reward or expecting a return or thanks is the opposite of rejection. We give without seeking favour and we receive without feeling beholden.

Pride is a major reason that people reject offers of help. We may not wish to appear weak or open ourselves up to the opinion of others and therefore expose ourselves to judgement. It is not wrong to be concerned about these things, but we must also consider what opportunities for friendship are lost if we continue to reject. If we develop a habit of saying no to offers of help, then we can end up in the cold because eventually those offers of help and assistance are withdrawn and we no longer have that interaction.

Rejection that often hurts the deepest is the rejection of a child for the parent. A child as it grows can become stubborn if they have a strong will and decide that they do not want the parent to intrude into their lives. This can make a parent feel rejected and unwanted by those they love the most. This is a prime example of how hurtful the act of rejecting someone can be.

We live in a world where we have very many choices. Dependent upon the society we live in, we may discriminate and divide people into groups by their dress, colour or even religion. By seeing someone as different, we can be suspicious and therefore fearful of their difference, leading us to reject passively or with hostility. In the eyes of, God, we should not reject anyone. In the bigger plan of things we are all here to learn to get on with one another.

Ultimately, had we all learned to offer unconditional love, we would accept everyone for who they are. However, we are in many ways children learning to live with each other. We each have a level of acceptance of behaviour, of other people and of situations. Within our own restrictions, we should look to keep an open mind and treat our fellow man kindly and with the same level of respect we would want for ourselves. **Making an effort to understand others makes us more tolerant and opens the doorway for us to develop.**

10. You should give without thought of what you will receive in return.

Giving freely is putting someone else first and at the very least, having consideration for their needs. Giving is sacrificing something of our own and sharing it with someone else, even if it is merely our good will. Giving is the ultimate expression of God's will.

To be truly free in our own minds we must give with an open and clear heart; a true willingness to help the other person. The true gift of giving is the joy and emotional healing we receive for helping others. By giving without thought for what we might receive in return, we are making ourselves open to the universe and teaching ourselves unconditional love. Unconditional love is one of the hardest things to learn, but remember that none of us are perfect and unconditional love is open to abuse, so if we do not expect a return on our giving, we are less likely to be hurt if we do not receive thanks or recompense. Nowadays, it is not uncommon, no matter whether we have enough money or not, to not have enough time to enjoy life, therefore our time can be one of the greatest gifts we are able to give.

There are many things that we can give to one another. Time is the most important, because our time here on Earth is the one thing we know is finite. Choosing to give our time to another is a statement that we care about them.

By choosing to spend our time with someone and perhaps listen to their problems, we allow them to feel wanted and needed. Importantly, being listened to means we feel valued and that someone cares about us. **By giving time and spending it with others we are able to form bonds that other types of gifts do not necessarily forge.**

Chapter Sixteen - Learning on the Pathway

No matter what direction we choose to develop in, spirituality can offer us a way forward in our lives and yet because we can have so many inner and outer pressures, this pathway can often become neglected. So it is very important that we find a way forward that suits our individual temperament. Spirituality is a personal search for answers to the questions of life and if we apply effort it can be a journey of awakening to who we really are, a journey from confusion to meaning and from fear to faith, so that we no longer feel alone in what can be a hostile world; pursued to its ultimate conclusion, it offers us the hope of being at one with everyone and everything.

Spirituality opens the doorway to knowledge that, if we work with it, applying it to our own situation can help us to understand life and ourselves that much better. Knowing that life is a journey and that each of us is experiencing variations on the same range of emotions, problems and situations helps us to understand that we are not alone. Knowing that each of us are searching for happiness helps us on the pathway to developing our wisdom, because it puts everyone's actions, even our own, into perspective.

If we develop clear vision within a spiritual perspective, then our insight can be applied not only to our own lives, but also to the lives and situations of others around us.

This life is full of pressures and we do well to remember that there are many that have trodden this pathway, met their challenges and succeeded in building a happier more meaningful life for themselves. We can have many things in our life, the work we do, pastimes that we enjoy, family, friends and responsibilities. All of these can be put into perspective by treading a spiritual pathway, lending more importance and meaning to those elements that are fulfilling of themselves such as family and friendships. Where we are called upon to face what feels like pressure and stress, spiritual thought and action can help us apply ourselves so that we develop as individuals and work for the best outcome.

Knowledge can come from a book, but does not offer us experience. We may read an account of an explorer making a perilous journey, but even if we know the physical reactions and hardships their bodies are going through, we have not done it ourselves. "I know" can often be a phrase that makes us feel superior or separate from others. It can come with a feeling of being better informed, with greater capacity of understanding or merely a bigger ego! If we feel superior, it is one indication that we are going wrong. If we are feeling superior, it shows we are lacking in compassion or understanding of how and why a person came to be in a particular situation. Better to know than to say it.

Meditation - The Inner Sanctuary

This exercise can aid you in understanding how you relate to others. It can help you to find out how you feel about another person and how you might interact together. The Inner Sanctuary technique can provide you with a perspective that is not dependent on you ingrained ways of reacting that might otherwise dictate how you feel.

The technique is based on visualisation and will spiritually bring out both your own view of your 'self' and how you might interact with another. It can be used to gain an insight into your relationship with anyone, be they a potential partner, friend, work colleague, family member or acquaintance.

Preparation
Put yourself in a place where you feel at ease. Sitting comfortably or lying down, put on some relaxing music. Take some nice deep breaths and close your eyes. Move your mind-energy to the

backs of your eyelids and, keeping your eyelids closed, look through them into the darkness beyond. Letting your shoulders relax, listen to the music and breathe peacefully. Let go of your Earthly vision and any distracting sounds around you. Focus your attention outward into the darkness and allow your mind to clear of all thoughts and worries.

You may wish to have pen and paper to hand to write down any images, feelings or impressions that you encounter after the exercise is complete.

Relax your body and sit with arms relaxed, hands on thighs with feet flat on the floor. If this position is uncomfortable in any way just take some time to relax get in a position that is best for you. Let yourself settle and just let your mind be at ease.

Now, in your mind's eye visualise yourself standing in front of a large ornate sanctuary with a door set within it. Walk up to the door and open it. Step inside and find brightly coloured satin cushions scattered on the floor all around you. Make yourself comfortable on the cushions, sitting or laying down so that you feel safe and secure. Just feel comfortable. This room is your Inner Sanctuary.

In your mind's eye look around and get a feel for the space within your Inner Sanctuary. Look at the door and picture the person you wish to enter into your space in the doorway. How do you feel about them being there? Do you want to let them in? If so, let them in and see how you now feel about it. How do they act? Do you feel comfortable or uncomfortable? Look to see how you are getting on. Do they take over and change things or is it a nice feeling of equality? See what happens as they arrive.

How comfortable you are with them in your space will reveal whether there are potential relationship issues to address.

You can also imagine yourself at the door of that person's Sanctuary and see how the interaction takes place. Do they let you in? What do you experience in their space? It is how you feel emotionally as well as what you visualise that will give you the key to any issues. If you feel threatened they may simply be a very imposing character, while if you feel a bit disappointed, they may not have enough to offer you, or your expectations may be too high.

Once you have a feel for the interaction, ask the person to leave (or if you are in their Sanctuary - return to your own). Allow yourself to sit in your own Sanctuary for a while and then, when you are ready, allow yourself to return from your visualisation. Have a stretch - take some water if you need it and write down anything you want to. Once you have finished, look at the results. You have now completed the exercise.

This tool will enable you to get a clearer picture of any underlying issues your intuition may be hinting at and will also enable you to gain an impression of how you really feel about any other relationship in your life, either potential or existing.

We can look at examples of how this works in practice. For example, a young man used this exercise to see whether he was compatible with an acquaintance he had just met. In his mind's eye he invited this new friend into his Inner Sanctuary. He was happy to see that his new friend brought in food and drink and that they both felt very comfortable in each other's company. However, the exercise also revealed that his new friend had no intention of leaving and left a mess of food remnants and packaging. The exercise in this instance showed that this pleasant, amicable young man had a hidden agenda, intending to stay and impose himself without consideration. This stranger, bearing gifts of food, was not good news and the man in question managed to nip this situation in the bud because he used The Inner Sanctuary exercise.

Another situation that was revealed by The Inner Sanctuary involves a lady called Sarah and her sister. In life and reality, Sarah did not get on with her sister and therefore used this exercise to find out what was going on in the relationship that she was not aware of. So Sarah invited her sister into her Inner Sanctuary. Her sister immediately tidied and rearranged the cushions in The Inner Sanctuary to suit her own taste. In other words, Sarah's sister was taking over, which is why the relationship in real life was uncomfortable. Yet, when she reversed the situation and went into her sister's Inner Sanctuary, she was made totally welcome. Sarah realised that her sister was not trying to take over, but rather felt inadequate to Sarah and so wanted to feel useful to her. Armed with this knowledge, Sarah was able to welcome her sister into her life, letting her feel useful. Aided by this greater understanding, their relationship grew closer.

Meditation - The Cleansing Room

The Cleansing Room provides you with a way to clear your mind and allow new thoughts and ideas to come in, uncluttered by pre-judgement, negativities and self-doubt. In this way, regularly using this exercise allows us to develop the ability to see clearly, free of our past conditioning.

The aim of the exercise is to leave the Cleansing Room totally clear, by taking out any clutter you find and leaving it sparklingly clean.

The Cleansing Room is unique. You are entering the domain of your own thoughts. It may appear the same to you each time you enter it, or it may constantly change. Either is fine. Whatever appears is merely a reflection of your current state-of-mind.

Picture a door in front of you. With your hand, reach out and trace the lettering on the door, feeling the contours and reading each letter in turn as your fingers trace their outline. The words spelled out are "Your name" and "My Cleansing Room".

Looking down the door, feel with your hand until you come across a handle, turn the handle and open the door. Look inside and see what is in your room. Is it cluttered and full or is it relatively clear? Sometimes you will see furniture, sometimes junk. Whatever is there, you will need to clear away.

Once you have a picture of your Cleansing Room in your mind, get ready to clear it out, allowing your mind to become clear. You can elicit whatever help you need to do this. The universal energy can provide whatever you need; shovels, dusters, vacuum cleaners, even rubbish collection vans, all can be waiting for you outside the door to your mind room. Whatever you need to clear out your Cleansing Room, make it available to yourself. Put yourself wholeheartedly to clearing and cleaning this space. Clean, scrape, dust, polish and make your Cleansing Room as wonderfully clear as you want it to be. The work you do here is very important. You are giving your mind greater space and clarity. Fixtures, fittings – all can be cleared away. Any windows can be polished to a state of sparkling clarity. And don't worry if there are gaps in the walls or ceilings, this shows you have a mind that is open! Just dust around any openings and make them as clear and clean as the rest!

Whatever rubbish you find is disposed of in whatever way works best for you. The important thing is that anything in that room gets sent off to be recycled by the universal energy. For instance, you can imagine a huge rubbish truck, ready to take all of your clutter away to infinity so that it never returns.

When you have finished, you should be left with just walls and ceilings and in some cases, the walls and ceilings may eventually disappear. Either way, this is fine. When you have finished cleaning, just sit within your Cleansing Room for a while. Enjoy the results of your hard work.

When you are ready to leave, go through the door and firmly close it, using the key in the lock to secure it behind you. Briefly trace the lettering on the door once more, feeling good about the work you have done and what you have achieved.

Comment

The Cleansing Room is a space you can visit at any time. You may return to your Cleansing Room whenever you feel the need to swiftly de-clutter your mind and make room for greater clarity, deeper levels of relaxation and the freedom for more positive thought. It is a good idea to do your Cleansing Room meditation every day and follow it with the Healing Energy Room. Practising both these meditations together can clear your mind and invite healing into your life, a good thing for each and every one of us!

The Cleansing Room can be a daily or weekly practice. However often you practice this exercise, allow yourself to get used to the feeling of the room and leaving it clear and clean after every visit. It may be that clutter or furniture reappears each time you go through the exercise. Do not be worried by this, some of the clutter we have in our minds may have been there for a long time. Eventually, with enough practice our Cleansing Room will be clear each time we visit it, so that we are free of the past and limiting thoughts that might otherwise remain with us.

Meditation - Recognising restrictions in life

Purpose of the meditation

This mediation will help you to recognise the restrictions in your own life and how they can alter our view of life itself. By practicing the meditation, we can see how changing our perspective can open up fresh options to us and help us maintain our equilibrium, despite life's limitations.

Preparation

Put yourself in a place where you feel at ease. Sitting comfortably or lying down, put on some relaxing music. Take some nice deep breaths and close your eyes. Move your mind-energy to the backs of your eyelids and, keeping your eyelids closed, look through them into the darkness beyond. Letting your shoulders relax, listen to the music and breathe peacefully. Let go of your Earthly vision and any distracting sounds around you. Focus your attention outward into the darkness and allow your mind to clear of all thoughts and worries.

The first thing we notice is a narrow uneven dirt path below our feet. The path is almost like a gully with bracken and stones upon it. On either side is a tall enclosing hedge with dark green foliage that grows above our head and overshadows us. The hedge is really close, we cannot see above it and it hems us in, so close that our elbows can touch it on either side. All we can see is the hedge and the precarious uneven pathway our feet are upon. To move forwards we must keep a careful eye on where our footsteps fall and steer our way with care.

We now decide to stand still, to look and take in the path and the hedge around us. Allow the feeling of being enclosed and restricted to come through. Feel what it is like and allow yourself to understand how different people could feel in this situation. Some of us may feel negative, restricted and become introverted, causing us to retreat within ourselves. Allow yourself to feel this reaction. Alternatively we may feel repressed and become angry, railing against the feeling of being restricted, wanting to break free from the confinement and to break out! We can allow ourselves to feel this, relating to how people can become enraged by frustrations. Now we can look again at the situation we are in; look outwardly at the restrictions and notice the details within the scene, the flowers within the hedge, the birds that nest there, the hedge reaching upwards to the sun and putting down roots to sustain itself, the flowers struggling to grow and the birds finding a place for themselves in the security the thick foliage provides. Everything around us has its place and despite the seeming lack of order, seeks to grow and live and is thriving despite the overwhelming density of the growth. There is beauty within life's struggle and every element has its purpose.

Recognise that within any situation where we are feeling restricted, uncomfortable or challenged, we can look for the positive within it. If we are not having such a nice time of it, we may choose to notice the person who took the time to say hello to us, or the nice things that happen in our day-to-day lives. We can use the visualisation to pick up on all these positive details, like blackberries growing within the hedge, beautifully formed and ripe, or small flowers growing at its base, finding the light and pushing upwards. We can look and see all of these positives within a potentially frustrating scene. It is our choice what we focus on.

Continue on your journey, treading carefully and feeling positive thoughts. Then look and you will see that the hedge on your left hand side has dropped away. In its place are the sky and the field and a lovely, open feeling. In seeing this we can forget that the hemmed in feeling of the other hedge is there at all and we can breathe freely and fully, now that this one side is cleared.

Carry on your journey until you notice that the hedge on your right hand side and with it the restrictions, has dropped away. Both sides are now open and we can feel how it is to have unrestricted vision and movement, totally free and at one with everything. This expansive openness is a very spiritual feeling; we are free of all the stress, the troubles and anxieties that feeling hemmed in and restricted brings.

When you are ready, allow yourself to come back to awareness of the room around you and gently come out of your meditation.

Comment

This visualisation illustrates the restrictions of life and how each and every one of us can experience different reactions to them. We all go through these feelings and situations at some time. By allowing ourselves to go through this visualisation, we can feel not only how different people react, but also how choosing to take a spiritual view we can overcome some of the pain. It can also help overcome our emotional reaction to the feeling of being restricted. Taking a spiritual view means we can introduce flexibility into our way of thinking and benefit from the freedom and positivity of recognising alternatives in our lives.

Learning for all ages

The exercises in this book can help us to develop, or at the very least, offer us the opportunity for some welcome relaxation. Their potential is to provide us with an insight into ourselves, our relationships and how our mind functions. It is our choice what we take on board; greater self-knowledge informs the choices we make so that we are better able to navigate our pathway according to what we feel is right for us.

One of the most important times for our progress is when we are children, yet as a child we are at the earliest stage of our human development and we are yet to learn to discern what is good for us. Instead, we must rely on the adult influences in our life to guide, protect, nurture, love and teach us. Therefore, our childhood is the foundation for our future growth and the most precious time to establish bonding and security.

What is true for adults is equally true for children, we all have emotional needs that, if met, can allow our unique personalities to evolve in the way that is right for the journey before us.

As in adult life, when we are children, we may become frustrated and thwarted in our goals. A child is vulnerable and in its infancy is yet to develop all the skills we may later take for granted. How much harder then is it for a child, with no life experience, where everything is new and yet to be learned.

As adults we can be supremely important in the development of our offspring. Offering security is key if our children are to grow without inner barriers towards love and affection. If love and affection and comfort are present, then that child will have perspective, knowing that it is secure. If they are absent, then that child will seek attention because it feels this absence of love as a void within and not knowing how else to find it, will express its frustration in tantrums or all manner of angry venting. If we are like this as a child, it will have ramifications for our behaviour as adults.

Love that is caring, non-judgemental, understanding and consistent gives our child the chance to develop their own wisdom, based on inner strength. Yet children may test us, as they learn how far they can go before there is a consequence and they meet with our disapproval.

Before the age of two, life is a playground and as children, we have no recognition that there is danger within it. Some children are naturally more inquisitive and will want to test the water. As adults, parents or carers, we can become scared on their behalf, take our concerns for their safety too far and perhaps overreact, shouting or becoming angry through worry. If we scream and rant and rave and are even violent towards our children, we become a problem in their lives, because whatever we do, we are leading by example. The replacement of our love with aggression can cause children to rebel against us. If we deal with unacceptable behaviour by withdrawing our love, then a child can be lead to seek our approval and instead of seeking to dominate the relationship through rebellion, can become lost and life will seem barren and empty. A child in this situation may spend their lives trying to find the love that was absent in their formative years, while a child that was treated with aggression and perhaps violence will be less able to express love in their lives, in their relationships and to their own children.

That is not to say we are to be modern day Saints and a child must learn to accept the boundaries that we lay out for their safety and guidance. Boundaries help a child recognise that which is acceptable and that which is not and enforcing those boundaries is very important. Bringing up a child can be very difficult and it is important we find a way of working with them that allows the child to develop and the parent to have a life, so that the relationship grows and feeds us both.

Recognising that a child is seeking to learn, we can appreciate that they are expressing this thirst for knowledge and seeking love, so there is no such thing as a naughty child. None of us are born into this world naughty. It is through the situations and interactions that children encounter in their early lives that they are shaped. Children are not born intentionally disruptive or ill-behaved. In the same way that a child comes into this world with an individual face and unique DNA, they each have their own personalities seeking expression; we may have a child that is stubborn or wilful, just as we may have a child that is insecure and sensitive. The role of parenting is to meet our child's emotional needs, playing with the child and bonding so that they feel safe and secure within our love. Out of this partnership comes balance and we can develop a healthy discipline by offering interaction, alternatives to harmful behaviour and communicating what is acceptable and what is not, all the while recognising that with the right guidance we can allow the best parts of their personality to come forward.

Routine is very helpful in the parent child relationship, it helps to build a sense of purpose and provides the child with the additional security of knowing both what is expected and what to expect in return. Likewise, if our situation allows it, working as a team with your partner in the child's interest will help them recognise how family life helps build a happy life. Even for separated couples, fulfilling responsibilities to the child can help to build trust and lessens the feeling of rejection that can otherwise plague a child if one parent is absent.

Trust is dependent on honesty and therefore being clear and open is a key part of our relationship with children. We should always consider how open we can be with a child and be guided by what the child can understand, but never fudge an issue so that we are telling untruths. If we do lie, then a child's trust will diminish.

Offering this support, we at least know we have given the best we can to ensure that a child is secure and steadfast in adult life.

The key to dealing with children who are behaving badly is to identify why. If a child is being naughty and throwing a tantrum, why is it doing this? It may be that the child is feeling neglected or ignored, or it could be that they are merely seeking their own way. If it is the latter then we are best to ignore them. If there is another reason behind the outburst, we can only find it through communication. Often a child is seeking security and bonding, so the answer is to offer as much love and affection as we are able. Alongside our love, time is the most precious thing we can bring to any relationship and giving our attention can show our children that they are wanted and that we value them.

Chapter Seventeen - Using your clear vision

In this chapter we are going to look at how we can learn to use our mind to apply our clear vision, how to conduct a reading for ourselves and how we can interpret what we perceive.

To do this, we will look at visualisation techniques that if learned correctly, can teach us to tune in to the energy that surrounds us all and find what is relevant to a person's life. To properly use these techniques, we must understand the way information presents itself to our mind and how to interpret that information.

Before we start, it is important to know that we cannot promise you this book alone will give you perfect clear vision. While we can present the basics (and results can be immediate) it may take time to get to a stage where you are of good enough calibre to give a well-rounded reading. If your mind is ready and you are willing to apply yourself, you can start to develop these abilities and even surprise yourself and have fun with the results you achieve.

Clear vision is an innate faculty we are born with, yet this ability is not recognised by everyone and is the subject of much debate. Therefore, it can be seen by society as being divorced, separate and even alien to what is accepted as part of our everyday life. In reality, the energy we are connecting with when we use our clear vision surrounds us all and we are all part of it. So depending on your viewpoint, the ability to use clear vision can seem normal, strange or the most magical thing in the world.

No matter what our view, we all do well to remember that we are born into human bodies and we must learn to keep our spiritual journey in perspective of this physical existence. If you find you are perceiving life in a different way because of your clear vision, it can make you take stock and even turn your view of what is important in life on its head. It may give you the urge or the impulse to change your way of living to concentrate on the spiritual. Many of us want to abandon our seemingly mundane everyday life in preference for one that puts spirituality to the forefront. Yet we can still enjoy all the benefits and rewards of living a spiritual existence, while maintaining our physical life. Life can carry on normally when we discover ourselves. By learning to place spirituality at the core of what we do, it need not take over, but rather the changes can come subtly from within.

So whatever change we feel drawn towards, we are best advised to temper our wishes with our common sense. If we develop the ability to see things that others may not, we are all still subject to the laws of karma and the universe. Spiritual riches are accessible by us all, but they will not put food on the table, nor will they pay the mortgage or the rent. So please don't get so swept up by your development that you give your spiritual side more importance than life's basic needs. If you need to earn money to provide for yourself and family, then you will need to make sure those needs are catered for in some way. The majority of us are here to learn through our physical journey and to abandon it entirely to pursue our spirituality can carry quite serious implications. The day job that seems boring in comparison to our clear vision, the house that may seem less important once you have found spiritual wealth, all of these things may be necessary to your life, so remember your responsibility to yourself and any who depend upon you and keep any abilities you learn in perspective.

During the early stages of development, in all likelihood, our thought is merely thought. That is to say, we are only familiar with our own thoughts and imagination. We do not necessarily have a feel of where or how to focus the brain to receive information other than that from our five senses, or that generated through thought or emotion. We should not worry if at first we merely get a vague feeling or pictures in our mind that may be very limited. As we take our first steps in development, even perceiving nothing at all increases our awareness, because we are recognising the frequency on which our clear vision manifests and distinguishing between it and other thoughts.

With this in mind, we can look forward to learning how to tune into our own clear vision and how to interpret what we perceive so that it works for the benefit of all.

The language of symbolics

Images are the language of the mind. We dream in them, can think in them and those we see with our physical eyes can greatly influence us.

Our clear vision comes to us through our mind's ability to sense energy. Usually the primary way this energy manifests is as images in the mind, while we can also experience corresponding feelings and perhaps even sounds, smells, tastes, or tactile sensations. However, in most of us, it will be the visual images and their symbolic meanings that are the predominant language of the mind. The reason we don't see the spoken word or written language with our clear vision is partly because it is limited and difficult to perceive clearly. If you choose to visualise a bright red apple, you should see it almost immediately and perhaps even gain a feeling of its taste and smell. Now try visualising the words 'red apple'; for most of us this is more difficult and those two words alone don't provide the feeling that comes with visualisation. Words tell, but we need to read them to understand what image and feeling they are seeking to convey. It can take many words to express the feeling of being in a situation, while symbols can swiftly provide insight and depth. Also, if we are perceiving words with our clear vision, they need to be spelled out in our mind's eye one by one and words therefore are a slow and unwieldy way of getting the feel of a situation.

Negating the need for intellectual analysis, a symbolic image can convey an association instantly. Words do not give an insight of themselves, yet an image brings feelings with it and, through interpretation, allows us to empathise and understand a person's situation. Therefore, the language of our clear vision is made up of symbolic images that, of themselves, provide us with the basis to interpret their many layers of meaning.

Just as symbolic images are the language of clear vision, so the mind can only work with images that are relevant to it. We can only relate to the things we have encountered in life, as experience is our reference point, both for information and interpretation. For instance, if we are shown the image of a spade, then for some readers this image may indicate someone who is down to Earth and hard working, while for others it may show that someone is currently involved in a search for some meaning or information – because they are 'digging' for it! Yet all of us recognise the image of a spade and eventually we will learn to interpret images in a way that we personally understand. Two people using their clear vision may receive the same images, or different ones that convey similar meanings or nuances of information. However, if we had been raised in a society where there were no spades and we had never come across one, our mind could not relate to that image. Instead our mind might 'see' an image of something we might recognise, such as a garden fork or a trowel. Therefore, we can only interpret what we know and we will also only see images that we, in turn, have the ability to learn to interpret.

The power of symbolic images is recognised throughout society, through national flags, the logos of businesses and brands and even sporting teams. These carry all manner of meanings, dependent upon how we relate to them, in a condensed image. So not only does a symbolic image convey meaning, but the nuances of that meaning will differ greatly depending on who we are. The devout Christian will identify positively with an image of a crucifix, because of their knowledge of what it represents, while a committed agnostic may feel ambivalent about such an image and its associations.

In our meditations we use visualisation as a way of accessing and influencing our minds' deeper levels, the levels below logic, conditioning and rationalisation. As we progress and learn to use our clear vision, we can perceive all manner of images. These can be common place objects, but like logos and brand names, they can hold levels of meaning far beyond the obvious. Learning to interpret these images is the basis of giving a clear interpretation of someone's situation and, if we progress, the skill of interpreting these images can become second nature and as natural as if we were reading the written word. One picture, as the saying goes, can paint a thousand words and convey to us, in our minds, an instant grasp of what is going on in a person's life.

Therefore, when we are looking at a person or a situation with our clear vision, it is essential we learn to understand any images or symbolics that present themselves. They are the language of our clear vision, the key to developing an understanding of our mind and ultimately, life itself.

In the initial stages of our learning when we seek to access our clear vision, we may find the images we see in our mind's eye difficult to interpret. This is because symbolics are a language in their own right. The good news is that the language of symbolics has a consistent vocabulary. Here are a few examples to illustrate the point and help you understand how to work with symbolic images.

If, for instance, we visualise a person in a canoe, going down the rapids, we can understand that the meaning of the image is that person is going through a very emotional situation that is carrying them along in one direction, while they are desperately trying to keep control within it. Just as a canoeist will fight to keep their direction and avoid the rocks, so a person in this emotional situation will be avoiding the worst and strive to keep themselves 'afloat.'

Another example is if we see a tiger, this can represent a lively, solitary and sometimes ferocious character. It does not indicate that they own a tiger, nor that they have black and orange stripes! Likewise, an elephant may indicate strength for a person, not that they have a menagerie of exotic animals or are going on safari!

Symbolics are normally not literal. To illustrate this, if we were to use another animal as an example – a mouse for instance, if we looked at it literally we would think that the person was perhaps weak or timid. However, in reality, a mouse is a canny animal that avoids confrontation and is a survivor. By sensing the feeling that comes with an image, we can learn to interpret the correct meaning. Not all symbolics are animals however, these are merely examples we can all relate to.

To develop our minds so that we can receive and interpret symbolics, we need to stretch and strengthen them. All the exercises and meditations in this book, with practice, can help us exercise the area of our brains that interpret energy. This area of our brain is usually, to a greater or lesser degree, in a relatively dormant state. Using exercises helps us stretch our minds and can build our abilities so that we are able to achieve more with our clear vision. In the same way that we develop muscles by exercise and stretching, we are developing the mind through techniques that broaden and deepen our mental awareness. As with any exercise, what may at first feel tiring and a drain on our resources, can blossom into an activity that actually leaves us feeling energised. Using our minds in this way can build our energy levels.

There are three distinct stages to developing our clear vision. When we reach the stage that we are ready to use it to look and read situations for ourselves and others, we will find that while some information is easy to interpret and understand, we may not be able to translate all of the impressions and images we see. It is therefore a good idea to keep a regular record of images we encounter and to write them all down. Later on in our development we can look at what we recorded and see how far we have progressed. Also images that we were unable to successfully interpret at the time may become clearer to us later on. If we have seen and written down things that we felt were in the future we can check to see whether they have come to pass and therefore whether we have been correct in our clear vision. We can translate the images in our mind by applying our knowledge of symbolics, so for instance we know that if we see an image of water it represents an emotional situation. While we are learning, it may be that we don't pick up every element of a situation. So when we return to read our notes, perhaps having given subsequent readings or knowing a situation for what it is, we can then compare the reality with what we saw and interpreted.

Eventually, we will become accustomed to the feelings that come with our clear vision. As we progress, we will also refine our interpretation of what we see and feel and know when it is our imagination that is manifesting itself. Also, through the exercises in this book, we can clear our minds of the negativities and bias that obstruct our reading of situations and people.

The significance of colours
When we use our clear vision, we can see colours and these can provide an indication of a person's situation. Each and every colour has a correspondence to an emotion, reaction or situation that is taking place; the deeper the colour, the deeper the corresponding association being experienced. Before we go on to use the visualisation techniques that can open our minds to clear vision, we should first take a look at the colours we might come across when we do so.

A light yellow, for instance, would indicate someone who is learning, but perhaps not involved in deep study. A dark blue would indicate deep emotions, perhaps deep enough to overwhelm, while a light blue would mean that there were lighter emotions present.

Colours can be seen as permeating every area of a person's life, or symbolic images can be shown where a colour is strongly present. For instance a bridge might signify that someone is moving forwards in life and taking steps to address their fears (by crossing a chasm they are crossing over fears). If the bridge is red, then we can read it as being that there will be stress and if it is partly yellow, we know the corresponding association is with learning. As we develop, we can come to directly recognise the feelings that come with each colour that, in turn, will help us to recognise their significance and where they sit in someone's life. What follows here is a list of colours and their associated meanings. It is important to recognise that with each colour, there are degrees of depth and they may not relate to the whole of a person's life but purely to the area we perceive them in. The exercises further on help us to determine what situation colours relate to and how strong the related emotion is.

Summary of colour associations

Blue indicates the emotions
Brown indicates grounding and being down to Earth
Green indicates growth
Orange indicates vitality and happiness
Pink indicates unconditional love
Purple indicates healing
Red indicates stress
Yellow indicates learning
White is a neutral colour indicating a lack of colour in one's life.
Grey signifies a lack of joy or depression. The darker the grey the deeper the depression. A light grey may just indicate that the person is feeling low and out of sorts

Black severe deep depression and negativity.

Below are some examples of colour combinations that might appear in a reading and how we can interpret them:

Examples

In each instance, we are assuming we are looking with our clear vision at someone's life situation and we have a sight of the following colours in our mind's eye. Alongside each colour there is an example of how it can be interpreted. The fact that we are seeing colours, in a particular order can help us to build a picture of what is going on with the person we are reading for:

Example One

In front of us is our first candidate and the first colour we see for this person is blue. Knowing that blue is associated with the emotions, we recognise that this person is experiencing an emotional time. We look for a second colour to go with it and in this case the colour we see is yellow, which is associated with learning. The third colour we see is red which is associated with stress.

Having seen these three colours, we know that the person is going through an emotional time and is in the course of learning – because the yellow we are seeing is very deep, we can see that there is intense study. This may be on a study programme, through formal education or through a life situation. This, in turn, is leading to a very deep red, which is also associated with stress. So from three colours, we have picked up the main things going on in a person's life.

Example Two

In front of us is our second candidate. The first colour we see for this person is brown, which tells us we have a grounded and practical-minded person with us. The next colour is yellow, which tells us this person is learning, but this yellow is very light. The third colour is green, the colour of growth.

Looking at these three colours in relationship to each other, we can see that this person is down to Earth and practical minded. They are learning, but it is not taking over their lives because it is light in colour. The green is the outcome, which is growth and that growth is occurring within the context of this practical-minded outlook.

Example Three
Our notional third candidate is in front of us. The first colour we see for this person is orange, indicating vitality and joy. The second colour we see is pink and the third colour we perceive in our mind's eye is grey.

This colour combination tells us that this person is in a situation that has given them great happiness and joy. The pink indicates that they have moved on to give unconditionally within that situation. However, in this case, the person has moved on to grey, which signifies they have become lightly depressed.

At the initial stages of developing our clear vision, we will experience and find colours. From this start, we can move on to perceive the feelings and situations around them. In this way, we can progress from merely 'seeing' a colour to feeling the emotion around it and eventually clearly knowing the situation in as much detail as we are able to discern.

Example Four
In this example we shall look at how an experienced person can use colours and interpretation with a well-developed insight, to give a more complete assessment of the situation and to put the information in context. Once we are familiar with reading the colours, we shall see that a feeling will come with each one to help guide us as to its meaning and where it sits in a person's life.

Our notional fourth candidate sits down in front of us and the first colour we can see is green which indicates growth. With this green comes the feeling of success, the kind of buzz we feel when things are improving around us and so we can tell the person that their life is improving and growing. The second colour we perceive is pink and with this pink comes the feeling of the person giving more than they are receiving. The third colour is a dark grey. This person is giving unconditionally and not receiving rewards or recognition in return. Because our experienced reader feels this is related to a work situation, we are able to tell that this person has grown within a job and yet, even though they are making a huge amount of effort, they are becoming depressed with the situation because they are working too hard. This means that the joy that would otherwise be there is lacking and this person has no sense of fulfilment. Therefore, at the present time, their life is all work and no play.

Initially, when we see these colours in a reading, it may be that we do not get the feel for their association one for the other. As we learn, we can begin to recognise and eventually intuitively know what they represent.

Visualisations to access our clear vision

Now that we have a feeling for the colours that can appear when we look in our mind's eye in a reading, we can begin to get a feel for combining them with symbolics and how the two elements can provide a well-rounded picture and clearer meaning. These visualisations can be used by you for yourself or for the benefit of anyone you know, such as a family member or a friend.

We will now look at three exercises in turn that enable us to access our clear vision. We will then go on to combine these elements into one exercise to provide ourselves with a tool that can enable us to give a more complete reading.

Step One: The Doorway

Visualize a door in front of you. Feel the door in your mind and with your hands. What type and colour of door is it, is it modern or old fashioned, decorated or plain? Accept the first thought that comes into your mind. Now open the door. Does it open inwards towards you so that you might have to step backwards, or does it open outwards away from you so that you can walk straight forward and through?

The colour of the door represents something within the chosen person's life. If the door opens inwards towards you, then that means that something in life is coming towards them and they need not necessarily make changes for it to happen, while if the door is opening outwards and away from you, that means that they will need to move forwards towards life, proactively finding and working towards their goal.

For instance, if you see a yellow doorway opening towards you, then that person is already on a path where progress will happen for them and they won't necessarily have to do anything further to make it happen. We know that there will be learning on the path because that is the symbolic meaning of the colour yellow. Whereas for the person where we see a green door opening outwards and away from them, they will have to seek and find and make things happen for their future, otherwise things won't happen for them. Because the doorway is green, it shows that they will grow, but the direction of the door shows that they have to find their own way forward. The first person does not necessarily need to put in new effort or changes, whereas the second person does.

Step Two: The Ground
Regardless of which way the door opens, the next step is to use our clear vision to move forward through the doorway. Step through and see what ground is beneath your feet. As ever, accept the first thing that comes into your mind. It can be

anything; take the image that first comes to mind and use the glossary of symbolics and colours to interpret the image.

For instance, if you find yourself on nice, even, short grass that feels comfortable to walk on, this represents even and controlled growth in that person's life, because the colour green and flourishing plant life each represent growth. If you find yourself on a concrete pathway, then this may mean that person has stability and direction, but presently no growth around them.

Step Three: The Sky
The next step is to look at the sky above us. Look up in your mind's eye and once more take your first impression. If you see an unobstructed blue sky, that indicates that the person has a sunny outlook and is dealing with life well. A cloudy sky with rain falling means that there are unhelpful influences intruding, outside this person's control.

Combining the doorway, ground and sky visualisations to give a complete picture
Visualise all three elements, the doorway, the ground and the sky in order and note your readings, then use the glossary of symbolic meanings to interpret each element. Putting all three together will enable you to create a very basic reading for the person you have in mind.

It is very important to get used to taking the first image you receive or which comes to you during your visualisation. Don't analyse it, or brush it off as imagination either, just take what you see and then interpret it. You may at first want to work with someone who is also learning or open to the idea of clear vision and give each other honest feedback and encouragement.

Meditation - The Pathway

There are many visualisations we can use to gain access to our clear vision, yet in reality we need comparatively few of these techniques and therefore just a few are presented in this book. Which techniques we use is less important than the function they serve to open our mind and tune us into the underlying energy, so that we see situations from this clear perspective. Eventually, we can open our mind to the extent that the visualisation techniques are no longer necessary.

Each of us is on a particular path in life and to see our immediate situation and our past and present life journey, we can use a technique called The Pathway.

The Pathway enables us to tune into what is happening in our lives and how it is affecting us. As with all clear vision, the visualisation gives us tools to access the right area of our lives in a way that we can relate to. Eventually, as with all these exercises, after much practice, we may find that we no longer need the visualisation technique and we can access our clear vision just by turning our mind to it. This is by no means the case for everyone, yet at the same time it is a possibility that we can develop this far.

Pathways provide basic insight. The solidity, the construction, the width, the colour and the structure of a pathway can tell us as a reader enough to establish the present situation in a person's journey of life.

The exercise
In your mind's eye, visualise either your own feet or the feet of the person for whom you are reading. You should immediately get an impression of the ground their feet are standing on. Look with your mind's eye until you have it. Once you have this in your mind, accept what you see and look to see the details of this ground. Is it concrete, carpet, water, sand, gravel, grass or even bare earth? Using the language of symbolics, each of the

different types of ground tells us something about that person's situation. In simple terms, a good solid pathway indicates that life is quite sound for that person, while if we saw someone up to their ankles in mud, then we would know that they are stuck in an unpleasant situation and it may require effort to extricate themselves. We will look at different pathways in more detail later on.

Once you have looked and understood what is going on for that person on their immediate pathway, we can then look to the pathway ahead so that we understand what that person is facing in the future. To do this, in your mind's eye, simply raise your gaze and look forward, what appears to you will indicate what is facing that person in their future, be it difficulty or opportunity. The immediate pathway ahead is the immediate future, while the further along the pathway we look, the further forward in the future we are going. So if we see a long upward climb for a person, we can see that they are improving their situation and literally 'going up in the world', while the steepness of the pathway indicates how difficult that journey might be for them. Conversely, if we see a person's pathway is blocked by a cliff, we know that they have a particularly difficult journey ahead of them (climbing a cliff isn't usually easy!) and our job as a clear-reader is to see if there are more convenient ways forward for them, as well as whether they are up to the challenge and how undertaking it might affect them. To do this, we can look around the cliff in our mind and see if there are easier pathways to pursue. If there are not, then mentally put yourself in their shoes and visualise yourself making the climb. Do you complete the climb and if so, how do you then feel?

We are just learning this technique and as we do, we should get feelings associated with each element of the pathway. We may, for instance, study the cliff and get a feeling that it is to do with the person's work. The reading is not a guessing game however and we must only interpret and pass on what we find on the pathway.

So for instance, if we see a certificate pinned to the top of the cliff, we would read that the cliff is a journey of study and that there would be a qualification or certificate at the end of it. If the cliff were coloured yellow, then this would indicate learning and if there were splashes of red on the cliff face, we would know that there will be periods of stress associated with the studying. By contrast, if we see a nice gentle pathway with a cottage at the end of it, that comes with a comfortable relaxed feeling, we could read that someone has modest aspirations for getting the house of their dreams (symbolised by the cottage) and that their journey will be easily achievable (as it is not a steep climb). There are infinite pathways with an infinite number of symbolics we can find on them and these are just given as examples of what we may find.

On The Pathway visualisation, we can also look to the sky. In life, the sky and the weather has a mind of its own; we cannot control or interrupt it, we can only seek to protect ourselves from its worst conditions and enjoy the weather when it is warm and balmy. The ground or pathway indicates what a person is now experiencing and feeling and how they are progressing tells us how they are coping with what we find in the visualisation. The sky and the weather conditions tell us the nature of the outside influences in that person's life. Rain (as it is water) would tell us that there are a lot of outside emotions coming to that person from others; it could be someone around them is trying to off-load their emotions on to them, for instance, and we would then have to look to see how our subject is coping. If they are wearing waterproof clothing, then that indicates that they are able to protect themselves, while if their clothing is instead saturated, then we know that this outside emotional pressure is getting through. The nature and quality of the rain will tell us just how intense this outside pressure is. A heavy thunderstorm will show us that it is intense, while light showers indicate that it is sporadic and not such a cause for concern. Clouds in the sky will indicate negative influences, while sunshine speaks for itself as a nice environment around the person indicates a sunny disposition.

There is a whole library of symbolics, hundreds of symbols that spirit world use because we can relate to them. Symbolics are based on common sense and, once learnt, are an easy way of describing a situation appertaining to the person being read.

What we are looking to achieve in a reading is to tune into the person being read and provide evidence that there is more to life than just the physical world we perceive with our five senses and therefore help them to see their own way forward more clearly. The desired result, therefore, is to demonstrate proof of what is taking place around the person being read. This proof can only be accepted when you are ready for it, even the most amazing clear vision readings can be explained away by a cynic, while quite mundane information can serve as proof to someone whose mind is open and doesn't think they are being duped. The proof of the pudding is in the eating and nowhere else.

Situations and images we can encounter on the pathway

When we look with our clear vision, there are limitless situations we can encounter. The key to interpretation is once more not to look literally but to interpret the image by immersing ourselves in the visualisation and understanding what it feels like to be presented with what you find. Once you have this feeling, learn to go with the flow and experience will tell you which feeling puts you on the right track.

A pathway with a lack of Vegetation and growth Means that this person is receiving few returns, or is not yet in a situation to receive recognition for their work. This can be shown as a desert, bog, quicksand, rocks, concrete oceans, tar or asphalt roadways.
A rug pulled from under the feet This is a common situation and the person may be emotionally winded and may need guidance and help in their situation. The next step in their reading would be to look and guide them to get back on their feet.
Ball and Chain Carrying responsibilities.

Blizzard Lost with a lack of emotional warmth and support around them.

Blue Skies A warm blue sky means that this person has an optimistic and positive attitude.

Blindfold Someone who is blind to the obvious and therefore needs to awaken to the situation around them.

A Wall An obstruction! It is important to check whether there is the possibility of going around it, climbing over it or going through it. However, the wall may be that person's insecurities presenting themselves and is therefore representing a challenge that they may readily overcome as it could be paper thin. What do we feel the wall is made of? A wall represents an obstruction in one's life and if we cannot overcome it then we need to rethink our life situation and what is causing this obstacle.

Bright light Blinded to the obvious situation around them.

Butterfly Someone who flits around from topic to topic, unsettled and in need of grounding.

Clouds (grey) A grey cloudy sky means that this person has a lack of warmth in their life. This person may feel grey like the sky or is perhaps becoming negative.

Clouds (white) A white cloudy sky means that there is a lack of warmth as in our grey sky but they are more able to be positive than if the clouds were seen as being grey.

Concrete Boots Unable to move. Therefore this person is in a position where they will not move on.

Concrete Pathways A pathway where there is direction but an absence of growth.

Corners Corners in the pathway ahead mean that one is potentially blind to where one is heading and therefore unable to see a way forward in life.

Crutches Needing emotional support.

Crystals Crystals represent a spiritual association and the enhancement of life with energy and colour. If we see an environment with crystals this represents someone who is developing spiritually, with healing and positive energy present.

Dark skies Continuous depression. A person who had black skies would be in deep depression and should seek guidance from a medical professional.

Deckchair Retirement or rest and relaxation.

Desert Massive irritations all around and no growth in their life.

Elephant Someone with strength and the ability to carry life's heavy burdens.

Empty pockets Lacks ready cash.

River across the pathway Blocked by emotions. May be overwhelming and difficult to overcome.

Fences Restrictions and boundaries.

Fire Debt! A big fire indicates some form of financial crisis because fire is destructive and all consuming. A smaller fire could be credit or financial loan situations.

Flowers Flowers of any type in a reading indicate colourful growth in life with choices. Alternatively they may signify an anniversary such as a Birthday.

Forest Can't see the wood for the trees. Needs to differentiate between problems. This person may feel lost.

Grass Growth! Longer grass may mean uncontrolled growth, whereas a neatly trimmed lawn means that the growth is well under control

Hammer Someone who is quick and direct and to the point. "Hitting the nail on the head."

Hands over the eyes Hiding from a situation around them. They are blocking it out. If they are wearing a blindfold, then the situation is being held from them or they may not be ready to see the obvious.

Head in the sand Needs to face life and stand up for own convictions.

Hills Hills on a person's pathway - going uphill can be hard going dependent upon the gradient. Going downhill can mean that life is in danger of running out of control.

Holes Areas of depression.

Lack of emotional warmth in life Represented by images of clouds, rain, winter, lack of fire, no coat being worn, a lack of sunshine, or by snow.

Lame Someone who is 'limping along', needing emotional and physical support.

Losing balance Need emotional and physical support.

Mud Means verbal accusations are being directed at the person and are sticking, therefore affecting them emotionally.

Puddles On and off outside emotional influences that can be avoided or the person can get themselves involved.

Rain Represents emotions that are not in your control.

Rainbow Someone heading towards a very emotional time with each corresponding colour coming up. We should check the position of the rainbow i.e. is it ahead of us, or is it already behind us or are we in it and what colour are we in at the moment?

Rapids in a river Life is totally out of control. Fast flowing water represents painful emotions that are in danger of taking us over, with nothing seemingly straightforward. Rapids represent a fearful situation that we are caught up in where life may be running away with us until we are out of that situation.

Road – narrow Restrictions & frustrations.

Road – wide Choices and opportunities.

Rug pulled from underfoot A person who has been taken by surprise and winded without warning, by someone or something in their life. Any shocking news can come across this way. Needing guidance and understanding.

Running and jumping along a road Avoiding situations (by jumping over them).

Sand Is indicative of different forms of irritations – as one would feel sand on the skin.

Sandy beach A life full of irritations.

Scorpion Someone who does not hold back in an argument (because they have a sting in their tail!).

Sitting still Needing encouragement (to get moving in life).

Snake A snake indicates a female who may have bad intentions. 'A venomous natured person.'

Snow Snow obscures the ground beneath your feet. Despite appearing bright and appealing life is treacherous. If the snow is melting, this indicates water and emotions.

Stampeding elephants Impending threat from destructive outside influences beyond your control.

Shifting from one foot to the other Needs guidance in knowing where to start (not able to make a decision as to which direction to take).

Stepping into fog Someone who needs guidance with their current situation. They may feel things are wrong with their situation, but they cannot see their way out of it and don't know when it will end. We can step mentally into the image and feel what it is like for them and find a way forward.

Stepping off a cliff Drawing strength to achieve the impossible (by taking a step of faith and walking forwards into the unknown).

Stile in a field Undergoing a transition from one situation to another. Check to see if the grass is greener in the next field!

Straight pathway with plants A good future with lots of opportunity and controlled growth within their lives.

Sunflowers Stature and presence, a person who is upright, stands out and has a sunny disposition.

Sunny Day See Blue Skies.

Sunsets A sunset with darkening skies and flashes of red and different colours means that there is emotional trauma ahead in this person's life.

Swimming with dolphins A very spiritual person.

Teddy Bear Childlike personality and fond of comfort or with a need for comfort.

Tightrope A situation where one needs to balance oneself.

Trees in a park A nice, open situation with the opportunity to rest and enjoy the growth in one's life.

Walking stick Needing temporary balance with support.

Water on the pathway at a person's feet This will represent emotional pain in one form or another. However, as the water is only as high as the feet, it is merely uncomfortable. As water signifies upset emotions, the higher we see the water rising, the worse the situation is for that person. To understand this, imagine what it is like if water is at waist height, it would be very difficult to move forward. If it were up to our noses then we would almost be drowning in our emotions. There are limitless permutations.

Zigzagging on a pathway Someone who is constantly changing their mind and will not commit to one course of action. A pathway is there to be walked so this person should be advised to stay on track and pursue ideas to their conclusion.

Exercises

Another way of developing our clear vision is to tune into the emotions. In each of these exercises, visualise the pathway of the person you are reading for. In your mind's eye, place yourself in their situation and experience their reactions to the pathway they are on. In each example below, we will focus on one state-of-mind. Some people will have an excess of one feeling within them, while for others you will need to look harder to find if it is present. Of course we won't be experiencing all of these emotions at once, rather we are using these exercises to get a feeling for someone's emotional background. This will help you recognise and familiarise yourself with each feeling and voice your interpretation of it:

Sadness Concentrate on the sadness of the person sitting in front of you. How long or how short a time has the sadness been with them? How deep or shallow is that sadness?

Emotional pain Concentrate on the pain within the person in front of you. How are they reacting to it and how do they deal with any past traumas. How deep were they and do they bottle them up or have they learnt from them? Look to see how they are coping.

Anger Look for anger and get the feeling of it. How are they coping with the anger? What triggers it and where do these feelings originate from? Are they short-fused, rebelling, slamming doors or suppressing it? Have they developed hatred? How deep and for how long have they had these feelings?

Insecurities Look and feel the insecurities within the person in front of you. What makes them feel this way and how do they express and cope with these feelings? Are they clinging or rejecting? When did the insecurities start and who brought the insecurities into their life? Is it family or relationship bonding? What are your findings?

Loneliness How deep and how long has this loneliness been with them? What has made them feel this way? Are they mentally or physically isolated from people? Do they feel rejected in some way and is this happening now, or is it a reaction to something that happened in the past?

Fear How long has it been with them and where did it start from? How are they coping? Do you see a mask? Do you find them going inward or outward and wanting to run? Are they standing still in fear? How does it affect their lives now?

Jealousy Where did the jealousy originate from? How and why did insecurities form into jealousy in adulthood? Look to see how destructive jealousy can be and how it is affecting their life now.

Control Control in this sense refers not to self-control, but the desire to control life and the situations and people around us. Look and see how and why they have the desire, or need, to have things their way and their way alone? How damaging is it? How does it affect them and others? Why and when did this start? Feel how difficult it is to trust while the necessity to control is present.

Mistrust Look to see where they lost trust in their lives. Which parent or which situation started it? Observe how this lack of mental freedom restricts their life. Are they rejecting others before they are rejected or are they clinging emotionally to their own opinions to feel safe?

We can now look at some examples of how we can use every element of the exercises together. We are still only looking at giving very basic readings in the examples, but eventually, our clear vision can take us beyond, firstly into knowing what the symbolic images represent and then onwards to a point where we directly 'know' without needing symbolics. With enough practice, it is possible to reach a point where our insight will come naturally without our having to try too hard.

Below are several scenarios that we can engage with to show how we can use our developing clear vision to help and guide yourself and others.

Within each example tune in with your clear vision to the following colours and symbolics given. When you have a feel for each example, write down your findings. While you are gaining familiarity and when need be, use the glossary to help you.

Picture these scenarios in your mind's eye and experience what each feels like. Placing yourself fully into the visualisation is the key to accessing your clear vision.

In a reading, we have to put ourselves totally into the other person's situation and feel what it is like for them before we speak. Do not analyse! How you personally react to a situation may be totally different to the person you are reading for. Keep a distinction between your own feelings and your findings. We should only ever pass on what we can feel through using the exercises and not how we would react or deal with a situation ourselves. Developing the ability to differentiate is a key part of our education and using symbolics is key. Interpreting the images you perceive, rather than leaping to conclusions, teaches us to distinguish between assumption and clear vision.

The golden rule is, if you haven't seen and felt it with your clear vision, then don't say it. Learning this pathway opens you up so that you have options beyond just your own opinions, so that you may read for others with a clear agenda. Therefore, always test what you are saying in your mind's eye before you say it, in that way you know you are delivering something far clearer than just your own imagination or opinions.

Now we can practice using some scenarios. In each one, we have to imagine that there is a person with you who you will read for, therefore you can undertake these scenarios whenever and wherever you like. Write down your interpretation in each case and check it against the interpretation we have placed below it. Once you have completed them, we recommend that you test on yourself or a friend who understands that you are learning and therefore not to act on the advice you give.

For instance, if you see that someone is having doubts about a work position, you can look and see whether they would be successful in seeking a job elsewhere. You may see the situation as a fork in the pathway with two options ahead of them. You may also see them hopping from one foot to the other. The first image tells us that there is a choice of direction, and the second image tells us that this person does not know which one to take. If they did know which way to go, or were set on a course regardless of advice, you would see them walking forward along one fork in the road and would be unable to see them walking along the other fork they could have taken. If you are able to place them equally comfortable on either pathway, it is an indication that there are choices that can be made.

Before you choose, you will need mentally to take that person on either pathway, identify which one it is that leads them forwards in their existing role and which one involves change and a new job. Then put yourself on that person's pathway and in their shoes, how do they feel? Are they nervous, excited, fearful? Walk them along the pathway of seeking a new role, how do they feel now? Logically you may see it as an exciting challenge, but for someone who is not so self-assured, their lack of confidence could be a major block, stopping them even from contemplating looking for a new position.

What you see and feel with your clear vision will inform you of their feelings and, therefore, what advice is going to be the most appropriate for them. For instance, if you cannot mentally get the person to walk their pathway that represents change, this means that something is holding them back. Feel what it is, look at them on the pathway and feel what emotions come with this immobility. You may find that walking along the pathway of choosing to look for a new role fills them with fear, but may also be a pathway that, once this initial barrier is crossed, provides them with a great deal of personal fulfilment. You will know only once you have mentally walked that pathway in your mind's eye. Taking a long-term view is always a key to success in reading, as it enables you to look beyond the immediate reactions and deliver a reading that considers the bigger picture.

Scenario One

Our notional person sits down in front of us. Tuning in with your mind's eye you immediately find the following:
- The colour red
- A barren pathway
- Fences on either side of the pathway
- That the person you are reading for is hopping from foot one foot to the other

Interpretation

From the symbolics and colours, we can see that this person is undergoing stress in a life journey that is lacking in growth and they are restricted by situations that hem them in. They are indecisive and don't know what decision to make to achieve the best outcome.

The colour red indicates that stress is present, while a pathway with no growth, surrounded by fences, tells us that restrictions and lack of development are present. Hopping from one foot to another shows their indecisiveness as to what to do next.

Scenario Two

Our notional person sits down in front of us. We tune in with our mind's eye and find the following:

- The colour yellow
- A canoe careering down rapids in a raging river with no paddles.
- A rainbow

Interpretation

This person is totally out of control, with no ability to steer a direction in their life. Their situation is very threatening and they could easily find themselves overcome by life, the problems within it and their emotional reaction to it. But also remember that the colour yellow is present and this person is therefore learning what could be valuable lessons from the situation they are in. Hopefully, they are learning never to allow themselves to be drawn into this kind of situation again! The rainbow is quite a common image to see after the rapids, because when life is at its most out of control and we are in the rapids ourselves, we are putting all of our effort into just dealing with situations and keeping ourselves afloat emotionally and perhaps financially as well. A rainbow represents our experiencing the full spectrum of emotions we can feel ourselves going through once the immediate situation has passed. Quite often, after having gone through a challenging time we can experience a huge range of emotions, from grief to anger. We may go through stress, relief, fear, insecurity; any of which we know from our study of colours can be in the rainbow. If we see a person in such a situation as this, it is always a good idea to look forward for that person to see the outcome. It may be that after the rapids and the rainbow's emotional backlash, they enter a new phase of calmness and growth that is far more rewarding and comfortable. This may be shown as a quiet river-bank where they can disembark or a peaceful lagoon where they can relax and find their bearings again.

Scenario Three
Our notional person sits down in front of us. We tune in with our mind's eye and find the following:
- A clear blue sky
- A yellow brick road
- A cave full of crystals

Interpretation
This is someone who has a positive outlook and a clear mental environment. They are learning from life and taking everything in their stride as they move forwards. There is also a spiritual side to this person which is providing positive, healing and creative energy to sustain them.

The blue skies represent someone who is able to keep their thoughts free from clutter, even if they are experiencing difficulties to be overcome. The yellow on their pathway indicates a road of learning and the bricks show firm supportive footing that enables them to move safely forwards. The crystal cave is a haven for healing that will yield up many positive energies and colours, showing that they have a spiritual element within.

Exercise - The brown sack

The 'brown sack' is another exercise that allows us to access our clear vision and provide an interpretation. It can be good fun, but it also has a deeper and more profound meaning. This exercise provides you with a very quick method to read for a person, describing their personality and traits.

When we first meet someone, we will normally react to their physical appearance and demeanour, which initially is all that we have to work with. If we get the opportunity to understand them more deeply, we may get a clearer idea of what they are about. However, the brown sack is another way of gaining a quick understanding of what a person is like, while developing our understanding and feel for symbolic language.

You can use this exercise to gain an insight into yourself or others. The brown sack involves your taking objects out of a sack that you visualise in your mind's eye. Typically you will take three objects to gain an insight into a person's character. Each object informs us about that person's personality, outlook on life and the nature of their character. It is also an ideal prop if you find yourself stuck or unable to see a person's pathway clearly. Lastly, it can be used to enable even someone who is totally new to the practice of clear vision to read for themselves, as it is simple, direct and only requires a limited knowledge of the subject.

How to practice the exercise
Sit and make yourself comfortable, as you would for meditation. Have a pen and paper to hand to note your findings. In your mind's eye, picture a brown sack in front of you or in the middle of the room. Now see your hand reaching into the sack and alighting upon an object within it. Whatever you first encounter should be taken out of the sack for you to examine. Go with whatever presents itself, no matter how bizarre or mundane it initially appears. It could be any object, a toy a train, a spade, a house or a boat; anything at all.

The exercise provides insight because it is spontaneous, therefore interpreting what you pull out of the sack is easy once you get the hang of it. Firstly, you should always remember that the object represents something directly relevant to that person. So if we pull out a hammer, then we may have lit upon someone who is direct and to the point, 'hitting the nail on the head'. If we pull out a teddy bear, then we know that that person has a childlike quality and that they are fond of their comforts, because a teddy bear is a symbol of youth and comfort. Likewise, a teddy bear is cuddled, therefore this person has a need to be loved. A trumpet will signify someone with an ability to make themselves heard – because you cannot avoid hearing a trumpet. As our ability to see clearly develops, we may get feelings alongside these images, but initially we should directly associate with the function of the object we pull out of the sack. It is the function of the object and its direct associations that determine how we interpret it. So a scorpion has a sting in its tail, an elephant is someone with a very big presence and a butterfly is someone who flits around, perhaps with a very light touch and changing often from topic to topic or place to place. When you have pulled out as many objects as you need, having voiced your findings, finish the exercise.

Remember that the object is a representation of the person you are reading for. It does not represent their life or what is happening around them, it is them. Below are just few examples of what can be found in the brown sack alongside the way in which they can be interpreted:

A bomber aeroplane Has the ability to destroy, perhaps unexpectedly (bombs can fall from the sky without warning).

A book Someone with the ability to focus and hold that focus. They may be educating themselves in life and have the ability to hold someone's interest, as does a book. A book with blank pages means that person has not yet found meaning in their life or perhaps not yet found their chosen direction.

A Buddha Searching for meaning or security through enlightenment.

A clock Someone who is a good time-keeper or who is working to tight schedules.

A coat Someone who likes to feel secure (because a coat offers warmth and protection from outside influences).

A crystal ball An intuitive person who can see situations clearly and throw light upon them through their insight, perhaps seeing outcomes that others do not.

Floorboards Someone who is practical minded and thinks of practicalities first (because a floor is brown which represents being down to earth and floorboards are made from wood and are physically the ground on which we walk).

A Giraffe Someone who can see beyond the immediate and obvious and is able to take the long view (as a Giraffe can see further because of its height). This person will also have high aspirations (as a giraffe

A gorilla Represents someone who is strong, unpredictable, protective, very conscious of their own space and therefore territorial. Family orientated and able to put on a great show of aggression to protect their space (as would a gorilla).

A lollipop A person who is appealing and can provide sustenance that lasts for a short while. This person may be delightful giving us enjoyment but not have the staying power to hang around for long (as lollipops last only a short while).

A medallion or medal Works hard in the background and deserves to be rewarded (as a medal is being offered to them).

A mirror Someone who is conscious of their image, either with vanity or insecurity. (Because when we look in a mirror we see only ourselves).

A needle Someone who has the ability to hold things together (a needle will stitch two pieces of cloth together that would otherwise remain separate).

A nest of baby spiders An adaptable jack of all trades and is perhaps yet to find a single vocation or grow in their existing one, but is likely to produce results that spread.

A pen A person able to make their mark on people's lives.

A plant in a pot Someone who is contained in a situation that is limiting their growth. (A pot plant can only spread its roots as far as the pot allows). This person may also feel stifled because of the situation they are in and need nurturing from others to survive (as a pot plant needs watering and feeding to survive).

will sustain itself from sources out of the reach of others).

A scaffold on a building Able to deal with people on many levels (levels such as you would find on a scaffold) and in many walks of life, but keeps those relationships at a distance (a scaffold is outside a building and not within it).

One shoe Someone who is unbalanced in that they are protected in one area of their life (where they have a shoe on), but on the other side are vulnerable and open to hurt (because they are barefooted). Typically this would be someone who is tough and strong minded, at work for instance, but can be taken advantage of in other areas, such as their relationships.

A wedding ring Someone who is able to form a commitment in any area and dedicate themselves to it for life.

Reading blind

A great exercise is to 'read blind.' When you are reading blind you are reading the subject without any visual contact, so you may simply close your eyes so that you cannot be distracted by their body language or facial expression, or use any barrier that blocks your view. Using this technique means that you can only read what appears to your clear vision and you cannot interpret in any other way other than what you perceive with your mind. This helps you to use clear vision alone without any interference or outside input. You can 'read blind' using any of the exercises in this chapter and you may even find it a better way to focus, as you will be untroubled by visual input.

Chapter Eighteen – A Summarising Note from the Authors

This book is written in the hope that it will provide ways for you to develop your personal understanding of spirituality, while delivering tools you can use to benefit your state-of-mind and open you to the world of clear vision.

We are, each of us, a spiritual being in an Earthly body and our soul harbours all the knowledge and wisdom that we glean from this life, gaining understanding and knowledge, that we can then take back when we pass over to the spirit world. Therefore, life is not a journey that is there to serve the Earthly body but rather a journey of learning for our soul.

To achieve inner harmony we need merely recognise the soul and allow it a role in guiding our lives. In so doing, we need to value ourselves, to recognise that everything exists for a reason and to respect those around us, all of whom are on their own journey.

While our soul chooses where and when to be born, from the moment we are here, we are subject to life's challenges and that which confronts us within those challenges. Therefore, the only true choice we have in our physical body is to how to express our will, knowing that what we do will shape who we are and that we are accountable for our actions. By allowing this recognition to guide us, we gain true freedom, because life becomes honest, accountable and worthwhile, rather than an ill-considered reaction to what challenges us. Because it helps us access greater clarity, clear vision can help us find our spirituality and incorporate it into our everyday lives.

The soul chooses its own time of birth and death. Yet, in modern society we are not necessarily in tune enough to recognise this spiritually chosen journey. By encouraging our own spiritual growth, we are better able to identify what feelings originate from our conditioning and intellect and distinguish those that are in accord with our conscience. Another way of looking at this is to see the soul as a lodger in our body. The brain will often argue with this tenant, creating an inner struggle, the outcome of which dictates what direction we take in life. Without inner guidance, the brain reacts in accordance with the thought-pattern we have developed through conditioning. In contrast, the soul carries all our learning and has a connection with a higher source. The soul, therefore, is able to provide us with wisdom which we can choose to access, but may sometimes seem at odds with our immediate wishes. Therefore, at times, we may find ourselves wrestling with the feelings of desire generated by our reaction to life and the soul's need for fulfilment and knowledge. To gain the most from our journey we must find balance between the brain and the soul, which means learning to prioritise our spiritual life so that it can find expression through the physical.

A spiritual pathway should give voice to our soul, giving us freedom to become one and to have peace and harmony within. To achieve this state, we need to firstly recognise when our thoughts and actions are being governed by our conditioned brain. If we then listen to our inner feelings, our brain too will listen and learn from them, rather than attempt to ignore them. This is vital if we are to be guided from within. Spirituality offers us the opportunity to embody what we are born with, freedom within ourselves and the ability to be who we truly are. We need not claim ourselves to be spiritually motivated. Many people follow not only a moral or ethical code, but possess an inner compass that instinctively guides them in a spiritual direction.

The soul can come here for many reasons. It can come to bond in family love, to set examples or show the way, yet whatever the chosen pathway, it comes to learn from experiences and to expand awareness. The soul may live through both pain and love and may bond as a friend or in a family as a mother, father, sister or brother. It may come here to experience handicaps, or just to learn and grow, enhancing itself through the knowledge it gains. Therefore we can come to leave our mark here, having a positive influence, perhaps as a teacher, nurse, hairdresser, writer or leader. Whatever our physical pathway, the soul's journey is inevitable. It can be a journey of hardship, misery, love, giving, gaining strength or perhaps making amends and living out its karma. The soul can choose to come here to save another or to feel the joy of living and to flourish in life itself. Alternatively, it may be here to pursue a cause, to help save the planet, to help the children of this world, the animals, our forests or to express itself through art or music.

Freedom of choice is always ours and it is our prerogative whether we seek awareness of our soul's journey. Whatever we choose, the one certainty is that death will come at the end of our physical life. It is then that our soul returns to its spiritual home and finds light and release.

Initially, we are children in a playground, progressing and growing through our lives here on Earth. Each of us are playing roles and learning, both the good lessons and the bad, experiencing the conflicts and the closeness with our fellow mankind.

For those of us who choose a spiritual pathway, the ultimate goal is to develop a union between the physical body and the spiritual, that realises peace within ourselves and with each other. Rather than pushing and shoving to gain advantage over each other, the pathway can guide us to work together.

It is up to each of us to choose. If we work in concord rather than competition, treating our neighbours as we ourselves would wish to be treated, we can have a positive impact on ourselves and on one another. This brings benefits, shaping the communities in which we live and creating a sense of community. If we work cooperatively, which is a great thing in itself, we are achieving something positive and we can rest easier in our own world, knowing that we are doing what we can to improve it.

Regrettably, there is a lack of common understanding and spiritual cohesion in society and many of our children are born into a culture that teaches us to live for the moment, without respect or ultimate purpose other than to satisfy our own needs and desires. Spirituality begins with ourselves and with those who are within our families and circle of friends. Just as we are responsible for ourselves, it is the responsibility of every parent to invest in their child's development. If we all worked to develop ourselves, our families and friendships, then imagine what a better environment we would live in.

Once we have an understanding of ourselves spiritually, it can help us understand others. Life is not an even playing field, but despite this, choice means that either we can open our minds and become actively engaged, or shut ourselves off from the world around us.

A lot of people are doing their very best in life, putting effort into seeking happiness and fulfilment, or helping and caring for those who are near or dear to them. Likewise, there are many people doing things that are detrimental, with the potential to harm themselves and others. If life feels too difficult to bear, we will often seek some form of release. The people who do this regularly, losing themselves to drugs and alcohol, can make their own lives miserable. The personal disorder this brings can permeate into the society around us. With no values or respect for ourselves, we can lose perspective and at the extreme we see this spill over into violence, intimidation and theft that ultimately pushes communities into their individual homes and behind closed doors. Spirituality can give us a helping hand when we encounter this chaos and the people who are in it. It provides us with inner strength, promotes understanding and a recognition that things can change. To reclaim our lives and encourage something better than this potential mayhem, we need to join with like minds, so that a common understanding can create a lasting common purpose. It is our choice which path we follow and which path we create.

Achieving our goals in the knowledge of life's wider purpose and despite its trials and tribulations, helps us to develop both self-worth and wisdom. For society to have a common purpose, we must all understand where we are aiming and what our commonly accepted boundaries are. This allows us to then live in community with solidarity and share the good feelings that come from respecting one another in thought and deed.

A culture that seeks personal gratification at the cost of others is not one that we have to buy into. Some people go to the extreme, attempting short cuts such as stealing and therefore what they have they do not value. In previous centuries, much of the world offered us far more living space. Countries, cities and the planet are now increasingly crowded, meaning we are often living in very close proximity to each other. These conditions lead to us being packed into flats and apartments, our traffic congested and our travel delayed. With so much pressure, spiritual or even moral reference points can be lost and disagreements find fertile ground.

Work demands and material aspirations mean that the traditional family structure has changed and in many families, no longer does the housewife work solely at home and the man solely at his job. These days, we may have aspirations for a lifestyle that few enjoyed in the past and the financial pressures of sustaining it mean that both partners have the responsibility of jobs and carrying out the household chores. Therefore role of a house-person is seen as an occupation with less value. With both parents working, man and woman have equal responsibility and yet structure in social communities is being lost and some children are left to fend for themselves or are cared for by relatives or child-carers. A side effect of this, is that there is no longer a structure where one person runs the household and responsibility is divided. Just as self-discipline is necessary for self-respect to flourish, so nowadays there is a need for both parents to bring discipline to the family structure, for the sake of all our children.

Man is born with physical strength but women have an emotional outlook and awareness. Women are mentally stronger, in that they have the ability to do more than one thing at once, while a man may be more single minded. Yet, because of our familiarity with a traditional social structure, women can have a heavier burden to carry – with the expectation that they both have a job, do the housework and care for the children. Because of the diverse burdens women carry, many are looking for their emotional needs to be answered. However, many women feel that men are not equipped to respond to their needs because they do not have the skills or they do not have the sensitivity to engage emotionally. Much as we might love our partner, this gap in emotional communication means the love we are seeking can seem elusive or even impossible. Clear vision can show us how our partner feels. It can teach us how to remain true to our own feelings, understanding their emotional responses without seeking to control them.

Spirituality can be sought and embodied without the need for great complexity. The very possession of life means that we have so much potential and the fact that life does have meaning and purpose creates the cause for us all to be happy. Yet, not everyone in life responds well to it, but neither are we all foolish or aggressive or petty minded. In this world we can easily find those who are full of the milk of human kindness, or even just nice people who are easy to get along with. It is our ignorance that means the pathway can seem full of lessons to learn. Once understood however, the message is simplicity itself. Therefore, in this book we have sought to convey our perspective of this way of life, so that it is understandable by us all.

The spiritual pathway does not necessarily demand that we live a contemplative life. We cannot all be preachers, priests or even parishioners. Life offers all of us enough experiences to expand our thoughts, to teach us patience and embrace us with love. We can develop wisdom and compassion and understanding and all the higher achievements just by living a normal life.

Love is the eternal possibility that permeates all of creation, yet so few of our lives embody it in its totality. Cynicism, by contrast, is a man made attitude and a product of past experience that distorts our outlook because it assumes the worst motivations or outcomes. It stops analytical thought in its tracks, limits our potential to see a positive outcome and twists our point of view so that it is at odds with reality.

So why do we insist on expecting the worst? There is the potential for good and bad in everyone. Being cynical we do not expose ourselves to emotional risk, because our hopes cannot be shattered. This may make us feel more secure in ourselves, as having learnt to expect little from people and from life, we can act accordingly and give little in return. Yet, this dangerous state-of-mind does not armour us against disappointment because as a cynic we are already living in a constant state of dissatisfaction and having seemingly armoured ourselves, we are closed to much of the joy that life offers.

If we allow ourselves to focus on the positive, we can see what we have, how far we have journeyed and what we have learnt and achieved. This mind-set will enable us to move forwards in life, without dwelling on our disappointments, nor colouring our judgement of others. A positive outlook allows room for positive outcomes and widens our mind, because it recognises the possibility of success, despite life's challenges.

Yet some people have had too many disappointments and positivity seems out of reach. If we allow this attitude to continue for too long, we can find ourselves depressed and lonely and even feel hopeless or helplessly lost. From this perspective, we cannot see the wood for the trees because we do not have the mental space to take a step back and gain perspective. Instead, our emotions overwhelm us. Casting about in this situation, we might end up throwing ourselves in any direction that we think offers hope. This could be a relationship or anything we see as a lifeline, but because of our limited viewpoint, it could be entirely wrong for us and unable to meet our long-term needs.

There may be many of us who wish to help others in need, yet have not learnt how to react to someone's cry for help. Also, we may feel we cannot reach out because we are stifled by feelings of negativity or embarrassment and are fearful of the possibility of rejection. Our own awkwardness may stop us from reaching out to offer support to the bereaved or those who are bereft. Likewise, we may see people who are old and in need of help or kind words and we fail to respond because our lives are too busy to take on any level of commitment, perhaps because of the boundaries we have set ourselves. Developing spiritually means we are better able to look outside of our own concerns and recognise situations that might otherwise go unnoticed, put our embarrassment to the side and reach out to others.

Without the empathy and support of other people, life can be lonely and painful. Yet, when we have been through a distressing situation, we can understand those who are suffering similar experiences. It is sad that to gain a sense of solidarity, we may need to go through harrowing experiences. Often it is disasters, wars and the trying times that affect us as a community that serve to bring us together and help each other. Having lived through an emotionally trying time means we can truly empathise with someone in the same situation and be sensitive to their suffering.

Many of us experience the consequences of another human being's choices, be it through military, economic or political decisions made on our behalf. Wherever we turn in life, what others do affects us, in the same way that what we do has an impact on other people. Knowing this, we should recognise where our own boundaries lie, where we feel we have been wronged and whether we are making any of those same mistakes ourselves. The past is a great teacher if we pay it heed. For instance, if we suffer abuse, then that should teach us not to be a source of pain to others.

There are many situations when we are thrown together with people from different groups and in these circumstances we have no choice other than to get on with one another. Sitting on a bus or a park bench, did we but know it, we are each only one conversation away from getting to know someone and making the world a better place for it. Relating to other people will always show us that there are those who are better or worse off than ourselves and recognise that perhaps our own lives aren't so bad, or that there is room for hope.

Sometimes, how we act doesn't feel like it is born out of choice. In some situations, we may feel we have no option. Our search for love leads us into making mistakes born out of loneliness. We may feel barren without recognising why, feeling an absence of love as a need that we cannot satisfy. Try as we might and no matter what our situation, we cannot guarantee we will find love here on Earth. Though this may sound bleak, if we look to a spiritual source, we will find love far greater than any other, permeating us from within and more than we need to fulfil us. If we are loved, then we can, in turn, recognise we are loveable and find ourselves more emotionally at ease, for love brings the best from us. The greater inner peace we find, enables us to be generous with ourselves and each other. Finding the ultimate source of love in the universal energy can fulfil us spiritually and emotionally and allow us to be the best we can be.

In the same way that our bodies are vehicles for our spiritual growth, so our planet Earth is the vehicle for all of us to make life's journey. Each of us has an everlasting life and Earth provides us with a physical place to be born into, time and time again. Respecting our bodies is our personal responsibility and respecting the planet is our duty, both to ourselves and each other.

If we think in terms of all of our lives and those of the people around us, then we can see the requirement we have to treat the environment as well as we are able. Practically, we can help the planet for ourselves and for future generations and so that we have a decent place to come back to in future lives. This obligation should not be treated lightly.

We are held in place by gravity, on an Earth that is lit by a sun and orbited by a moon that affects our tides and rhythms, yet overpopulation is making the planet uninhabitable. As we look to our own interests and our own development and our own spirituality and how we live here, so we need to look at how we nurture and look after our planet. Knowing that this may not last forever, if the Earth is so mistreated that it becomes uninhabitable, it could take many thousands of years for it to revitalise itself and our spiritual journey can be put on hold until such time as it is renewed. In the meantime, those of us who choose to live here and keep genetic human life going so that we do not die off as a species, will have to live on a planet in turmoil, facing untold physical hardships.

Our good will to others is a key part of the spiritual journey and purpose can play a great role in our lives. There are still communities where collective responsibilities and goals are at their core. Developing positive thoughts to those around us and truly believing in the potential for good within us, means that we are all worth saving and if we are worth saving, then so is our planet. We may not, each of us, individually be able to save the world but we can all contribute with the right kind of thoughts and even a helping hand to nature. All our natural environment; the parklands, animals, birds and everything around us can benefit in some small way if we do our bit. The natural world can have a nurturing effect on us and we owe it to ourselves and each other to make it a better place for everyone and everything.

Society lacks structure and yet we all feel better for finding ways of bonding. Spirituality can provide an answer to this quest for cohesion. By treating others as we would hope to be treated, we receive a greater sense of self-worth and unite in friendship.

The spiritual pathway is not dictated. You are encouraged to develop your way, using what you learn as a guide. Each of us will react in different ways, accepting and rejecting as we progress through our own experience. Clear vision gives you better ability to recognise what is right or wrong for you. It opens us up to a wider perspective so that whatever confronts us in life is not necessarily a barrier to happiness. Clear vision gives us options and we can become wrapped up in the thoughts and fears of the moment, or use our enhanced perspective to guide us.

With the spread of the media and communications, we are able to access many points of view, with information on everything that is going on in the world today. Each of us uses the media in different ways, but we would all do well to remember it does not always paint the whole picture. Much of what we are exposed to can trivialise life or create fear and anxiety.

The more we saturate ourselves in the negativity, violence and pain of this world, the more we attract it and we can become negative, angry, or things other than that which we are within.
If we have a natural curiosity, of course we can learn about what is going on around us, but be mindful of the effect this can have. Remember that we have free-will. We must ask what purpose we are seeking to achieve. Taking on board too much of what we

read can also convince us that life is complicated. Fear breeds fear and with the threat of violence, we can become suspicious and paranoid. If we are seeking peace in our lives, then we should put time aside to focus on things that are both positive and peaceful.

Our will may be directed toward personal ambitions for recognition and material achievements, or to furthering our spiritual journey. Yet whatever wealth we amass, it will only serve a purpose in the physical world, we cannot take it with us and therefore it has no ultimate worth. Nothing lasts forever and sometimes life can seem like 'Mission Impossible'. Yet, the soul is here to teach us life's true value, providing a sense of purpose as it guides us towards peace and fulfilment. Therefore, spirituality is concerned with developing ourselves as human beings, helping us along our road of life and progressing positively so that our negativities have less of a hold over us. This learning process is a journey that changes us for the better. By embracing compassion, truth and love, we can feel the nourishment they provide. By allowing ourselves to question who we really are and our role in the universe, we can recognise those behaviours that are programmed into us through culture, habit and society's expectations. Spirituality offers us the opportunity to think freely and choose, so we can develop the positive characteristics we value and embody the feelings we are all seeking.

In conclusion
Whatever situation we are in, we will do well to remember that everything changes and moves on. Nothing stays the same forever.

Our love and best efforts are here in the writing of this book and all the many years of Carolann's experience are committed to print, for the very first time, so that they are now available to everyone who wishes to engage with this spiritual journey. Our hope is that what is offered will provide benefit to all those who read it and choose to practice the meditations and exercises herein. Our wish is that it will serve to further self-knowledge and pass on what we have learned from the world of spirit.

Spirituality is a personal search for answers to the most profound questions of life and a journey of awakening to who we really are. This can be a lifelong pathway, from confusion to meaning, from fear to faith, from feeling alone to being at one with everyone and everything.

Prayer is a communication of our inner self and an outlet for our spiritual expression. It offers us a lifeline to a higher source. It refines our inner wishes and, if we know for ourselves that we are being listened to, it can bring peace, love and humility through our openness with God.

Practicing the exercises correctly can provide you with access to a whole new spiritual universe, while putting your thoughts towards someone close and understanding how they feel means your clear vision can help you, your family, your friends and beyond.

Meditation can give us space so that our thoughts are clearer and we feel more open and even allow us peace of mind. Visualisations can offer us access to the world of spirit and God and this can help us to find direction. Your pathway is your own, as is what you choose to guide you. Clear vision can offer a personal experience that opens your perspective. What we find for ourselves can serve as personal enlightenment.

Our love goes with you on your own personal pathway to enlightenment.

Carolann and Roland

Glossary of Terms

Clairvoyant - Someone who has developed or is born with the ability to perceive information beyond their physical senses. In this book this term is used to include the ability to see, hear, touch, feel and taste, independent of those physical senses Therefore, we use the term clairvoyance to include Clairaudience, Clairalience, Claircognizance, Clairgustance and Clairsentience. These gifts are often referred to as psychic abilities or by the generic term of Extra-Sensory Perception (ESP).

Colours in exercises - Colours are used to express and identify emotions and situations. Each colour has an associated emotion and can therefore indicate what needs to be addressed. Emotions can also be signified by water.

God - The supreme ultimate energy from where all life-forms originate and to where we will all eventually return. A totally unconditional energy that is the womb to us all. God is the life-force that keeps the world and the universe together and personifies compassion and forgiveness. When we encounter Him, God is the overarching example of everything we would like to be and be part of. He is the light and to Him we are children. It is because of this relationship to Him that in some religions he is referred to as 'Our Father.' There are many questions we can ask about the nature of God that may help us to grasp an understanding. Ultimately, words cannot describe what it is like to be in His presence, they are merely a guide towards comprehending His purpose and the all-encompassing all-knowing, all-seeing ultimate of all knowledge. God is both the beginning and end of all things known; like the circumference of a sphere, He has no beginning and no end. God is an energy that encompasses all dimensions of existence. This energy holds together all of our known universe and beyond. We grow in a pattern of evolution, God is the one that drives and directs it. God gives us life, an environment to develop and grow in, free-will and freedom of choice.

Meditation - The act of putting ourselves in a quiet mental place. A way of dealing with our stress and learning to cope, so that we can achieve greater calmness within our lives. Meditation is the doorway to developing our spirituality.

Medium - A medium is someone able to relate to and communicate with the energy within us that dwells in the world of spirit once our physical body has died.

Soul - The inner part of us that is also an extension of us in spirit world and learns through our physical body here on Earth. We are a Spiritual Energy within a physical body. Without the physical, the soul could not take its journey into this world. Our driving force is our soul and the body is its physical vehicle. The soul exists for a purpose, its origin is spirit world. Each new soul is born from God, lacking physical experience, like a sponge ready to absorb. Each physical life provides it with sensations and experiences that build knowledge, fuelling the soul with information in the same way that a child's brain is fuelled with knowledge to enable it to develop along its natural path.

Spirit - The spirit is our energy, our life force, the conscious manifestation of soul that exists to sustain soul and body for the duration of each physical life. Like the body, the Spirit is merely a vehicle for the soul to live a physical existence. In the same way that the body cannot function without the brain, the 'Spirit' has no existence without a soul.

Spirit world - Spirit world is the energy plane where our soul dwells between lives and the souls that live in spirit world are an extension of us. When we pass over into spirit world we take with us all the things we have learned, along with the memories and links with loved-ones. There, we join with all of those that we know and love and have passed before us as part of our everlasting life.

Spiritual Pathway - Our conscious journey to a better inner life. The spiritual path of clear vision is guided by our clairvoyance and intuition. A spiritual pathway aids us in recognising our purpose, developing a greater awareness and our true potential for personal enlightenment, so that we are able to help ourselves and others. The true function of our spiritual path is to develop knowledge and take it home to spirit world, so that our souls may develop and ascend. If we are good people then what we return home with will have served its purpose and we will learn positive lessons for self-betterment.

Spirituality - Our spirituality is our inner wealth of positive spiritual traits such as understanding, compassion, unconditional love, a willingness to help others and patience. It is something we naturally possess and we can choose to develop.

The other side - This is a common phrase used for spirit world where our soul energy originates from and returns to on our journey of everlasting life.

Universal energy - Each of us has physical, spiritual and mental energy. Universal energy is a part of God, the energy that radiates from God like an aura and encompasses the world, the universe and everything within it. By going with the flow of the universal energy, we are going with the flow of God's Energy.

Upstairs - Another term for Spirit World, used because it conveys the sense of another higher level that we are all able to reach, but that remains above us and our usual 'ground level' day to day lives on Earth. Upstairs also conveys the association with bedrooms, which are usually located on the upper storeys; places of rest and relaxation where we recuperate after each day, while in spirit world we recuperate after each life.

Appendix - Ghosts

There has always been media interest in ghosts and of late there has been a focus on the sensationalist and frightening aspects of ghostly apparitions and presences. Traditionally ghost stories have been used to scare us and excite our interest in the paranormal world, intriguing us perhaps with unanswered questions as to the truth of their existence and their purpose. While it is a fascinating part of psychic phenomena, there is much misunderstanding as to what a ghost is and what it is not.

A ghost is a residual image, a dispossessed shadow with no substance nor ability to identify with the world around it. Ghosts are not entities, nor individuals; they are merely residual energy, reflections of what was. Therefore, like an image cast on film, they are not capable of communication, nor do they have an existence as we understand it. They are unchanging shadows of the past, mere silhouettes that serve no spiritual purpose.

Just as we can sense the atmosphere in a room shortly after someone has argued, the image of a ghost is created because energy remains from a particular event, either one that was extremely traumatic, or one that was repeated many times with emotional intensity. If you imagine a worst case scenario such as a murder, where there was huge fear and trauma, then the intense energy of that event can be left as an imprint. Likewise, if someone were to pray time after time in the same spot, putting heart and soul into the act, they may create an entirely different but equally powerful impression. This is why a ghost can be seen replaying the same actions time after time, it is just the image of the event that remains, while the soul in question has passed over. When the right circumstances occur, we can glimpse that energy and 'see a ghost.'

A ghost is an entirely separate and different thing to a soul, or what is commonly referred to as a 'spirit'. Our soul is what naturally passes over to spirit world when our physical body dies and yet there are soul- related phenomena that are confused with ghosts. If, at the time of physical death, the soul remains attached to the Earth, this is referred to as an 'Earthbound spirit.' It will have conscious thought patterns whereas a ghost will not. What we think of as ghostly goings on, where there are physical manifestations such as noises, poltergeist activity etc., can only be manifested by an Earthbound spirit. Ghosts are seen and not heard!

In recent times, more of us have opened up to the idea of ghosts. They can appear in castles and very old properties and we tend to think of them inhabiting old stately homes or crumbling ruins, although they can inhabit not so old and new premises alike. If we take, as a hypothetical example, a person who died living in a castle, then the ghost of their image may remain on the physical plane after death, perhaps because they repeated the same actions time and time again. This image will repeat those same patterns over the years, decades and centuries. Regardless of what has physically changed, they will still tread the same fixed patterns as when they were alive on the Earth plane. Ghosts may travel through walls, because those walls did not exist in their lifetime. If the level of the earth or the floors changes, then we may see their image pass through these too, seemingly walking in mid-air, or with just their upper torso visible above a floor.

Ghosts permeate the environment they are in, they are like old wallpaper that becomes part of the wall and is very difficult to remove or separate. A ghost is a reflection of what was, not what is and, in many ways, is irrelevant to clairvoyance, mediumship and spirituality because the soul of the person who left that image has passed over to spirit world.

If, on the other hand, our soul remains Earthbound, our whole consciousness is not open to us, as we have left our bodies, it is like a recurring breathless dream from which we do not awaken. Earthbound souls are often trapped in the memory of their previous existence, perhaps locked in the last few moments, or within an important part of their lives here on Earth. They are relating to their past Earthly existence and not what is now around them, so that changes in the environment will have no impact on them at all because they do not recognise anything other than how things were for them during life. This residual soul energy is something entirely different to a soul in spirit world, which will have knowledge of its past and present existence and a level of self-awareness according to its level of development.

The reasons that souls stay connected to this plane are numerous. Their passage over to the other side may be postponed if they are confused by the manner of their passing. Alternatively, the soul may have been so attached to a person, loved one, or place that they could not imagine themselves in any other situation and therefore stayed put when they first had the opportunity to be taken across, instead remaining with whatever or whomever they could not let go of. Earthbound souls can be anchored to the Earth by a loved one's grief or they find themselves unable to relate to their own death, so that they do not move on, trapped in a timeless moment of attachment to the situation they were familiar with here on Earth. Remember, this is a rare occurrence, our soul's natural dwelling place outside of the body is spirit world and the vast majority of souls will pass over naturally. When our body dies, no matter how strong our love for those on Earth, nor how much they are missed, our soul will be pulled upwards. It is only an infinitesimal number that remain and they will all eventually move on.

The consciousness of a soul trapped here on Earth will have a thinking pattern that controls its actions and will be able to consciously affect the environment around it. For instance, it is able to use its energy to tap on walls, meddle with electrical equipment or engineer noises to attract our attention to its situation and it will, in all probability, feel lost, alone and isolated. There is no reason to be afraid of this disembodied energy.

Another reason for the soul to remain here is a fear of joining with the wider energy in spirit world and going through the natural process of meeting our Maker being answerable for their actions in life. So when we talk of a bad 'spirit' it is normally an Earthbound soul we are dealing with, that remains here through dread of the consequences of moving on. Not all Earthbound souls are 'bad', this is merely the case for those who will not move on through apprehension of the unknown. There are spiritual practitioners who can communicate with any Earthbound spirit so that it may be freed to join the light of spirit world.

By contrast, the soul of a loved one who has passed can choose to visit us. Be it family, friends or even a pet, they can manifest here. When we receive such a visit from spirit world, it is usually intended to help us and the visiting loved one will project their once-human form to our mind. These 'apparitions' are not ghosts, but soul energy. In this instance, we can be grateful that our loved-ones are still concerned enough about us to visit in such a way that we can see them. With these visits, we will normally be aware of the feelings of love and understanding that come with them. We have no reason to be afraid even when we pass into another dimension our love never dies and can influence us to return to those we love.

Sometimes we may experience a feeling of cold which alerts us to the presence of a soul and we may assume from this that it is a bad energy or feeling. However, it can just be a reflection of the emotional energy of a soul visiting us, or be a side effect of the accompanying change in energy. For instance, we may have a grandparent who was not particularly warm as a personality in this life and even if they had feelings for us, if their soul energy visits, it may come with a feeling of cold. Again, there is no reason to be afraid of this sort of visitation. We may experience a child returning in spirit form that is mischievous, perhaps moving objects and turning lights on and off, fiddling with switches as children will do. This is not a malicious 'haunting', but rather a reflection of their love of adventure. If we can look beyond our initial fear and annoyance and understand the nature of this visit, we may recognise the reason that a soul is with us. Some souls will bring with them a feeling of physical presence that we sense beside us. This can indicate that the person's energy is present and we feel it as a pressure in the air, as if a physical body is present. Often, the visit is merely there to show us the love that is available and to reassure us that we are not alone and that help is on hand if we are willing to ask for it.

For more information on our work, please visit
www.carolannspathway.co.uk or email
info@carolannspathway.co.uk

4799883R00191

Printed in Germany
by Amazon Distribution
GmbH, Leipzig